Rape Justice

Rape Justice

Beyond the Criminal Law

Edited by

Anastasia Powell
RMIT University, Australia

Nicola Henry
La Trobe University, Australia

Asher Flynn
Monash University, Australia

palgrave
macmillan

First published 2015 by
PALGRAVE MACMILLAN

Palgrave Macmillan in the UK is an imprint of Macmillan Publishers Limited, registered in England, company number 785998, of Houndmills, Basingstoke, Hampshire RG21 6XS.

Palgrave Macmillan in the US is a division of St Martin's Press LLC, 175 Fifth Avenue, New York, NY 10010.

Palgrave Macmillan is the global academic imprint of the above companies and has companies and representatives throughout the world.

Palgrave® and Macmillan® are registered trademarks in the United States, the United Kingdom, Europe and other countries.

ISBN 978–1–137–47614–2

This book is printed on paper suitable for recycling and made from fully managed and sustained forest sources. Logging, pulping and manufacturing processes are expected to conform to the environmental regulations of the country of origin.

A catalogue record for this book is available from the British Library.

A catalog record for this book is available from the Library of Congress.

Contents

Tables

Acknowledgements

Despite decades of concerted activism, policy and legal reform, achieving justice for victim-survivors of sexual violence remains a pressing and unfinished ordeal.

This unique collection brings together expertise from across Australia, Canada, Croatia, Norway and the United Kingdom, to critically reflect on *Rape Justice: Beyond the Criminal Law.* Working with these scholars whose passion and practice reveals the limits and possibilities of justice has been a thoroughly humbling and rewarding experience. We have also had the great privilege of exploring and discussing the themes of this book with many of our contributors over the last few years, including at the 2013 colloquium of the Violence and Discrimination Against Women Research Network (VDAWnet) kindly supported by RMIT University and La Trobe University, Melbourne, Australia. It is a rare opportunity to bring together academics and practitioners from different practice backgrounds and theoretical perspectives to interrogate the social and political issues that this book explores, and we are very grateful for the conversations that have provided a basis for many of the chapters included here. We would like to thank each of our contributing authors for their diligence and their patience; for responding so graciously and positively to feedback on earlier drafts; and overall, for the tremendous contributions that their work both within and beyond this book makes to progress justice for victim-survivors.

We would like to also express our sincere gratitude to the editorial team at Palgrave Macmillan: in particular, Julia Willan, Harriet Barker and Dominic Walker, who have been constant sources of enthusiasm and support for this book throughout its journey from concept, to proposal, to publication. Thank you also to Susie Elliott for her magnificent editorial assistance. We are also very grateful to our peers and colleagues who have provided advice and guidance on the content of this book, and who also generously reviewed our own chapter contributions.

Finally, we would like to thank our families, friends and colleagues for their ongoing support and encouragement. In particular, Anastasia would like to thank her partner Matthew Weston and son Alexander. It is not easy to be a support to an academic whose work never seems to stay at work. Thank you also to her friends and colleagues including her head of discipline, Michele Ruyters, who is a constant source of encouragement and all-important resources, and most especially to her co-editors Nicola and Asher with whom it continues to be an absolute pleasure to work. Nicola would like to thank her loving, caring and supportive partner Brent and her sweet, adorable and cute little Frederick. Thanks also to her wonderful family, especially Mum, Dad, Justine, Emma and Matt, and to friends and colleagues who have supported her immensely, in particular to Tarryn and Nesam for their constant support, advice and friendship. Lastly, Asher would like to thank Pamela and Allen for their ongoing support, unconditional love and encouragement. Thanks also to her Monash criminology colleagues for their valued support on this (and many other) research endeavours. Asher dedicates this book to her partner, Mark, and his colleagues, who are challenging stereotypes and seeking to make a real difference from within the realm of law.

Contributors

Haley Clark is a social worker and counsellor at Southland Help Rape and Abuse Support Centre, New Zealand. She has worked in research, policy and practice in the area of sexual violence for more than a decade. This includes having worked as a senior researcher at the Australian Centre for the Study of Sexual Assault and for the Victorian Department of Justice during the implementation of sexual offences law reforms, as well as for non-government organisations. She holds a MApplSW (Hons) and a PhD in criminology from the University of Melbourne. Her doctoral research examined the concept of justice from the perspectives of victim-survivors of sexual violence. She has written a number of articles and reports in the area of sexual violence and justice, and continues to provide support, education and advocacy in this area.

Kathleen Daly is Professor of Criminology and Criminal Justice, Griffith University, Brisbane, Australia. She writes on gender, race, crime and criminal justice; and on restorative, indigenous and transitional justice. Her recent work is on conventional and innovative justice responses to sexual and violent victimisation in different contexts of violence; and on redress, restoration and reparation. Her recent book, *Redressing Institutional Abuse of Children* (2014), analyses 19 major Australian and Canadian cases of historical institutional abuse. She is the editor or author of six books and over 85 journal articles or book chapters, past President of the Australian and New Zealand Society of Criminology (2005–2009) and Fellow of the Academy of the Social Sciences in Australia (2007) and the American Society of Criminology (2014).

Sara E. Davies is an Australian Research Council (ARC) Future Fellow, based at the Health Law Research Centre, Queensland University of Technology, Australia. She is the recipient of an ARC Discovery Project with Professor Jacqui True (Monash University) that examines the prevention of sexual violence in conflict and post-conflict situations in the Asia-Pacific region (PSV-AP). This ARC Discovery Project builds on her previous work on the prevention of mass atrocities and the Responsibility to Protect (co-editor, *Women Peace and Security and the Responsibility to Protect* (2013)). She has written two books, *Global Politics of Health*

(2010) and *Legitimising Rejection: International Refugee Law in Southeast Asia* (2007). She is the co-founder and co-editor of the quarterly journal *Global Responsibility to Protect.*

Benjamin de Carvalho is a senior research fellow at the Norwegian Institute of International Affairs, NUPI, Norway. His work on peacekeeping has focused on the protection of civilians (PoC) and sexual and gender-based violence (SGBV). He has undertaken fieldwork in Liberia, the Sudans and Chad.

Asher Flynn is Senior Lecturer in Criminology within the School of Social Sciences at Monash University, Melbourne, Australia, and a Research Fellow in Law within the Criminal Justice Centre at the University of Warwick, England. Her research utilises a socio-legal framework to understand, critique and transform legal policy and practice. Informed by national and international context, her research examines how accessing justice is negotiated, and the gendered, class-based application and practice of law. She has been awarded a number of prestigious international research fellowships and national awards in recognition of her work in the access to justice and plea negotiation fields, which has allowed her to spend time at the University of Manchester (Research Fellow in Law, 2013), the University of Warwick (Research Fellow in Law, 2014 – ongoing; Visiting Fellow in Criminal Justice, 2013) and Mannix College (Research Fellow in Social Sciences, 2014 – ongoing). She is a chief investigator with Emeritus Professor Arie Freiberg on a Criminology Research Council Project (2014–2016) analysing the plea negotiation process in Victoria.

Nikki Godden-Rasul is a feminist legal scholar whose research focuses on seeking justice for rape victim-survivors through unconventional legal responses. She has written on tort law and civil claims for rape in *King's Law Journal* and in *Feminist Perspectives on Tort Law* (edited by Erika Rackley and Janice Richardson), and she has also written on restorative justice and rape (with Clare McGlynn and Nicole Westmarland) in the *Journal of Law and Society*. She is the co-creator, editor and contributor of the blog *Inherently Human: Critical Perspectives on Law, Gender & Sexuality*.

Lise Gotell is Professor and Chair of Women's and Gender Studies at the University of Alberta, Canada. Her research expertise is in the area of gender and law, and she has written on such topics as equality litigation, constitutional jurisprudence, obscenity law and sexual assault. She is a co-author of *Bad Attitude/s on Trial: Feminism, Pornography and the Butler Decision* (1997) and a co-editor (together with Barbara Crow) of *Open Boundaries: A Canadian Women's Studies Reader* (2009). For the past several years, her published work has focused on the implications of Canadian sexual assault reforms, including interrogating the legal standard for consent and evaluating the effectiveness of legislative restrictions on sexual history evidence and confidential records. Gotell is a founding member of Sexual Assault Voices of Edmonton, a community–police–academic collaboration that uses social marketing to educate about consent and to change attitudes that contribute to sexual assault.

Nicola Henry is Senior Lecturer in Legal Studies in the Department of Social Inquiry at La Trobe University, Melbourne, Australia. Her research focuses on justice responses to sexual violence in both international and domestic spaces. Her books include *War and Rape: Law, Memory and Justice* (2011) and *Preventing Sexual Violence: Interdisciplinary Approaches to Overcoming a Rape Culture*, co-edited with Anastasia Powell (2014). She is a chief investigator (with Anastasia Powell) on an Australian Research Council (ARC) Discovery Project on technology-facilitated sexual violence and harassment.

Rosemary Nagy is Associate Professor of Gender Equality and Social Justice in the Faculty of Arts and Sciences, Nipissing University, Canada. Her research interests have to do with the scopes and bounds of an internationalised transitional justice. This includes the task of engendering transitional justice, the relationship between transitional justice and social or distributive justice, and legal pluralism in transitional context, in particular, the use of 'traditional' mechanisms. Rosemary's current research project is about the Canadian Truth and Reconciliation Commission on residential schools.

Niels Nagelhus Schia is an anthropologist and research fellow at the Norwegian Institute of International Affairs, NUPI, Norway, focusing on organisational culture, international organisations and peacebuilding. He has previously worked as a visiting researcher in a policy-producing section in the UN Department of Peacekeeping Operations HQ in New York and has written several peer-reviewed articles on peacebuilding.

Anastasia Powell is Senior Lecturer in Justice and Legal Studies at RMIT University, Melbourne, Australia. Her research has specialised on policy and prevention concerning violence against women. She has written widely in these fields including three books: *Sex, Power and Consent: Youth Culture and the Unwritten Rules* (2010); *Domestic Violence: Australian Public Policy*, co-authored with Suellen Murray (2011); and *Preventing Sexual Violence: Interdisciplinary Approaches to Overcoming a Rape Culture*, co-edited with Nicola Henry (2014). Her research has also focused more particularly on the interdisciplinary field of technology, sexual violence and justice, and she is currently a chief investigator (with Nicola Henry) on an Australian Research Council (ARC) Discovery Project grant *Technology-Facilitated Sexual Violence and Harassment: Violence Against Women in Cyberspace and the Implications for Reform* (2013–2016).

Ivana Radačić is a senior research associate at Ivo Pilar Institute of Social Sciences in Zagreb, working in the area of human rights and feminism. She is also a visiting lecturer at the University of Zagreb, the University of Osijek, the European Inter-University Centre for Human Rights and Democratisation, Venice, and University College London. She was a visiting lecturer at UN University for Peace, Costa Rica, and a fellow at the University of Kent and the University of Melbourne. She worked at the European Court of Human Rights, and she cooperates with a number of NGOs on strategic litigation and human rights education. She has written widely in the area of feminism and human rights, in particular on women's rights jurisprudence of the European Court of Human Rights. Her latest book analyses rape myths and gender stereotypes in the Croatian rape laws and judicial practice.

James A. Roffee is Lecturer in Criminology at Monash University, Melbourne, Australia. He holds a PhD in law from the University of Leicester. Prior to joining Monash University, he taught law part-time at De Montfort University and the University of Leicester in the United Kingdom. His field of expertise concerns legal responses to sexual offences, especially relating to familial sexual activity. He has worked on legal responses to incest in England, Wales and Scotland as well as chairing the Incest and Sexual Abuse Survivors Trust. His interdisciplinary research has involved both a historical and contemporary review of the way in which familial sexual activity has been managed in the legal sphere. This has involved reviewing punitive responses to familial sexual activity, and understanding a human-rights based approach to the problem as well as community responses to incest.

Jacqui True is Professor of Politics and International Relations and an Australian Research Council Future Fellow at Monash University, Melbourne, Australia. She is a specialist in gender and international relations and critical international political economy, with a focus on the social dimensions of globalisation and feminist research methodologies. Her articles on gender mainstreaming and global governance rank among the most highly cited in the field. Her latest book, *The Political Economy of Violence Against Women*, was published in 2012. She is chair of the Australian Political Science Association's International Relations Standing Committee and is an editor of *International Studies Perspectives*. She is a member of the editorial boards of *International Feminist Journal of Politics, Foreign Policy Analysis, Women, Politics & Policy, Political Science* and the Palgrave Macmillan *Gender and Politics Series*.

1

The Promise and Paradox of Justice

Rape Justice Beyond the Criminal Law

Nicola Henry, Asher Flynn and Anastasia Powell

Introduction

Justice for victim-survivors of sexual violence is marred by a series of intersecting paradoxes, predicaments and contradictions. On the one hand, sexual violence is commonly understood as a 'trauma' under increasingly medicalised and individualised psychological frameworks (see Gavey & Schmidt, 2011). Rape is often rendered incomprehensible and taboo to others; seen as the 'worst of crimes', 'an assault on the soul' (Sharratt & Kaschak, 2013) or 'the ultimate violation' (Rowland, 1985). Yet on the other hand, victim-blaming cultural attitudes, stereotypes and myths continue to normalise sexual violence and trivialise victim experiences (Heenan & Murray, 2006), particularly when the perpetrator is a person known to the victim and/or when the victim is in an intoxicated state (Lynch et al., 2013; Richardson & Campbell, 1982). Indeed, cultural, structural, institutional and social values about sexual violence have been identified as part of a phenomenon which is commonly yet controversially referred to as 'rape culture', defined as 'a complex set of beliefs that encourage male sexual aggression and supports violence against women' (Buchwald et al., 2005, p. xi; see also Brownmiller, 1975; Horvarth & Brown, 2009). Arguably an outcome of these prevailing forces – between the pathological trauma of rape and the minimisation and trivialisation of rape – is to contribute to the construction of a 'spoiled identity' (Gavey & Schmidt, 2011, p. 451) and a reinforcement of stranger rape as the prototype of 'real rape' (Estrich, 1987; Williams, 1984) – both a form of misrecognition and representational injustice (Fraser, 1998).

Scholars, activists and practitioners continue to decry the perpetual silence surrounding sexual violence in public discourse and the dismal failure of domestic and international legal courts to adequately prosecute rape, secure convictions and ensure proportionate sentences (see e.g. Mardorossian, 2002). Yet this critique of silence can be juxtaposed to the unprecedented global attention to sexual violence that has amassed in more recent times due to a number of events, including the gang rape and murder of a 23-year-old physiotherapy student in South Delhi, India, in 2012; the rape and murder of 29-year-old Irish woman and ABC employee Jill Meagher in Melbourne, Australia, in 2012; the 2014 Global Summit to End Sexual Violence in Conflict, co-chaired by UK Foreign Secretary William Hague and Special Envoy for the UN High Commissioner for Refugees, Angelina Jolie; and the dramatic profusion of online anti-rape websites offering victim-survivors a space to tell their stories to global audiences (see Powell, 2015; Rentschler, 2014). Alongside populist and intergovernmental attention, scholars, activists and victim-survivors have extensively written and campaigned about sexual violence in both peacetime and wartime contexts, culminating, amongst other things, in the recognition of rape as a crime against humanity, a war crime and a crime of genocide under international law. Yet conversely, others have questioned the desirability of fixating on rape as the 'worst of crimes', arguing that such rhetoric can be used to advance political interests and ideologies, and to present women as perpetually powerless, vulnerable, 'sexed' and in need of protection by a heroic band of 'international saviours' (Halley, 2008; Marcus, 1992; see also Henry, 2014).

Moreover, feminist academics and practitioners are divided over the extent to which '*gender* inequality should be framed as one factor among many in prevention work, or as *the* central, contributing factor underlying sexual violence in our society' (Powell & Henry, 2014, p. 11, original emphasis). The largest North American anti-sexual violence organisation RAINN (Rape, Abuse & Incest National Network), for example, expressed concern about the 'unfortunate trend towards blaming "rape culture" for the extensive problem of sexual violence on [college] campuses'. They noted that:

> While it is helpful to point out the systemic barriers to addressing the problem, it is important to not lose sight of the simple fact: *Rape is caused not by cultural factors but by the conscious decisions, of a small percentage of the community, to commit a violent crime.*
>
> (Emphasis added)

The issue is whether sexual violence and the diverse justice responses to it should be understood as an individual or collective problem. In other words, should justice mechanisms be directed towards ensuring individual culpability and responsibility, or should energy instead be invested in tackling deep-seated gender inequality as one of the underlying causes of sexual violence?

These aforementioned paradoxes are also reflected in debates about the efficacy of rape law reform. Since the latter part of the 20th century, a raft of legislative and procedural changes to rape law across jurisdictions globally have included innovative procedures and measures to address the 'justice gap' (Temkin & Krahé, 2008), which has come to characterise the prosecution of sexual offences in diverse criminal justice systems (see McGlynn & Munro, 2010). These reforms include, *inter alia*, changes to the definition of rape and sexual consent; amendments to jury directions; the abolishment of the requirement for witness corroboration; restrictions on the admission of evidence at trial about a complainant's sexual history; protective measures for vulnerable witnesses; the establishment of witness and victim support services with specialist expertise on sexual violence; various types of legal representation for victims; reparations, compensation, restitution and rehabilitation; specialist courts; and the criminalisation of marital rape. However, although recognised as progressive measures, many scholars, legal professionals and activists argue that the impact of rape law reform has been negligible, with little change to reporting, prosecution and conviction rates, and little improvement in procedural justice for both victims and accused persons (Daly, 2011; Larcombe, 2011; Stubbs, 2003). Indeed, despite the global momentum surrounding sexual violence, and the various feminist academic debates about the impacts and hierarchies of sexual violence in diverse contexts, there is little doubt that victim-survivors continue to face insurmountable obstacles in seeking justice through the criminal law in the aftermath of sexual violence.

The above-mentioned intersecting paradoxes and predicaments underscore the discursive construction of rape or sexual violence as simultaneously *inevitable* yet *unspeakable* (Henry, 2011). These paradoxes, we contend, are ultimately concerned with the complex notion of 'justice', leading us to ask: What constitutes justice for victim-survivors of sexual violence? Is justice *recognition* of a wrong? Is justice the *primary prevention* of that wrong? Should justice responses focus on individual criminal responsibility, or instead tackle deep-seated, underlying structural inequalities? Or is justice something far more ephemeral or nebulous to victim-survivors of these harms? To date, much of the excellent work on justice for sexual violence victim-survivors has been focused foremost on criminal justice systems in both domestic and international contexts (see McGlynn & Munro, 2010; Temkin & Krahé, 2008; Westmarland & Gangoli, 2011). Adding to this body of literature, this current collection critically examines the diverse assemblage of justice responses to sexual violence, encompassing criminal law, civil law, restorative justice mechanisms, international human rights law, civil society initiatives, customary law and online anti-rape activism. The book attempts to provide a reconceptualisation of justice both within and beyond the criminal law and to insist, as Kathleen Daly (2011, p. 2) does, that '[r]ather than one justice pathway for victim/survivors, a menu of options and varied pathways is required'. The collection is thus situated within a burgeoning interest in alternative and innovative justice responses to sexual violence both within and outside of the legal system (see e.g. Daly, 2011; Koss, 2010; McGlynn, 2011; McGlynn et al., 2012; Naylor, 2010). It addresses key debates regarding the false dichotomy between restorative and retributive justice, as well as the desirability and efficacy of legal redress for sexual violence. The book as a whole moves beyond a narrow treatment of justice through the criminal law, and instead focuses on different institutional, individualised and community-based mechanisms that are constantly changing in an age of expanding digital communication, information saturation, new forms of social activism and shifting 'imagined communities' (see also McGlynn, 2011).

In this chapter, we argue that these alternative justice sites, measures and mechanisms have potential empowering effects for individuals and groups, such as giving victim-survivors of sexual violence greater control over their narratives, challenging gendered rape myths and fostering collective, solidarity-building consensus. More broadly, creative, inventive or subaltern measures can serve to challenge the very idea that justice can and should be sought exclusively through formal legal channels. The first section of this chapter examines the philosophical and practical problematic notion of 'justice' and the array of justice mechanisms for responding to multiple forms of sexual violence in contemporary contexts. The second section provides an overview of the collection as a whole, focusing on the key themes of justice, context and moving beyond the realm of law.

The problem of justice: Beyond criminal law

Justice, according to many influential philosophers, is sacrosanct, compelling and inviolable: a 'word of magic evocations' (Cahn, 1964, p. 13). John Rawls (1976) described justice as the 'first virtue', but noted that what is just and unjust is perpetually in dispute. Justice prompts creative forms of energy; it is a power that both drives and impassions – but it remains perpetually elusive and impossible to define. The eternal, alluring expectation of justice as 'the basis for sovereignty, the source of political authority' keeps us, as subjects of law, always 'obedient, patient and hopeful' (Martel, 2011, pp. 158–159). As Jacques Derrida (1990) acutely notes, we are *always* waiting for justice. Justice is, Derrida claims, the experience of the impossible; it is 'always to come'.

Law remains the dominant frame for thinking about justice, but the law–justice relationship is characterised by a set of paradoxes. While it is true that victims of crime often turn to law as the normative remedy for injury, law at times can engender oppressive and deleterious effects, serving as a tool of further injustice. Relatedly, although law has the power to pronounce judgement and to construct the truth about an event, it can also silence and/or suppress other narratives and 'truths' (Finley, 1989). Law can empower individuals and groups in asserting their rights, providing a benchmark from which to check the abuse of interpersonal, organisational and state power, but it can also be used by the powerful to exert more power. Law's power is itself full of complexities and contingencies (Douzinas et al., 1994). Law, disguised as justice, may bring some satisfaction and other therapeutic gains to victim-survivors and the community more generally, but law can never fully erase the injury or long-term impacts of violence. Law ultimately promises, but fails to deliver, justice.

Despite the frustrations, mysteries and impossibilities of justice, law remains compellingly central to understandings of justice. This is particularly the case with criminal law. The criminal law, and the rituals of the justice system within which it operates, carries important symbolic meanings, as well as having practical effects that extend beyond the individuals directly involved, into the broader society (Murray & Powell, 2011). If, as Durkheim (1893) famously argued, criminal law and punishment is expressive of a society's collective vengeance for the violation of a shared core value, then seeking justice through the criminal courts represents more than seeking accountability and punishment for an individual's wrongdoing. Rather, criminal justice, when successful in terms of conviction and punishment for rape, represents society's public acknowledgement not only of the harm, but also that it *should not* occur; that rape is fundamentally an outrage to our collective values. In short, criminal law is a fundamental means of both establishing and communicating normative standards of sexual conduct (Larcombe, 2014). As David Garland (1990, p. 67) suggests:

> Rituals – including the rituals of criminal justice – are ceremonies, which, through the manipulation of emotion, prompt particular value commitments on the part of the participants and the audience and thus act as a kind of sentimental education, generating and regenerating a particular mentality and a particular sensibility.

It is perhaps a reflection of this core expressive function of the criminal law that for many victim-survivors, feminist scholars and activists, 'justice' in response to sexual violence has been pursued with specific reference to criminal convictions and carceral punishment (see Lewis et al., 2001; and for a critique, see Chapter 4). Nonetheless, there is growing acknowledgement that such measures and understandings of justice are considerably narrow (see Larcombe, 2011), and frequently fail to meet the varied justice needs of victim-survivors of sexual violence (Chapter 2). For example, feminist scholarship has long identified the criminal justice trial as analogous to a 'second rape' (Madigan & Gamble, 1989); an additional trauma endured by victim-survivors, rather than a process that offers either acknowledgement or healing. Furthermore, as Judith Herman (2005) notes, many of the processes of the criminal trial 'ritual' are antithetical to justice from the victim's perspective. At a time when victim-survivors require the opportunity to be heard, believed and regain control over their narrative, the criminal trial frequently silences, doubts and disinherits victims and renders them to the role of mere 'witnesses' (Herman, 2005). In light of such critiques, it is important to problematise the domination of criminal law in the imaginative space of justice.

As demonstrated throughout the collection, alternative sites of justice are indicative of a shift away from both the law and the state as the remedy for social injury. They signal a shift towards justice as a 'relational and contextual practice', away from institutionalisation, individualisation and libertarianism (Brown, 1995, p. 6). Thus new global and civil society configurations create new opportunities for disenfranchised groups and towards subaltern justice discourses that are capable of contesting and resisting contemporary forms of power and domination.

Differing forms of justice that move beyond the criminal law include customary law; online and offline activism and consciousness-raising; truth and reconciliation commissions; civil remedies; memorials and other forms of commemorations; film, art and literature; reparations through compensation and restitution; public apologies; royal commissions; and other formalised independent investigations. These differing avenues offer alternative understandings, approaches and forms of justice, both formal and informal. To varying degrees, these avenues respond to the needs and contexts of *individualised* lived experiences of sexual violence victim-survivors, as well as seeking to respond to the broader *societal* contexts and collective expectations of justice. What these differing avenues, mechanisms and measures of attaining, achieving, providing, approaching and engaging with justice demonstrate is the complexity of justice, and importantly, that there is a need to move towards a more multivalent approach to justice that is not solely reliant upon the state or the criminal law as the adjudicator of wrongdoing, or the sole provider of justice.

As Nancy Fraser (1998) advocates, justice must be about both redistribution and recognition, and above all, about 'parity of participation' in social life. Drawing on Fraser's justice model, we argue that redressing the misrecognition of the law of sexual violence not only requires changing the rules within law, to achieve this 'parity of participation', but it also requires an exploration of the emerging avenues outside of law – the 'counterpublic spaces' for seeking justice for sexual violence as both redistribution and recognition (Fraser, 1998). It is important to point out that these counterpublic spaces are not immune from deeply embedded cultural, socio-economic and racial hierarchies and there are dangers, limitations and potentials that must also be examined here too. However, we contend that although law continues to dominate the imaginative space of justice, there are possibilities for expanding how we think about justice in the aftermath of sexual violence. The vexed, complex and varied ideals of justice cannot be attained through one formal mechanism of acknowledging and responding to wrongdoing. Instead, we must be prepared to work within and move beyond the realm of criminal law and recognise the importance of context in responding and preventing sexual violence (see Chapter 3).

A note on terminology

Rape Justice is a deliberately provocative title for this book, and it is not without criticism. The term 'rape' and indeed associated definitions of 'sexual assault' and 'sexual violence' are widely divergent across criminal jurisdictions, as well as within public policy and scholarly discourses. In some instances, rape is defined as a penetrative offence;

for instance, the FBI now defines rape as '[t]he penetration, no matter how slight, of the vagina or anus with any body part or object, or oral penetration by a sex organ of another person, without the consent of the victim' (similar to the International Criminal Court's (ICC) definition). This is in contrast to the much broader definition of rape at the International Criminal Tribunal for Rwanda (ICTR), where rape was defined as 'a physical invasion of a sexual nature committed on a person under circumstances which are coercive'. The World Health Organization (WHO, 2011) meanwhile defines sexual violence as 'any sexual act, attempt to obtain a sexual act, unwanted sexual comments or advances, or acts to traffic, or otherwise directed, against a person's sexuality using coercion, by any person regardless of their relationship to the victim, in any setting, including but not limited to home and work'. Some definitions thus treat sexual assault, sexual violence and rape interchangeably, whereas definitions that focus on the penetrative element of the offence tend to treat sexual violence as the broad umbrella term that includes sexual assault as a non-penetrative sexual offence and rape as a separate penetrative offence. In some instances, sexual assault is used interchangeably with rape as a penetrative offence.

In light of these definitional dilemmas and divergences, it is interesting to note Liz Kelly's (1987, p. 54) contention that rather than discrete categories of violence and non-violence, women's experiences of violence exist along a continuum from 'choice to pressure to coercion to force'. Thus women's experiences of sexual violence are not disconnected from other coercive and discriminatory experiences, including sexual harassment, poverty and other gender-based inequalities. In line with a conceptualisation of a continuum of sexual violence in which the language of 'rape' may describe a variety of experiences of violation and abuse, throughout this book the terms rape, sexual violence and sexual assault are used sometimes interchangeably, and sometimes in the specific contexts in which the chapter authors define them.

However, it is not only in the context of a diversity of definitions and experiences that we have elected to draw together the chapters in this collection under the banner of 'rape justice'. 'Rape' and 'rape culture' are terms that have also been increasingly used in public discourse and debate, as a global community seeks to understand the basis for our shared societal epidemic of sexual violence. The dual term 'rape culture', rather than its longer counterpart referring to the 'cultural explanations or causes of rape', has become a powerful shorthand in popular discourse – instantly recognisable and attributable to a feminist-informed analysis of the collective, attitudinal, institutional and societal underpinnings of women's experiences of sexual violence. Critiques of 'rape culture' have thus become a focal point for renewed emphasis within feminist movements and scholarship. In a similar vein, this book places 'rape justice' front and centre, though each of the chapters here elaborates on the complexity, context and contributions of justice that occur within, through and outside of criminal law responses to sexual violence.

The chapters in this book are primarily concerned with the meanings and mechanisms for achieving justice for women victims of sexual violence. In gathering together contributing authors whose work focuses foremost on women (and girls) as victims, it is not our intention to suggest that men (and boys) do not experience sexual violence, nor that they do not have justice needs and face challenges that are similar to those faced by women and girls. Yet the broad critique and conceptualisation of justice that is developed within these pages is framed within an understanding of the fundamentally gender-based nature of sexual violence. Some chapters, for example by Haley Clark (Chapter 2), Kathleen Daly (Chapter 3) and James A. Roffee (Chapter 5), specifically acknowledge both women and men as victims, the broader context to sexual violence victimisation, and the over-regulation of some sexual practices as 'harmful' by the state. However overall, and in the context of women's overwhelming sexual victimisation at the hands of men, this book unapologetically places sexual violence against women at the core of debates regarding 'rape justice'.

The structure of the book

The chapters in this book explore conceptual themes that engage with the potentials and limitations of the law and its processes for responding to women's lived experiences of sexual violence. The chapters examine the complexities and associated problems of individualised versus collective needs in considering justice responses to sexual violence, and the differing expectations of what constitutes a 'justice' outcome, within an international context. Of significance, this collection moves beyond a critique of existing mechanisms to also highlight the importance of understanding context when discussing rape and justice, by specifically taking into consideration broader gendered inequalities and wider social, economic, cultural, physiological and ecological factors. In doing so, the chapters move beyond a focus on the criminal law and legal reform as the only mechanisms for achieving justice for victim-survivors of rape.

In Chapter 2, Haley Clark places the voices and experiences of victim-survivors of sexual violence front and centre in conceptualising the meanings of justice. Drawing on interviews with women and men, Clark develops an account of victim-survivors' justice needs, including acknowledgment and validation, perpetrator responsibility and accountability, and the role of retributive and punitive responses. Not only does Clark argue that there is a need for a reconsideration of criminal justice system processes in order to be more responsive to individual needs, but that ultimately, justice for many victim-survivors requires a broader social justice agenda. Clark's chapter contextualises the challenge which is a central theme underpinning this book: how to achieve justice for victim-survivors of sexual violence.

Understanding victim-survivors' justice needs also requires a widened understanding of what constitutes justice, and an illumination of the varied contexts in which sexual violence occurs. This is a key theme developed in Kathleen Daly's discussion (Chapter 3), where she elaborates on a number of confronting case studies to challenge us to move beyond stereotypical understandings of justice, redress, retribution and restoration, and to 'not assume there is one (or perhaps a handful) of desirable justice responses'. In the same way that feminists have challenged one form of rape ('real rape') and one form of victim (the 'ideal victim'), Daly argues that we should no longer accept one form of justice. In fact, she suggests we should challenge this very idea. An equally important point emerging from Daly's chapter is the need to focus on context. As she argues, 'context matters for justice'.

This theme of 'context matters' is an important one, and like the idea of moving beyond accepting one form of justice, it permeates the entire collection in relation to arguments around meanings of justice; formal and informal responses to sexual violence; and addressing victim-survivors' justice needs. Through a discussion of criminal law and legal reforms, Lise Gotell (Chapter 4) offers an important criticism of the existing critiques of 'carceral feminism'. Gotell argues that the debates around law reform need to return their focus to the best response for victims and move away from the highly flawed presumption that feminist critiques of rape law align with 'law and order' punitivism. Drawing from Canadian examples, Gotell argues that feminist calls for legal change have always focused on increasing recognition for victims, reducing the prevalence and acceptance of rape myths and providing fair treatment for complainants. Yet some scholars, as identified by Gotell, have fused advocating for victims' rights, with carceral justice. Gotell engages with a significant body of evidence to show there is a difference between punitivism and feminism, and suggests that feminists need to 'publicly disengage from the politics of punishment and to rearticulate...critiques of the law and order state'. Expanding from criminal conviction and carceral punishment as the key markers of 'justice', Gotell advocates for the success of rape law to be measured against victim-survivor outcomes and levels of satisfaction, including the extent to which the law actually reflects and responds to women's lived experiences of sexual violence.

The dominant critique of relying upon rape law to frame and attain justice is also present in James A. Roffee's chapter (Chapter 5), in which he argues that law does not 'cope well with shades of grey'. Drawing on examples of homosexuality, young people and incest, Roffee argues that the law's inability to act as an all-encompassing response to sexual violence presents challenges when it attempts to regulate those who practise non-traditional sexual scripts. Somewhat controversially, Roffee suggests that a response to this situation could involve the creation of offence levels (or some might argue, an offence hierarchy) for rape crimes. Roffee supports this argument by drawing on examples of sexual violence involving deception. While potentially having the effect of introducing a hierarchy of victimisation experiences which can reaffirm rape myths and prioritise 'real rape' above other experiences of sexual violence, Roffee contends that considering new ways of understanding consent in law, beyond what he deems an 'overly simplistic consent/non-consent binary', will go some way towards better recognising the individualised experiences of victim-survivors. In this way, Roffee engages with the 'context matters' theme, suggesting that clarifying levels of rape will assist the law in better recognising the varied contexts and situations in which sexual violence occurs.

In her analysis of innovative responses to sexual violence, Asher Flynn (Chapter 6) argues that the failings of conventional legal and prosecution processes have created an opportunity for the narratives around 'real rape' and carceral justice to be interrupted. In presenting examples of such opportunities, including shifts in rape awareness campaigns away from the actions of women victims to those of potential perpetrators, Flynn engages with two initiatives – specialist courts/prosecution units, and restorative justice models – to demonstrate a move away from a 'one size fits all' approach to justice. Supporting Daly's argument to challenge widespread acceptance of one form of justice, Flynn highlights the potential for further justice developments that operate within, alongside and beyond the criminal legal realm.

Expanding on ideas about context and moving beyond conventional measures of justice, Nikki Godden-Rasul (Chapter 7) considers how tort law can provide an alternate process for attaining justice beyond the criminal law, given its capacity to incorporate a procedure that considers the harms of rape and 'victim-survivor hopes for justice'. While acknowledging the potential limitations – primarily those associated with costs and the traditional favouring of male values in settlements – Godden uses case studies from the UK to demonstrate how social and legal responses continually fail to account for the diversity of women's lived experiences of rape; while tort law provides a way to individualise each case and thus recognise these individual experiences. In a similar vein to both Daly and Flynn, Godden argues that it is essential to look beyond the criminal law as the only form of justice.

The limitations of state-based criminal law to act as the sole remedy for sexual violence experiences are also explored by Ivana Radačić (Chapter 8), who considers the potential for international human rights laws, via the European Court of Human Rights, to assist victim-survivors where state-based mechanisms have failed. Radačić presents a compelling argument as to how international human rights law offers the potential to hold states accountable for failing victim-survivors in a way that does not appear to occur simply through state-based appeals courts. Engaging with several case studies, Radačić explores the efficacy of this additional form of official justice, suggesting that it provides a clear challenge to established rape myths, with the European Court openly criticising state justice systems for failing to prosecute cases that fall outside the 'real rape' setting. Additionally, Radačić highlights the potential for approaching sexual violence through a human rights lens to reconceptualise rape as a serious violation of human rights that exists in addition to a criminal violation, thereby recognising not only the physical and psychological damage, but also the damage to an individual's personal autonomy.

The politicisation of sexual violence is presented in Niels Nagelhus Schia and Benjamin de Carvalho's (Chapter 9) examination of sexual violence in Liberia, wherein they suggest responses to gendered and sexual violence in post-conflict societies often presume a prior functioning state, which is rarely reflective of the pre-conflict situation. Echoing Daly's argument that it is important not to accept all sexual violence as fitting into one form, Schia and de Carvalho similarly reiterate the importance of understanding context. In particular, they argue that in post-conflict settings, sexual and gender-based violence and wide tolerance of gender inequality must be dealt with in the building (or rebuilding) of legal, social and state institutions. Schia and de Carvalho present a thought-provoking discussion of the difficulties that can exist when multiple systems of justice attempt to work together. This discussion is framed around the development of a formal legal institution in Liberia that operates alongside a customary system of justice. While recognising some of the problems arising from these two models working in tandem, Schia and de Carvalho also suggest that customary responses can offer some guidance and advancements for traditional legal processes by engaging with restorative ideals that allow for 'less egregious types of rape' to be responded to in an official way. In this sense, there is a benefit (an argument presented in an entirely different geographical context in Flynn's chapter) to dual systems of justice working together to respond to sexual violence.

In their chapter examining conflict-related sexual violence and gender-based crimes, Sara Davies and Jacqui True (Chapter 10) embrace the 'context matters' theme more specifically, drawing attention to the importance of addressing gender inequality if any significant changes to social and legal responses to sexual violence are to take place. Informed by Sri Lankan experiences, Davies and True suggest that much research examining post-conflict responses to sexual violence has failed to adequately address a key issue: the need to examine, expose and redress serious levels of societal gender inequality, which is permitted and encouraged by the state in both conflict and post-conflict societies. Davies and True argue that focusing solely on sexual violence as a strategic weapon of war allows for the dark figure of these crimes to amplify, and ignores the very ways in which these crimes can be a political act; an act that 'successfully denies political representation and reparations post-conflict to those groups who are subject to these crimes'.

Following a similar argument to that presented by Davies and True, the importance of redressing gender inequality and the complex landscape of violence against women – structural, physical, political and state based – is a key argument in Rosemary Nagy's (Chapter 11) analysis of the violence committed against Indigenous Women in Canada. In highlighting the importance of context, Nagy demonstrates how gender-based violence intersects with other forms of oppression, and thus in considering how justice can be attained for sexual violence victim-survivors, the conversation must begin with substantive and holistic social changes that seek to challenge dominant narratives and beliefs that embrace gender bias and inequalities. Nagy's chapter thus develops a further key theme woven throughout many of the chapters in this book, arguing that justice must include recognition and redress for societal-level and institutionalised harms.

The capacity of alternative mechanisms to respond to victim-survivors' justice needs is a key theme emerging in Nicola Henry's (Chapter 12) analysis of civil society tribunals as a response to conflict-related sexual violence. Focusing on the Women's International War Crimes Tribunal on Japan's Military Sexual Slavery, Henry challenges us to consider the aims and purposes of transitional justice in post-atrocity contexts, noting the importance of acknowledging misrecognition as an injustice experienced by victim-survivors. In highlighting the potentials and limitations of civil society tribunals, the importance of context and the acknowledgement of broader gendered inequalities, Henry argues that while having some significant shortcomings, civil society tribunals have the potential to recognise the individual and collective experiences of victim-survivors in a public forum, as well as addressing the needs of redistribution and representation. She argues, however, that civil society war crimes tribunals mirror that of conventional international criminal courts because legal redress in the form of individual criminal responsibility is presented as the dominant, if not sole, remedy to past historical wrongdoings. As such, civil society tribunals can tend to gloss over structural causes, redistribution efforts and representations that are capable of capturing the intersectionality of disadvantage, violence and oppression.

Finally, while Clark's chapter opened this book with a discussion of justice in conventional legal settings, Anastasia Powell (Chapter 13) examines online activism and vigilantism as potential mechanisms for victim-survivors to access *informal* justice outside of the state. Powell explores examples where state-based legal systems and alternative legal avenues (such as college-based rape investigations) have failed; and where victim-survivors choose not to engage in the formal system, but rather elect to seek an alternative mode of justice through online forms of truth-telling. Like Daly and Gotell, Powell suggests that justice cannot be defined only through formal court measures, and in the wake of emerging technologies, there exists the potential for new forms of online, informal justice mechanisms to present an avenue for the justice needs of victim-survivors – specifically the needs of participation, voice, recognition and validation – to be met.

Conclusion

Responding to sexual violence through mechanisms that recognise the harms, hold perpetrators to account and restore dignity to victim-survivors is fundamental to the attainment and achievement of justice.

Sadly, as the chapters in this collection attest, there are enormous justice gaps in both formal and informal responses to sexual violence. Victim-survivors of rape are too often met with silence, disbelief, scepticism and critique. Rarely are perpetrators held to account for their behaviour and victims frequently remain the targets of social censure, shame and stigma.

This book was conceived in order to capture the fascinating emergence of new justice initiatives in response to both the harms of sexual violence, and the continual failings of the criminal justice system to respond to such harms. While it seeks to challenge the domination of criminal law in the imaginative space of justice, collectively we are not advocating the abandonment of law. Rather, the collection as a whole offers a critique of existing configurations of justice both within and beyond the criminal law. A common theme is the need to widen understandings of what constitutes justice, and to widen perceptions of the contexts in which sexual violence occurs. The collection thus advocates a radical rethinking of justice through such questions as 'How is justice done? What justice do we owe others? And what does it mean to act in the name of justice?' (Butler, 2004).

References

Brown, W. (1995) *States of Injury: Power and Freedom in Late Modernity* (Princeton, NJ: Princeton University Press).

Brownmiller, S. (1975) *Against Our Will: Men, Women and Rape* (New York: Bantam Books).

Buchwald, E., Fletcher, P. R. and Roth, M. (eds.) (2005) *Transforming a Rape Culture* (revised edition) (Minneapolis, MA: Milkweed Editions).

Butler, J. (2004) 'Jacques Derrida: Commemorating "One of the Greatest Philosophers of the 20th Century"', *London Review of Books,* 26(21), 4 November; retrieved from http://www.lrb.co.uk/v26/n21/judith-butler/jacques-derrida

Cahn, E. N. (1964) *The Sense of Injustice* (Bloomington, IA: Indiana University Press).

Daly, K. (2011) 'Conventional and Innovative Justice Responses to Sexual Violence', *ACSSA Issues,* 12 (Melbourne: Australian Institute of Family Studies), 1–35.

Derrida, J. (1990) 'Force of Law: The "Mystical Foundation of Authority"', *Cardozo Law Review*, 11, 919–1045.

Douzinas, C., Goodrich, P. and Hachamovitch, Y. (eds.) (1994) *Politics, Postmodernity, and Critical Legal Studies: The Legality of the Contingent* (London; New York: Routledge).

Durkheim, E. (1893/1972) 'Forms of Social Solidarity', in A. Giddens (ed.) *Emile Durkheim: Selected Writings* (Cambridge: Cambridge University Press), pp. 119–136.

Estrich, S. (1987) *Real Rape: How the Legal System Victimizes Women Who Say No* (Cambridge, MA: Harvard University Press).
Finley, L. M. (1989) 'Breaking Women's Silence in Law: The Dilemma of the Gendered Nature of Legal Reasoning', *Notre Dame Law Review*, 64(5), 886–910.
Fraser, N. (1998) 'Social Justice in the Age of Identity Politics: Redistribution, Recognition and Participation', in G. Peterson (ed.) *The Tanner Lectures on Human Values XIX* (Salt Lake City: University of Utah Press), 1–67.
Garland, D. (1990) *Punishment and Modern Society: A Study in Social Theory* (Oxford: Clarendon).
Gavey, N. and Schmidt, J. (2011) ' "Trauma of Rape" Discourse: A Double-Edged Template for Everyday Understandings of the Impact of Rape?', *Violence Against Women*, 17(4), 433–456.
Halley, J. (2008) 'Rape in Berlin: Reconsidering the Criminalisation of Rape in the International Law of Armed Conflict', *Melbourne Journal of International Law*, 9, 78–124.
Heenan, M. and Murray, S. (2006) *Study of Reported Rapes in Victoria 2000–2003: Summary Research Report* (Melbourne: Office of Women's Policy, Department for Victorian Communities).
Henry, N. (2011) *War and Rape: Law, Memory and Justice* (London; New York: Routledge).
Henry, N. (2014) 'The Fixation on Wartime Rape: Feminist Critique and International Criminal Law', *Social & Legal Studies*, 23(1), 93–111.
Herman, J. L. (2005) 'Justice from the Victim's Perspective', *Violence Against Women,* 11(5), 571–602.
Horvath, M. A. H. and Brown, J. M. (eds.) (2009) *Rape: Challenging Contemporary Thinking* (Portland, OR: Willan Publishing).
Kelly, L. (1987) 'The Continuum of Sexual Violence', in J. Hanmer and M. Maynard (eds.) *Women, Violence and Social Control* (London: Macmillan Press), pp. 46–60.
Koss, M. (2010) 'Restorative Justice for Acquaintance Rape and Misdemeanor Sex Crimes', in J. Ptacek (ed.) *Restorative Justice and Violence Against Women* (New York: Oxford University Press), pp. 218–238.
Larcombe, W. (2011) 'Falling Rape Conviction Rates: (Some) Feminist Aims and Measures for Rape Law', *Feminist Legal Studies*, 19(1), 27–45.
Larcombe, W. (2014) 'Limits of the Criminal Law for Preventing Sexual Violence', in N. Henry and A. Powell (eds.) *Preventing Sexual Violence: Interdisciplinary Approaches to Overcoming a Rape Culture* (Basingstoke: Palgrave Macmillan), pp. 64–83.
Lewis, R., Dobash, R. E., Dobash, R. P. and Cavanagh, K. (2001) 'Law's Progressive Potential: The Value of Engagement with the Law for Domestic Violence', *Social & Legal Studies*, 10(1), 105–130.
Lynch, K. R., Wasarhaley, N. E., Golding, J. M. and Simcic, T. (2013) ' "Who Bought the Drinks?" Juror Perceptions of Intoxication in a Rape Trial', *Journal of Interpersonal Violence*, 28(16), 3205–3222.
Madigan, L. and Gamble, N. C. (1989) *The Second Rape: Society's Continued Betrayal of the Victim* (New York: Lexington Books).
Marcus, S. (1992) 'Fighting Bodies, Fighting Words: A Theory and Politics of Rape Prevention', in J. Butler and J. Scott (eds.) *Feminists Theorize the Political* (London; New York: Routledge), pp. 385–403.

Mardorossian, C. M. (2002) 'Toward a New Feminist Theory of Rape', *Signs*, 27(3), 743–775.
Martel, J. (2011) 'Waiting for Justice: Benjamin and Derrida on Sovereignty and Immanence', *Republics of Letters: A Journal for the Study of Knowledge, Politics, and the Arts*, 2(2), 158–172.
McGlynn, C. (2011) 'Feminism, Rape and the Search for Justice', *Oxford Journal of Legal Studies*, 31(4), 825–842.
McGlynn, C. and Munro, V. (eds.) (2010) *Rethinking Rape Law: International and Comparative Responses* (Abingdon, UK; New York: Routledge).
McGlynn, C., Westmarland, N. and Godden, N. (2012) '"I Just Wanted Him to Hear Me": Sexual Violence and the Possibilities of Restorative Justice', *Journal of Law and Society*, 39(2), 213–240.
Murray, S. and Powell, A. (2011) *Domestic Violence: Australian Public Policy* (Melbourne: Australian Scholarly Publishing).
Naylor, B. (2010) 'Effective Justice for Victims of Sexual Assault: Taking Up the Debate on Alternative Pathways', *University of New South Wales Law Journal*, 33(2), 662–684.
Powell, A. (2015) 'Seeking Rape Justice: Formal and Informal Responses to Sexual Violence Through Technosocial Counterpublics', *Theoretical Criminology*, Online First, 1–18.
Powell, A. and Henry, N. (2014) 'Framing Sexual Violence Prevention', in N. Henry and A. Powell (eds.) *Preventing Sexual Violence: Interdisciplinary Approaches to Overcoming a Rape Culture* (Basingstoke: Palgrave Macmillan), pp. 1–21.
Rawls, J. (1976) *A Theory of Justice* (London: Oxford University Press).
Rentschler, C. A. (2014) 'Rape Culture and the Feminist Politics of Social Media', *Girlhood Studies*, 7(1), 65–82.
Richardson, D. and Campbell, J. L. (1982) 'Alcohol and Rape: The Effect of Alcohol on Attributions of Blame for Rape', *Personality and Social Psychology Bulletin*, 8, 468–476.
Rowland, J. (1985) *The Ultimate Violation* (New York: Doubleday).
Sharratt, S. and Kaschak, E. (eds.) (2013) *Assault on the Soul: Women in the Former Yugoslavia* (New York: Routledge).
Stubbs, J. (2003) 'Sexual Assault, Criminal Justice and Law and Order', *Women Against Violence*, 14, 14–26.
Tempkin, J. and Krahé, B. (2008) *Sexual Assault and the Justice Gap: A Question of Attitude* (Oxford; Portland, OR: Hart Publishing).
Westmarland, N. and Gangoli, G. (eds.) (2011) *International Approaches to Rape* (Bristol, UK; Portland, OR: Policy Press).
Williams, L. S. (1984) 'The Classic Rape: When do Victims Report?', *Social Problems*, 31(4), 459–467.
World Health Organization (WHO) (2011) *Violence Against Women – Intimate Partner and Sexual Violence Against Women* (Geneva: World Health Organization).

2
A Fair Way to Go
Justice for Victim-Survivors of Sexual Violence

Haley Clark

Introduction

Internationally, there is increasing emphasis on responding to the needs of victim-survivors of sexual assault (and crime victims more broadly). This has been demonstrated through a myriad of procedural and substantive law reforms that have been introduced over the past 40 years, and through sustained government investment in offering justice and safety for victims and the community. Judgements as to whether the criminal justice system has provided 'justice' and 'fairness' for those who have experienced sexual violence have largely relied on predefined notions contained within existing frameworks of criminal justice. For example, the effectiveness of criminal justice systems in handling cases of sexual violence often relies on data about attrition and conviction rates, the impact of the process of victim-witnesses and sentencing outcomes, rather than the conceptualisation of justice (e.g. VLRC, 2001, 2004). Research in this area has found that decades of reform efforts have not translated into significant change at an operational level. Reporting and conviction rates remain low (ABS, 2003; AIC, 2005; Daly & Bouhours, 2010; Lievore, 2003; Mouzos & Makkai, 2004), and victim-survivors continue to report experiencing the justice system's procedures, particularly the trial, as re-traumatising and re-victimising (Heath, 2005; Koss & Achilles, 2008; Orth & Maercker, 2004; Taylor, 2004).

These aspects provide measures against which to discern whether the criminal justice system is delivering what it purports to achieve; however, they do not challenge the system's purposes and processes.

Ascertaining victim-survivors' perspectives of justice provides important learnings for criminal justice policy and practice direction, because it centralises the understandings of the concept of justice from the perspectives of those seeking legal remedy. This provides a pathway for debates about the effectiveness of the legal system to move beyond preconceived frameworks about what it means to seek 'justice', and provides greater scope within which to consider non-legal alternatives.

This chapter considers how justice is understood by victim-survivors of sexual violence. The chapter draws on excerpts in victim-survivors' own words, highlighting the importance conceptually and politically of placing the voices, narratives and experiences of victim-survivors first and foremost. These excerpts and the discussion that follows are derived from interviews conducted in Victoria (Australia) in 2009–2010, with 18 women and four men who had experienced sexual violence. In the next section, I will discuss the relevance of system responses in providing justice for victim-survivors before considering key aspects underlying victim-survivors' understandings of justice. These aspects include the crucial need for acknowledgement and validation in responding to victim-survivors, the desire for perpetrator responsibility and accountability, the role of retributive and punitive responses, and the relevance of a broader commitment to safety and prevention. I conclude that privileging the knowledge and insights of victim-survivors enables more robust understandings of justice to emerge and opens new possibilities to strengthen responses to sexual violence. This involves the need to be responsive to individual needs, reconsidering system procedures, and connecting with a wider social justice agenda.

Justice and system responses

Women and men who were interviewed in this study generally situated the criminal justice system as the primary setting for justice in response to sexual offences. As one participant, Mandy, pointed out, '[i]t's very hard to think outside the system when the system is what you've got'. This may not be surprising given the status that the criminal justice system is afforded in contemporary Australian society (and internationally). As Dasgupta (2003, p. 15) has argued: '[a]t this point, the criminal justice system's presence is so woven into the fabric of society that most of us cannot envision what society would look like otherwise'. Munro (2001, 2007) has also noted that legal power extends beyond the legal system and into various other domains of social life. She argues that legal discourse impacts on various forms of social activity and other institutional responses (Munro, 2007). The power and influence of the legal system was clear in the way participants constructed understandings of 'justice' and the institutions that should be responsible for responding to sexual violence.

Notions of conventional criminal justice and the options provided by the justice system did not, however, align with the needs or values of nearly all participants. The criminal justice system was considered to be largely disconnected from the victim-survivors' justice needs and its procedures far removed from their ideals of justice. Participants all described the system in negative terms: as 're-victimising', 'threatening', 'bludgeoning', 'a game about winning and losing' and 'certainly not about justice'. Participants' understandings and experiences of the system clearly contradicted the capacity they believed it ought to have in delivering justice.

Participants were confronted with a range of philosophical and ethical dilemmas relating to the idea of achieving justice through the criminal justice system. This included challenges to their anti-violence values, their perceptions of institutions and the impact of proceedings on their families. Many participants reiterated that individual justice in an absolute sense, as they understood it, could never really be achieved. They emphasised that any attempt at redress would ultimately fall short: nothing could undo what had been done to them and no process would be able to fully compensate for the crimes. As such, a system response was limited to providing symbolic gestures of 'justice' rather than as definitive form.

> If you think of justice as a re-writing of wrongs, you can never undo the abuse so there can never be [adequate] compensation or recourse or addressing of the wrongs in any form. It can never undo the injustice or the wrongdoing. So any form of justice that exists is an approximation, it's the best or the closest you can come to acknowledging the depth of damage from the original wrongdoing.
>
> Hannah

Hannah's reflections reiterate the subjective nature of the concept of 'justice'. She makes a significant point in distinguishing what justice means and the limits to its translation into practice. Nonetheless, being provided with an avenue to achieve, to draw from Hannah's words, an 'approximate' form of justice through a formal system response was considered important by all victim-survivors in the study.

Participants' understanding of justice was not static but rather changed, developed and evolved along with their healing, philosophising about justice and resource needs. Some observed a shift away from desiring harsh penalties to seeking fairer consequences. Some began to prioritise personal growth over a system response, while others became involved in advocacy, or participated in political agendas to challenge the constraints of the legal system. The meaning of 'justice' differed considerably according to individual participants. For some, justice involved acknowledgment and validation, while others sought perpetrator accountability or retribution; for others, community safety was their primary justice goal.

Acknowledgement and validation

While there have been a range of attempts to respond to victims' needs within the criminal justice system, particularly since the 1980s, the personal experiences and impacts of the crimes on individual victim-survivors is not the central focus of the criminal justice system. Participants in this study, in line with past research (Herman, 2005; Koss, 2006), were shocked and concerned when they realised that their interests were not a priority to the system and that they lacked control over critical decisions including whether and how their case was pursued.

> You know I'm a person being violated in, I would say, one of the worst ways a person could be violated, and I get this little letter to say sorry it's not really important. For the criminal justice system to say, 'Well it's not worth our pursuing' that's the bit that's been the hardest. Apart from the abuse itself, that part has been really hard. It almost felt like being abused again.
>
> Penny

> I was told that it was not in the public's best interest to proceed...I thought that was bizarre as well because I thought, when is it in the public's interest to proceed? It's an interesting notion, I think, to use.
>
> Sarah

As demonstrated in Penny and Sarah's comments, decisions about pursuing cases highlighted the disjuncture between the legal system's operation and their status as an individual that had been victimised. Sarah was sexually assaulted by a general medical practitioner later identified by authorities as offending against a number of his patients, which further added to her frustration that her victimisation was not considered in the 'public's interest' to proceed.

Sexual offences are processed by the criminal justice system as harms against the state, not against individual victim-survivors. As such, the state is represented as the adversary of the defendant in a criminal trial. In the system, victim-survivors are witnesses rather than clients, and complainants rather than victims. In referring to the position of victims in the justice system, as McBarnet (1983, p. 300) bluntly states: '[i]f victims feel that nobody cares about their suffering, it is in part because *institutionally* nobody does...' (original emphasis). Displacement within the system undermines the acknowledgement participants seek as victims of crime. This raises concerns about the need to ensure that victims' experiences of crime remain with them and are not appropriated by state institutions (Christie, 2010, p. 116). Such a position challenges the depersonalisation of conflicts that come with state-controlled interventions to crime, and instead reiterates the need to keep individual victim-survivors' experiences central to response processes.

Victim-survivors interpreted the progress and outcome of their case as reflecting judgements about their credibility and worth, whether the crimes were considered serious by the authorities, and the state's investment in responding to sexual offences. Kane, for instance, concluded that the system saw him as a 'nobody with a mental illness' and Josie noted that she 'was kind of the ideal victim so in that sense the police did everything that they could'. Participants' feelings of being personally judged or discredited are supported by past research which has associated the progression of sexual violence cases through the system with belief, credibility, stereotypical attributes and evidence (Heenan & Murray, 2006; Jordan, 2004a, 2004b; Lievore, 2004, 2005). These findings reflect the procedural inadequacies in achieving 'just' outcomes for victim-survivors of sexual violence, and the unfair distribution of cases (and of the victims and perpetrators) that proceed, against those that do not. Not pursuing cases considered likely to result in successful prosecution adds further to the harm of victim-survivors who perceive the system is treating them as less credible people and less worthy of a response. This ultimately reinforces the injustice faced by victim-survivors.

Nonetheless, in ascertaining acknowledgement of the crimes, the status of the criminal justice system in carrying a state sanction had currency for participants.

> At least idealistically or theoretically at the moment there is very much a sense that this is much bigger than just me and my father, and it's quite validating to have the people that our country nominates as those who enforce the law on my side and chanting my cause and paying for it.
>
> Hannah

> To me, [the legal system saying it was wrong] is really important because it sort of assists me with my community that acknowledges that what I experienced was wrong and that it had an enormous impact on me and on my family and, you know, on everybody in my whole social network.
>
> Penny

In these comments, Hannah and Penny both identified the importance of the broader political rhetoric of reporting sexual violence to the criminal justice system. Beyond individual validation, they saw the criminal justice system playing an active and instrumental role in reiterating societal concern and in denouncing the crimes to the offender, their families and wider social networks. Hannah demonstrates the power of the criminal justice system that is often absent in other forms of redress: the power of state representation and, in cases resulting in conviction, of state condemnation of the offending conduct. Hudson (1998, p. 245) supports this position, proposing that in censoring or 'moral-boundary-declaring', the criminal law can serve to demonstrate that the official organisation of society, and therefore society in general, disapproves of sexual violence.

Victim-survivors consistently emphasised that system responses should validate their experiences. They wanted an official acknowledgment that the crime occurred and that it had a profound impact on their life.

> I was pretty upset about that, I really wanted to have the criminal justice system acknowledge that the crime had been committed and the enormous impact that it had on my life. I didn't want the perpetrator to go to jail or anything like that, I just wanted an acknowledgment or *something*, but I didn't get it so I felt pretty ripped off.
>
> Brenda

> So, understanding, acknowledgment of not just the abuse, 'cause that was acknowledged in my case, but of the damage that it

> caused. And then support and nurture during that time, rather than abandonment and rejection, which is what I got.
>
> Carmen

> The focus in the legal system is on events that happened. He did this on this day to me. Whereas there wasn't much focus on the actual impact... But the impact that it's had on the victim and everyone else is enormous. I think there needs to be more consideration taken about that.
>
> Penny

As demonstrated in the comments of Brenda, Carmen and Penny, victim-survivors want the system to recognise and respond to the impacts of the assaults rather than primarily concentrate on gathering evidence or question their experience. The criminal justice system provides little space for the impact and nature of sexual violence to be considered, let alone captured; and the reality of the offence is decontextualised, misconstrued, discarded and replaced by legal versions of facts and truths (Breckenridge, 1999).

A limited number of victim-survivors in this study felt acknowledged and validated through the justice system, but for most, the reverse was the case – that is, they received messages that the offence was not serious or significant, that belief in their story was questioned and that the offender could get away with the crimes. These messages were received through not contacting or charging the perpetrator, not establishing a conviction, or by handing down a sentence that was perceived by the victim-survivor as lenient. Moreover, the exclusionary nature of the system, its focus on the defence and absence of formal mechanisms to validate individuals' experiences, obstructed victim-survivors from gaining a profoundly meaningful interaction.

Accountability and responsibility

According to participants, perpetrator accountability and responsibility were key aspects in facilitating justice through formal mechanisms – they were considered necessary for acknowledging the specific crimes and for engaging the offender in the consequences. Yet all victim-survivors experienced some level of denial or minimisation of the assaults by perpetrators. They also found that the system procedures were at odds with promoting perpetrator accountability and responsibility. Participants believed that the justice system ought to play an active role in holding perpetrators to account for the crimes they had committed.

> I guess it [justice] would be going to court and making him accountable for what he's done would be the justice.
>
> Olivia

> Then hopefully go through a program and realise the consequences and go, 'right I fucking do deserve to do jail time for what I've done', you know, and realise what they've done and realise how much they've fucked up people's lives.
>
> Lance

> I would really want him to get counselling and for him to admit that yes, he's a mongrel and he does these things and he needs help, so that's an important process for me – for him to admit that yes, he did do things and it's not right and 'yes I need help'.
>
> Brenda

Despite the desire for the perpetrator to make an admission and take accountability that has been expressed by the participants above, most victim-survivors in this study felt that their perpetrator required substantial assistance to admit fully to their crimes. This is supported by research that shows sexual offenders are reluctant to take full personal responsibility for their offending (Boyd, 2006; Chung et al., 2006). Instead, as evidenced in Brenda's comments above, participants believed that responsibility-taking could be facilitated by incorporating counselling and education for the perpetrator into standard legal responses.

Participants in this study found that even when their perpetrators pleaded or were otherwise found guilty, they were still not forced to take responsibility for their behaviour by the system. Indeed, victim-survivors observed that perpetrators avoided a level of responsibility even post-conviction, for example at the sentencing stage.

> One of the things I found somewhat unsatisfying in recent times was, um, how in sentencing this person, the picture that was painted of this poor pathetic man who had had a hard life and all that, and how that's taken into account in sentencing. And yet there'd been such denial of what he'd done for so long, till the last minute, and I just thought there was a contradiction there.
>
> Sarah

> Yeah, I don't know, they gave him six months because of the time that he did it and the time now and that he hasn't been re-caught and to me, so he hasn't been caught because of either luck, who knows if he did or he didn't do it. To me once is enough. Oh there's not a pattern here. So what? That hurt me. If anything I had to say bad about the day where he was sentenced it was, yeah you haven't done it to anyone else so we'll just give you six months.
>
> Evan

Evan and Sarah emphasised that the perpetrators were able to avoid full responsibility for their offending during sentencing despite pleading guilty to having sexually offended against them. Perpetrators are provided an opportunity to evade responsibility through legislation and criminal justice processes – to deny offences, minimise through plea bargaining, to remain silent and to introduce mitigating factors for sentencing (see Flynn, 2012). Where settlements are reached or a guilty verdict made, legal processes virtually universally exclude any acknowledgement of wrongdoing by the offender (Bublick, 2006; Des Rosiers et al., 1998; Herman, 2005; Koss, 2006). The system-driven denial impeded on victim-survivors' need to have the full extent and veracity of the crimes acknowledged by the criminal justice system.

Further to failing to hold offenders to account, there is a long-standing tradition of victim-blaming in cases of sexual violence – both socially and institutionally. Socially, women are blamed for their own sexual violence, often that they somehow deserved or provoked the offence; for example, by focusing on what she wore, where she was or how much she drank. At the institutional level, victim-blaming has been evident in judicial, legal and police responses to victims of sexual violence and family violence (Clark, 2007; Easteal, 1998; Henning & Bronnitt, 1998; Stewart & Maddren, 1997; Strang, 2004). Responses that indicate victim blame and responsibility have been associated with greater victim trauma (Flood & Pease, 2006) and lower likelihood of engaging in formal response systems (Strang, 2004). The participants' stories emphasised that there was a need to focus on the perpetrator's behaviour rather than to question their credibility and part in the offences.

Victim-survivors expressed the need for criminal justice system officials to make perpetrators answerable for their behaviour, and that the promotion of perpetrator accountability needed to be enforced from the outset of criminal justice system involvement. The police were identified by participants as playing a role in promoting accountability and denouncing the crimes.

> Hopefully it's put the fear of God into him that someone has finally stood up and spoke about it and that he'll be, you know he's had the police at his house and his name's on record and, yeah, hopefully that's enough to get him to stop doing it again.
>
> Kane

> ... In a lot of situations people don't even want someone to go to jail, they still have some concern because it's someone known to them or a family member or um but what they want is for the person to be held to account in some way. And even have the police knock on the door and question them about that for some people that is their aim in the whole process, or is the most valuable thing to them.
>
> Lesley

In this way, having the police make contact with the perpetrator was considered by participants to be in itself a punitive or deterrent experience. The use of the legal system was an active strategy to control and prevent further sexual offending by the perpetrators. Yet the effectiveness of police intervention as a deterrence from further sexual violence has not been demonstrated by research, and strengthening accountability and responsibility is limited within the present legal framework.

Promoting perpetrator accountability sets significant challenges to traditional adversarial processing of cases and legal philosophies which underpin the system (e.g. innocent until proven guilty). Given that the incidence of admissions from perpetrators and convictions is the lowest of any offence, at least in the Australian context (ABS, 2010), further consideration needs to be given to innovative strategies to overcome evidentiary burdens and that increase prosecution rates. This is supported by human rights and victim rights agendas that have imposed increasing pressure on the state to enhance responses to sexual violence (Radačić, Chapter 8; see also Flynn, Chapter 6). Greater consideration needs to be given to how to respond to contentions surrounding ways to encourage perpetrator accountability within due process. This may include developing more innovative approaches to legal procedures and rethinking the construction of fair and just procedures from not only the perspective of the accused but also of victim-survivors and of the community more broadly (Cossins, 2006a, 2006b).

Retribution

Many participants questioned the suitability of punishment as a response to their perpetrators, advocating instead for non-retributive responses. Seven participants sought retributive responses; they wanted their perpetrator to receive fair punitive consequences for the crimes. When advocating for retributive consequences for their perpetrators, victim-survivors in this study felt particularly vulnerable to criticism. They noted that it fed into public misconceptions that they were vengeful and/or deranged. The idea that victim-survivors would be excessively punitive is rarely questioned, yet research does not support the public perception that victim-survivors of sexual violence are particularly vengeful towards perpetrators compared with those who have not been victims (Herman, 2005; Lewis et al., 2000).

Participants who sought retribution assigned various meanings and purposes to it, including punishment as revenge, for the perpetrator to learn a lesson, and to inflict suffering.

> I just thought, no, we are gonna pursue this. He is not getting away with this and I am not just gonna let this go. I'm not just gonna write this off. I want consequences to this and I want him to be punished. There really are, or there should be, very drastic consequences for people who step outside that line.
>
> Danielle

> I think they do need to be punished. They need to know that they've done something wrong, that it isn't right and that this is the consequences... You know, if they're not getting punished for it, what's going to stop them?
>
> Anne

> I honestly would have liked to have seen him go to jail because, while it's impacted on him the fact that he's got no job, right, he's not really suffering because of it.
>
> Lucy

These understandings of criminal justice reflect retributivist values as outlined by Smilansky (2006, p. 513): in having committed sexual offences, the perpetrator has disobeyed the law (and seriously breached codes of moral conduct) and for doing so they deserve to receive just punishment in response. Participants expressed that sexual offences should be responded to proportionately to other crimes.

> It needs to be done on the same basis as it is for other crimes.
>
> Josie

> I guess they've committed a crime so it's about getting an adequate sentence. So in comparison to other crimes, so you know a murderer gets forever and a rapist gets nothing and they're out within a year or something. So the right sentence for the crime... Yeh, it's probably that the right sentence, the right time and the right kind of sentence, whether it's jail or whatever.
>
> Olivia

In this way, participants who sought punishment sought *fair* punishment, bringing forward principles of proportionality and just deserts, rather than a desire for excessively punitive sentences. Notions of retribution, desert-based responses and proportionality prevail in many criminal justice systems. These are reflected in the use of imprisonment and other punitive sanctions handed down to offenders by the courts, as well as sentencing legislation that gives precedence to providing the level of punishment that reflects the seriousness of the offending behaviour (Von Hirsch, 2007; Von Hirsch & Ashworth, 2005).

Participants who felt the perpetrator should be punished also expressed that imprisonment was the most appropriate response for the perpetrators.

> [They need to] realise that there are consequences of their actions, and if that means that they have to go to jail for six months or two years as long as they get this counselling, so be it.
>
> Lance

> Once it was finalised I found out that he had to go to jail and I remember feeling elated... I thought... he will be punished. He will be put away and his life will have repercussions because of this from now on. So yeah, there was some good in it.
>
> Danielle

These participants supported the use of imprisonment by the criminal justice system, and that the system provided, in theory at least, the possibility for achieving their primary justice goal: incarcerating the perpetrator. Many felt that the sentences handed down were inadequate, disproportionately lenient or mitigated by their perpetrator's 'good standing' and misconceptions about what constitutes 'real rape'. This sent messages to them that the crime was not as serious as other crimes, and that the gravity of the perpetrator's conduct was not as great as the conduct of perpetrators of other crimes.

Participants sought punitive consequences to send direct messages to the perpetrator that what they did 'is wrong', 'unacceptable', 'a crime' and to promote deterrence from future offending. Victim-survivors wanted the receipt of a punitive sentence to explicitly send these messages to perpetrators rather than responding with harm for no other purpose than to cause pain. This predicament faced by victim-survivors in this study is similarly reflected in theories of punishment. For example, Hudson (1998, p. 245) outlines punishment is simultaneously necessary to symbolise 'the state's authoritative disapproval of certain forms of behaviour and futile in its effects at controlling that behaviour', which Garland (1990, p. 80) has described as the 'tragic quality' of punishment. This emphasises the tensions between punishing wrongdoing and preventing further offending in contemporary criminal justice practice.

Safety and prevention

For a number of participants, individual justice was not a key priority; rather, these participants defined justice primarily in terms of eliciting a response from public authorities that demonstrated a commitment to prevent sexual offending and to prioritise community safety. Most often they engaged the system to identify a dangerous person to the authority for the protection of others.

> I kept quiet for 20 years so I wasn't so much after justice, I just wanted to protect others from him and that was my primary goal in going there.
>
> Justin

> You know, like, I really only just wanted them to know that there was a man out there with his problem and how they could protect other people.
>
> Felicity

> I wanted other people to be safe within the family. Any children that were born, like I felt a huge responsibility to keep them safe, anyone safe, because I knew what he was capable of and those that knew wouldn't do anything and other people didn't know.
>
> Carmel

These comments demonstrate that promoting theirs and others' safety through the prevention of further sexual offending was a high priority, and most participants believed that preventing sexual violence ought to be the state's concern and a function of the criminal justice system.

Several participants hoped that by reporting the crimes they could shift the individual burden of responsibility to a system with the power to respond with authority and resources.

> Yeah, so as far as justice is concerned, I didn't get any... but I did feel a great weight lift off my shoulders that I'd finally spoken up... I carried it all through my childhood and teenage years that I hadn't told anyone, therefore I'm responsible for any subsequent abuses that this man may have... perpetrated, but now at least this man's name is in the system and it'll get flagged.
>
> Kane

> We were kind of sitting on this information, if you like and that we weren't really protecting other people, because we knew that he was capable of doing that... I just kept saying to them, I can't live with this, knowing that he could possibly be doing to other people and haven't even let the authorities know.
>
> Felicity

Kane and Felicity's comments reflect how, by reporting the offences, they were able to transfer the responsibility to deal with the perpetrator from them to the state. Frustration continued when system authorities did not then lay charges, prosecute or convict the perpetrator, which sent messages to victim-survivors that there was a lack of investment in the safety of others.

While the criminal justice system can provide significant symbolic messages, its capacity to prevent sexual violence is limited (Carmody & Carrington, 2000; Stubbs, 2003). Some scholars have suggested moving away from criminal justice to better realise prevention efforts. Ptacek (2010, p. 6), for instance, argues that: '[f]eminists have raised many concerns in recent years about the limitations of the criminal legal system as a means of stopping violence against women. And a rich and growing feminist literature details how the state has co-opted antiviolence efforts'. In this way, Ptacek argues, too much reliance on the criminal justice system in sexual violence prevention efforts can detract from feminist visions of justice and the kinds of social actions that must be taken.

Stubbs (2003, p. 23) argues that criminal laws say much about our rights as citizens and must change to better reflect the experiences and aspirations of women. Stubbs emphasises that real changes in the level of sexual violence ultimately may be dependent upon significant changes in social values and understandings of gender and sexuality rather than the effectiveness of the criminal justice system. These sentiments have been put forward by Carmody and Carrington (2000), who have argued that an adequate approach to sexual violence prevention requires an understanding of women as sexually autonomous and the promotion of ethical sexual practices. Similarly, Dasgupta (2003, p. 19) advocates for governments to put effort into centralising responsibility for violence against women rather than putting efforts into criminal justice responses to deal with sexual (and other) violence:

> Rather than the narrow, punitive focus of criminal legal strategies, the idea that government must assume broader responsibility and accountability for guaranteeing the basic human, economic, civil, political, and cultural rights of all human beings, is a key theme for the 21st century. This is the next step in evolving our sophistication as a human race to secure safety and justice for all.

These arguments emphasise that the criminal justice system is recognised as forming only one avenue in responding to sexual violence and, in order to make significant steps towards justice and prevention, wider social changes about gender, sexuality and equality need to be realised. Participants in this study prioritised prevention and, for this to be achieved, there is a need to address societal conditions that promote sexual violence alongside attempts to improve the criminal justice system's responses to sexual offending.

Conclusion

The meaning of justice had considerable variation for the participants in this study, and a range of developments that rise above these differences is necessary in order to deliver justice to victim-survivors of sexual violence. What is required is the development of responses that strengthen the position of victim-survivors and evolve notions of justice in ways that are constructive and beneficial to individuals and that are conducive to a society that works to respond to sexual violence and to deliver justice. Subscribing to the criminal justice system's interpretation of justice risks prefacing universalised legal preferences over meaningful responses to those affected by sexual violence. Reforms and initiatives must address both individual needs within the system's procedures and connect with a wider social justice agenda. This includes challenging conventional understandings of justice, addressing system and social structures that reinforce victim-survivors' disempowered positions, and applying innovative procedures to overcome key barriers in addressing sexual offences. Doing so establishes an accessible reform agenda that embraces victim-survivors' contributions and provides new possibilities to responding to sexual violence.

References

ABS [Australian Bureau of Statistics] (2003) *Reporting Crime to Police: Crime and Facts Information* (No. 58) (Canberra, Australia: Australian Government Publishing Service).

ABS [Australian Bureau of Statistics] (2004) *Sexual Assault in Australia: A Statistical Overview* (Canberra, Australia: Australian Government Publishing Service).

ABS [Australian Bureau of Statistics] (2006) *Personal Safety Survey* (Canberra, Australia: Australian Government Publishing Service).

ABS [Australian Bureau of Statistics] (2010) *Criminal Courts, Australia* (Cat. no. 4513.0) (Canberra, Australia: Australian Government Publishing Service).

AIC [Australian Institute of Criminology] (2005) *Trends in Recorded Sexual Assault: Crime and Facts Information* (Cat. No. 105) (Canberra, Australia: Australian Government Publishing Service).

Boyd, C. (2006) 'Young People Who Sexually Abuse: Key Issues', *ACSSA Wrap* (No. 5) (Melbourne, Australia: Australian Institute of Family Studies).

Breckenridge, J. (1999) 'Subjugation and Silences: The Role of the Professions in Silencing Victims of Sexual and Domestic Violence', in J. Breckenridge and L. Laing (eds.) *Challenging Silence: Innovative Responses to Sexual and Domestic Violence* (St Leonards, Australia: Allen & Unwin), pp. 6–30.

Bublick, E. M. (2006) 'Tort Suits Filed by Rape and Sexual Assault Victims in Civil Courts: Lessons for Courts, Classrooms and Constituencies', *Southern Methodist University Law Review*, 59, 55–122.

Carmody, M. and Carrington, K. (2000) 'Preventing Sexual Violence?', *Australian and New Zealand Journal of Criminology*, 33(3 December), 341–361.

Christie, N. (2010) 'Victim Movements at a Crossroad', *Punishment & Society*, 12(2), 115–122.

Chung, D., O'Leary, P. J. and Hand, T. (2006) 'Sexual Violence Offenders', *ACSSA Issues Paper* (No. 5) (Melbourne, Australia: Australian Institute of Family Studies).

Clark, H. (2007) 'Judging Rape: Public Attitudes and Sentencing', *ACSSA Aware*, 14, 17–25 (Melbourne, Australia: Australian Institute of Family Studies).

Cossins, A. (2006a) 'Prosecuting Child Sexual Assault Cases: Are Vulnerable Witness Protections Enough?', *Current Issues in Criminal Justice*, 18, 299–317.

Cossins, A. (2006b) 'Prosecuting Child Sexual Assault Cases: To Specialise or Not, That is the Question', *Current Issues in Criminal Justice*, 18, 318–342.

Daly, K. and Bouhours, B. (2010) 'Rape and Attrition in the Legal Process: A Comparative Analysis of Five Countries', *Crime and Justice*, 39(1), 565–650.

Daly, K. and Stubbs, J. (2006) 'Feminist Engagement with Restorative Justice', *Theoretical Criminology*, 10(1), 9–28.

Dasgupta, S. D. (2003) *Safety and Justice for All: Examining the Relationship between the Women's Anti-Violence Movement and the Criminal Legal System* (New York: Ms. Foundation).

Des Rosiers, N., Feldthusen, B. and Hankivsky, O. A. R. (1998) 'Legal Compensation for Sexual Violence: Therapeutic Consequences and Consequences for the Judicial System', *Psychology, Public Policy & Law*, 4, 433–451.

Easteal, P. (1998) 'Beyond Balancing', in P. Easteal (ed.) *Balancing the Scales: Rape, Law Reform and Australian Culture* (Sydney, Australia: The Federation Press), pp. 203–220.

Flood, M. and Pease, B. (2006) *The Factors Influencing Community Attitudes in Relation to Violence Against Women: A Critical Review of the Literature* (Melbourne, Australia: Victorian Health Promotion Foundation).

Flynn, A. (2012) 'Bargaining with Justice: Victims, Plea Bargaining and the *Victims' Charter Act 2006* (Vic)', *Monash University Law Review*, 32(3), 73–96.

Garland, D. (1990) *Punishment and Modern Society: A Study in Social Theory* (Oxford: Clarendon Press).

Heath, M. A. (2005) 'The Law and Sexual Offences Against Adults in Australia', *ACSSA Issues Paper* (No. 4) (Melbourne, Australia: Australian Institute of Family Studies).

Heath, M. A. (2007) 'Lack of Conviction: A Proposal to Make Rape Illegal in South Australia', *The Australian Feminist Law Journal*, 27, 175–192.

Heenan, M. and Murray, S. (2006) *Study of Reported Rapes in Victoria 2000–2003: Summary Research Report* (Melbourne, Australia: Office for Women's Policy).

Henning, T. and Bronnitt, S. (1998) 'Rape Victims on Trial: Regulating the Use and Abuse of Sexual History Evidence', in P. Easteal (ed.) *Balancing the Scales: Rape, Law Reform and Australian Culture* (Sydney, Australia: Federation Press), pp. 76–93.

Herman, J. L. (2005) 'Justice from the Victim's Perspective', *Violence Against Women*, 11(5), 571–602.

Hudson, B. (1998) 'Restorative Justice: The Challenge of Sexual and Racial Violence', *Journal of Law and Society*, 25(2), 237–256.

Jordan, J. (2004a) 'Beyond Belief? Police, Rape and Women's Credibility', *Criminal Justice*, 4, 29–59.

Jordan, J. (2004b) *The Word of a Woman? Police, Rape and Belief* (Hampshire, UK: Palgrave MacMillan).

Koss, M. P. (2006) 'Restoring Rape Survivors: Justice, Advocacy, and a Call to Action', *Annals of the New York Academy of Sciences*, 1087, 206–234.

Koss, M. P. and Achilles, M. (2008) *Restorative Justice Responses to Sexual Assault* (VAWnet: The National Online Resource Center on Violence Against Women).

Lewis, R., Dobash, R. P., Dobash, R. E. and Cavanagh, K. (2000) 'Protection, Prevention, Rehabilitation or Justice? Women's Use of the Law to Challenge Domestic Violence', *International Review of Victimology*, 7(1–3), 179–205.

Lievore, D. (2003) *Non-Reporting and Hidden Recording of Sexual Assault: An International Literature Review* (Canberra, Australia: Office of the Status of Women).

Lievore, D. (2004) 'Victim Credibility in Adult Sexual Assault Cases', *Trends and Issues in Crime and Criminal Justice* (No. 288) (Canberra, Australia: Australian Institute of Criminology).

Lievore, D. (2005) 'Prosecutorial Decisions in Adult Sexual Assault Cases', *Trends and Issues in Crime and Criminal Justice* (No. 291) (January) (Canberra, Australia: Australian Institute of Criminology).

McBarnet, D. (1983) 'Victim in the Witness Box: Confronting Victimology's Stereotype', *Contemporary Crises*, 7(3), 279–303.

Mouzos, J. and Makkai, T. (2004) *Women's Experience of Male Violence: Findings from the Australian Component of the International Violence against Women Survey* (Canberra, Australia: Australian Institute of Criminology).

Munro, V. E. (2001) 'Legal Feminism and Foucault – A Critique of the Expulsion of Law', *Journal of Law and Society*, 28(4), 546–567.

Munro, V. E. (2007) *Law and Politics at the Perimeter: Re-Evaluating Key Debates in Feminist Theory. Legal Theory Today Series* (North America: Hartland Publishing).

Orth, U. (2002) 'Secondary Victimization of Crime Victims by Criminal Proceedings', *Social Justice Research*, 15(4), 313–325.

Orth, U. and Maercker, A. (2004, February) 'Do Trials of Perpetrators Retraumatize Crime Victims?', *Journal of Interpersonal Violence*, 19, 212–227.

Ptacek, J. (2010) 'Resisting Co-Optation: Three Feminist Challenges to Antiviolence Work', in J. Ptacek (ed.) *Restorative Justice and Violence against Women* (Oxford: University Press), pp. 5–78.

Sanday, P. R. (1996) *A Woman Scorned: Acquaintance Rape on Trial* (New York: Doubleday).

Smilansky, S. (2006) 'Control, Desert and the Difference between Distributive and Retributive Justice', *Philosophical Studies*, 131(3), 511–524.

Stewart, A. and Maddren, K. (1997) 'Police Officers' Judgements of Blame in Family Violence: The Impact of Gender and Alcohol', *Sex Roles*, 37(11/12), 921–933.

Strang, H. (2004) 'Is Restorative Justice Imposing its Agenda on Victims?', in H. Zehr and B. Toews (eds.) *Critical Issues in Restorative Justice* (New York: Criminal Justice Press), pp. 95–106.

Stubbs, J. (2003) 'Sexual Assault, Criminal Justice and Law and Order', *Women Against Violence*, 14, 14–26.

Taylor, S. C. (2004) *Court Licensed Abuse: Patriarchal Lore and the Legal Response to Intrafamilial Sexual Abuse of Children* (New York: Peter Lang Publishing Inc.).

Victorian Law Reform Commission (2001) *Sexual Offences: Discussion Paper* (Melbourne, Australia: Victorian Law Reform Commission).

Victorian Law Reform Commission (2004) *Sexual Offences: Law and Procedure: Final Report* (Melbourne, Australia: Victorian Law Reform Commission).

Von Hirsch, A. (2007) 'The "Desert" Model for Sentencing: Its Influences, Prospects and Alternatives', *Social Research*, 74(2), 413–434.

Von Hirsch, A. and Ashworth, A. (2005) *Proportionate Sentencing: Exploring the Principles* (Oxford: Oxford University Press).

World Health Organization (2002) *World Report on Violence and Health* (Geneva: World Health Organization).

3

Sexual Violence and Justice

How and Why Context Matters

Kathleen Daly

Introduction

Sexual violence is ubiquitous. It occurs everywhere: in all the places we live, work, sleep, travel, play and pray. Victims range from infants to the elderly.[1] Victim–offender relations are highly varied: among and by family members, peers and associates, and those unknown to each other; by those in positions of occupational and organisational authority; and by war combatants against civilians and each other. Sexual violence is committed by those in professional and working capacities as doctors, dentists, nurses, priests, nuns, teachers, government officials, managers, counsellors, lawyers, police officers, prison guards, soldiers, bus drivers, agricultural workers – indeed, no occupation is likely to be exempt. It can be 'ordinary' and 'extraordinary', referring respectively to everyday forms of sexual violence, and genocidal and mass atrocity violence. Sexual violence occurs everywhere imaginable, but depending on context and interpretation, it may not be considered a 'crime'. Sexual activity can be transactional: an exchange for money, protection, affection and gratification, although the parties may have unequal status and their circumstances range along a continuum from consenting to coercive. Thus, it may not be clear when sexual activity as transaction shades into sexual violence, or when 'agency' or 'choice' stops and coercion begins. The wrong of sexual violence is not absolute, but gradational and often ambiguous (see also Roffee, Chapter 5).[2]

The term 'rape' does not sufficiently capture the ubiquity, variability and ambiguity of sexual violence. When scholars or advocates use the term, they are typically referring to a particular victim–offender relationship, that is, adult females victimised by adult males. What, then, of boys or girls, who are sexually victimised by family members, including other children, youth or adults? Typically, this is called 'child sexual abuse', not rape. What of boys or girls (now adult survivors), who are sexually victimised by adults (or peers) while in residential care? Today, this is called 'historical institutional abuse of children', not rape.[3] When discussing responses to sexual violence, scholars and advocates often have in mind an *individual* context of violence, that is, an individual acting alone (or perhaps with several others) who victimises a family member, peer, acquaintance or person unknown. In doing so, other contexts of violence are overlooked, such as when individuals use positions of occupational or organisational power, or when sexual victimisation occurs in closed institutions or symbolically closed communities, or when it is carried out by loosely or well-organised groups. Furthermore, despite the extraordinary growth of research on sexual violence in conflict and post-conflict zones and in the developing world, the weight of research remains on responding to and preventing sexual violence in affluent democratic countries that have a strong rule of law and the capacity to enforce it.

In this chapter, I call for a reconceptualisation of sexual victimisation and justice, which widens the scope of inquiry beyond an individual context of victimisation in affluent democratic countries. When widening the scope, we see that the standard advice to victims – 'call the police' and engage criminal justice – may not be possible or realistic in most contexts of victimisation. Even in affluent democratic countries at peace and individual contexts of sexual violence, a low share (14 per cent) calls the police (Daly & Bouhours, 2010). Thus, even here, other responses and forms of justice need to be considered.

My chapter has three sections. The first sketches the components of my *Victimisation and Justice Model*: contexts of victimisation, justice mechanisms and victims' justice interests. In the second, I focus on contexts by presenting my *Sexual Victimisation and Justice Matrix* (hereafter, 'Matrix'), which arrays country contexts (developed, developing at war/post-conflict) by victimisation contexts (individual, occupational-organisational, institutional, institutional-symbolic and collective). The Matrix has 15 cells (or contexts) and, within each, we can identify the distinctive problems victim-survivors face in seeking justice, the different types of justice mechanisms available and victims' experiences with them. In the third section, I present case studies in two Matrix cells: intra-familial sexual violence (A1) and historical institutional abuse (A3). These examples challenge conventional ways of thinking about 'rape' and justice.

Victimisation and Justice Model

The Model's three components are contexts of victimisation, justice mechanisms and victims' justice interests. *Contexts of victimisation* will be described in the second section. *Justice mechanisms* reside on a continuum from conventional to innovative; the two categories are not mutually exclusive and can be combined in hybrid forms (see Daly, 2011, 2014a). Conventional mechanisms may be part of the legal process or work alongside of it; most assume reliance on formal legality, with a focus on criminal prosecution, trial and sentencing, and supports for victims in these legal contexts.[4] Innovative justice mechanisms may work alongside of or be integrated with criminal justice, be part of non-judicial (or administrative) procedures, or operate in civil society. They include mediated meetings or conferences with victims and offenders, other types of informal justice mechanisms, truth-telling or truth-seeking and redress schemes or reparations packages that have material and symbolic elements.[5]

Importantly, to assess responses to sexual victimisation, we should focus on justice mechanisms, not on 'types of justice'. By the latter I mean analyses that compare restorative justice, therapeutic jurisprudence or non-adversarial justice to standard or conventional police and court processes.[6] A 'types of justice' approach poorly specifies what actually occurs on the ground in justice practices. Moreover, responses to a single case of sexual violence may include a mix of conventional and innovative justice mechanisms (for example, criminal prosecution, civil litigation and a post-sentence conference). We need to understand how each is perceived and relates to the other, from the perspective of victim-survivors. Although I would encourage the use of innovative justice mechanisms, conventional justice mechanisms are important and cannot be disparaged as the 'punitive' justice, as often happens when researchers compare (what they inaccurately term) 'retributive and restorative justice'. Instead, the task should be to determine the degree to which a range of conventional and innovative justice mechanisms can address one or more victims' justice interests in the aftermath of sexual victimisation.[7]

I devised the construct of *victims' justice interests* to address a deficit in research on victims' experiences of justice practices. The dominant focus of this research is on the extent to which victims are 'satisfied'. However, the 'satisfaction variable' is overly simplified and largely uninterpretable (Pemberton & Reynaers, 2011, pp. 238–239). Recent research has also examined the socio-psychological benefits of justice practices to help victims recover from crime. Discussed elsewhere (Daly, 2014a, pp. 386–389), measures of satisfaction or recovery alone are limited. Better, I argue, to identify a set of reasonable expectations that victims as citizens have in seeking justice. Based on my research and that of others (see Herman, 2005; Koss, 2006), these interests are for participation, voice, validation, vindication and offender accountability.[8] To build a credible and useful body of research on effective responses to sexual violence, I propose that we *not simply* ask victims, 'are you satisfied?' with a justice activity. We should also ask, does a justice mechanism have the capacity to address one or more victims' justice interests, and to what extent does this occur? By applying the construct of victims' justice interests across a range of justice mechanisms, we can assess and compare them using a common metric. Another point should be made here: in the immediate or longer-term aftermath of sexual victimisation, many victim-survivors choose not to engage or participate in any justice activities at all; or they may initiate an activity and abandon it. This latter group forms the largest share of victim-survivors, and understanding their experiences is as important as understanding those who have participated in justice activities in some way.

Sexual Violence and Justice Matrix

The *Sexual Violence and Justice Matrix* depicts a broad sweep of places, positions and relationships. It arrays country contexts (developed, developing, at peace or conflict/post-conflict) and offending-victimisation contexts of violence (Table 3.1).[9] The country categories reflect differing legal, economic and political capacities to respond to sexual victimisation, along with differences in social organisation and cohesion for countries in conflict or relative peace. The offending-victimisation contexts are *individual* (row 1); *organisational-occupational*, that is, a person using a position of organisational or occupational power in a community setting (row 2); *institutional*, that is, a person using their position of power in a closed institution (this includes peer relations) (row 3); victimisation in a *symbolically closed community* such as geographically remote communities or segregated urban enclaves, based on race-ethnicity, nation or religion (row 4); and *collective*, that is, by loosely organised gangs or by state and quasi-state combatants (row 5). Thus, each cell in the Matrix identifies different social relations and place elements in a particular country context of violence. Of course, the Matrix's rows and columns could be expanded,

Table 3.1 Sexual Violence and Justice Matrix, A and C country contexts (B country contexts, developing country at peace, excluded for reasons of space)

Offending-victimisation context of sexual violence	**Country A Developed country at peace**	**Country C Conflict, post-conflict or post-authoritarian regime**
(1) Person acting alone	**A1** **Relations:** peer, familial, known and (atypically) stranger relations **Place:** mainly residential **Problem:** must fit 'real rape' template (stranger relations, injury)	**C1** **Relations:** peer, familial, known and (atypically) stranger relations **Place:** mainly residential **Problem:** must fit 'rape as weapon of war' template
(2) Person using position of organisational-occupational authority in community-based settings	**A2** **Relations:** religious, medical or state official (clergy, doctor, police) and child/adult victim **Place:** residential and occupational **Problem:** trusted person or state official is the abuser	**C2** **Relations:** foreign peacekeepers, aid workers and soldiers, in addition to A2 **Place:** residential and occupational **Problem:** legal jurisdiction, police or peacekeeper is the abuser, zero tolerance policy
(3) Person using position of organisational-occupational authority in closed institutions (includes peer relations in institutions)	**A3** **Relations:** religious or state official having duty of care and child/adult victims **Place:** residential schools, prisons, detention centres, armed forces facilities **Problem:** trusted person or state official is the abuser, unable to escape, inmate code of silence	**C3** **Relations:** state official having duty of care and refugee/prisoner **Place:** refugee camps and detention centres, in addition to A3 **Problem:** official is the abuser, unable to escape, inmate code of silence
(4) Offending in symbolically closed communities	**A4** **Relations:** peer, familial and known relations **Place:** remote communities or segregated urban enclaves **Problem:** fear and negative community consequences of disclosing; unable to escape	**C4** Limited documentation; but relations, place and problem are likely similar to A4

(5) Offending by loosely or well-organised groups	**A5** **Relations:** gangs, criminal enterprises, human trafficking groups **Place:** residential and occupational **Problem:** serious reprisals by offenders if reported, repatriation to home country	**C5** **Relations:** gangs, state or quasi-state combatants, militia, armed forces **Place:** everywhere **Problem:** scale of mass violence, civilian terror, no security presence, fear and negative consequences of disclosure

or subdivided further, as researchers identify specific contexts relevant to their research. Furthermore, a person can experience multiple contexts of victimisation in a day or over a short period of time; and still further, a person may be victimised one day and offend the next. The ubiquity and variability of sexual violence is such that we should not expect a two-dimensional matrix to accurately represent all forms of sexual victimisation and offending that occur (or have occurred) in human society. Rather, my aims in creating the Matrix are empirical and critical. Empirically, I am interested in devising a systematic way to name and compare victim-survivors' experiences of sexual victimisation and the distinctive problems they face in seeking justice. In addition, I wish to identify the justice mechanisms available and victim-survivors' experiences with them. Finally, by depicting a large canvas of sexual violence, I can identify similarities and differences across the varied contexts of victimisation by comparing what is learned in each Matrix cell.

My critical impulse is twofold. First, although sexual violence is ubiquitous, one matrix cell, A1 – an individual context in a developed country at peace – dominates the landscape of thought. In this context, an individual victimises another outside an institution or without using a position of occupational or organisational power. If you are sexually victimised in an A1 context, the standard advice is to 'call the police' and mobilise criminal law and criminal justice, although as we know, most victim-survivors do not do so. Virtually all efforts to reform rape laws in affluent democratic societies have focused exclusively on, or have assumed, an A1 context of victimisation. Other contexts of victimisation and other abusive relationships (even within an A1 context) are sidelined. Second, the legal or policy template forged from an A1 context of victimisation is often assumed to be relevant to other contexts, when this may not be so. Consider, for example, assaults in closed (or 'total') institutions such as detention centres, prisons, training schools, orphanages, immigration centres or military organisations (row 3); in symbolically closed communities such as racially or religiously segregated enclaves in urban areas or geographically remote Indigenous settlements (row 4); or in war and conflict zones (column C). Reflect on being a victim in these contexts. What are your options? Calling the police and mobilising criminal law may not be optimal, feasible or desirable. Thus, we need to pay attention to what is optimal and feasible in these contexts, and not assume there is just one (or a handful) of desirable justice responses.

A growing body of research has focused on C country contexts, and especially C5. Here, the work of international law and transitional justice scholars is relevant. Some are now challenging a 'top-down' rule of law perspective, which proposes particular recommendations and often sets unrealistic goals. Although international criminal justice responses may be appropriate, scholars are also calling for 'localizing' transitional justice (Shaw & Waldorf, 2010). In part, the problem is that those victimised may have few options, little or no voice, or limited participation in setting an agenda for justice and nation rebuilding; and in part, human rights advocates and organisations have used a highly Westernised, individualised concept of crime and justice, with a focus on 'legal justice' (Weinstein et al., 2010, p. 47). Translating this into the vernacular of the Sexual Violence and Justice Matrix, criminal justice responses that may be appropriate for A1 contexts are often thought to be the preferred or optimal mechanisms for C5.

Case studies of victimisation and justice

Each case study departs from what is assumed to be the standard sexual violence scenario in an A1 context. This scenario assumes that an adult male sexually victimises a female (adult or younger). In reflecting on how each case differs from the standard sexual violence scenario, the following words and images come to mind. Victims are in the shadows, on the periphery or largely excluded from research or policy discussions on experiences of sexual victimisation and optimal responses. Or, they may be recognised but placed in a separate category, which is not considered part of a 'general' analysis of victim-survivors. In presenting the case studies, my aim is to illustrate how and why context matters for justice. Context structures how (or whether) a person can report sexual victimisation to an authority, what justice mechanisms are available and how they might be engaged.

Sibling sexual abuse (A1 context)

I begin in an A1 context (or arguably, an A4 context)[10] by discussing sibling sexual abuse, an intra-familial abuse relationship that is infrequently considered. Victims of sibling sexual abuse are at the periphery in the following ways: compared with the standard scenario, they are very young, more likely to be male and are victimised by family members who are themselves children or adolescents. All analyses of rape and legal reform focus on questions of consent, specifically, on ways of changing evidentiary standards or burdens for proving consent (or lack of consent). However, and with reference to laws in Australia, 'children cannot legally consent to sexual activity if they are under the age of 10 to 13', depending on the jurisdiction and the age differentials of the parties (Stathopoulos, 2012, p. 12). Data from South Australia (Daly & Wade, 2012) and the United States (Krienert & Walsh, 2011) show that the average age of sibling sexual abuse victims is eight years. Thus, consent is not legally relevant in most of these cases.[11]

Although the prevalence of sibling sexual abuse is unknown (a problem compounded by different definitions used), it is believed to be the most common form of intra-familial sexual abuse, occurring three to five times more often than parental (father-to-daughter) sexual abuse (Ballantine, 2012). Although sibling sexual abuse is termed 'opportunistic' because of the physical proximity of siblings (Stathopoulos, 2012, p. 1), it is secretive, ongoing and can continue for many years; in this respect, it shares commonalities with adult partner violence and adult sexual abuse of children. Abused siblings worry about the consequences of disclosing victimisation to their parents or carers: they may be disbelieved, blamed or punished by their parents. Parents or carers, in turn, may deny, minimise or trivialise the abuse. They may be reluctant 'to report incidents to authorities' in part because they are concerned 'for the reputation and social standing of the family' (Krienert & Walsh, 2011, p. 356). Other dynamics make disclosure difficult for abused siblings: they do not want an abusive sibling taken away, they want to avoid family conflict, they may be threatened into silence by an abusive sibling and they may be unsure that what they are experiencing is 'abuse' (Stathopoulos, 2012, p. 11). Here, the ambiguity of sexual victimisation is complex and profound: children may turn to older siblings for what they perceive to be a source of affection not offered by their parents. Adding further complexity, abusive siblings may themselves have been physically or sexually abused.

To say more about these cases, I draw from two South Australian data sets: one is of all youths charged with sex offences in South Australia during a period of 6.5 years (385 youths), and a second is of all youths whose cases were referred to a youth justice conference (described below) during a six-month period (8 youths).[12] Of the 385 youths, 59 (15 per cent) were charged with offences against siblings[13] and 266 (69 per cent) were charged with non-sibling 'hands-on' offences. The rest (16 per cent) were charged with a variety of 'hands-off' offences (for example, public indecency and exposure). For the 'hands-on' cases only, sibling cases more likely involved ongoing violence, with multiple incidents over time compared with the non-sibling cases (64 and 23 per cent, respectively); and they more likely involved penetrative or oral sexual activity than the non-sibling cases (68 and 55 per cent, respectively). Abused siblings were younger (7.7 years) than those in non-sibling cases (12.6 years), and the male share of victims was higher in sibling (27 per cent) than non-sibling (18 per cent) cases. The offender–victim dyad was brother–brother in a higher share of sibling than non-sibling cases (27 and 17 per cent, respectively), although the typical dyad was brother–sister for both (Daly & Wade, 2012, pp. 90–91). For the United States, Krienert and Walsh (2011, p. 362) report nearly identical percentages: 29 per cent of sibling abuse victims were male and, although brothers abusing brothers represented 25 per cent of cases, two-thirds were brothers abusing sisters.

One objective of the South Australia research was to compare legal response to youth sexual offences. South Australia is an unusual jurisdiction in responding to youth sexual offending.[14] If a youth admits sexual offending to the police (fully or partly) early in the legal process, the police can divert the matter to a youth justice conference. In a conference, the victim, an admitted offender, their supporters and any other relevant parties meet to discuss the offence, its impact and how to address it. The conference is organised by a youth justice coordinator, with a police officer present. If a youth admits to an offence and completes the agreement, no conviction is recorded. Examining the 'touch' offences only, youth in the sibling cases were more likely to show remorse during the police interview, to make admissions to the police, to be referred to a conference and to be referred to a specialist programme for adolescent youth offenders, compared with non-sibling cases. Of cases referred to court, youth in the sibling cases were more likely to admit or plead guilty to offending and were more likely to be referred to the specialist treatment programme for adolescent sex offending. I cannot explain these differences. However, I suspect it may be more difficult for youths to deny offending that occurs in close proximity to their parent(s); and in addition, perhaps the 'carrot' of conference participation (no conviction recorded) encourages parents to address the problem, rather than minimise or deny it.

What, then, about victims in these cases? Research centres on the impact of abuse, and it shows patterns similar to other forms of child sexual abuse: trauma symptoms and lowered self-esteem, and longer-term effects into adulthood such as drug use, 'sexual dysfunction' and problems parenting (Stathopoulos, 2012, pp. 9, 14). For victims' experiences of justice, evidence is slim.[15] Distilling from our data on conferences in four sibling sexual abuse cases, which included police reports and interviews with the conference facilitator and parents (typically a mother), here is what we learned (Daly & Wade, 2012, 2014). Victims' ages ranged from five to eight years, and none attended the conference. In two cases, mothers were placed in a difficult dual role of representing their abused child and supporting their abusive child. Each conference focused largely on addressing the youth's (all were male) behaviour and on ways of reunifying him with family members or in the family home. Legal or justice aims for victims were secondary to rehabilitative or therapeutic aims: to ensure that victims and offenders received counselling. A significant finding was that although sexual abuse was disclosed and ultimately reported to the police, it remained hidden, except perhaps to counsellors. The 'full story' of what occurred was not clear in the police report or articulated in the conference setting.

Sibling sexual abuse is a recent area of inquiry, in part prompted by a shift from seeing it as benign and experimental, to seeing it as harmful. It is instructive that the term 'rape' is rarely used in this literature.[16] Indeed, in this context of offending and victimisation, ambiguity is everywhere apparent. Is the sexual behaviour thought to be 'developmentally appropriate', 'developmentally inappropriate' or 'problematic' (Stathopoulos, 2012, pp. 5–7)? The categories are not fixed, but a guide to interpretation by counsellors or psychologists. What, then, might child victims be thinking? Perhaps some are too young to 'know'. Thus, for how and why context matters, a key question turns on whose interpretation is decisive in depicting sexual behaviour as harmful or wrong: is it the child's, a parent's, another adult's or an expert's? Research suggests that when a child's disclosure is met with disbelief or minimisation by a parent or significant adult, more negative consequences to the victim may flow. Thus, seeking justice in this context means, in the first instance, that a child's account of being hurt is heard, believed and understood by a parent or family member. After that, it is up to a child's parent or significant adult to engage in legal or therapeutic activities that may promote a sense of justice, even if a child victim may not fully understand or be aware of what has occurred. Ultimately, justice is not only responding to a wrong, but for many victim-survivors, the ability to recreate a relationship of trust and safety with a (formerly abusive) sibling in the future.

Historical institutional abuse (A3 context)

Victimisation of children and youth in 'closed' (or total) institutions was 'discovered' as a social problem in the 1980s in affluent democratic countries. The United States was the first country to examine 'institutional abuse' as a named social problem, with a 1979 Senate Subcommittee hearing. Other early inquiries were established in Northern Ireland, England and Wales, and Canada in the 1980s. Sexual abuse of children by Catholic clergy in churches, rectories and other community-based contexts first became subject to intense media attention, litigation and prosecution in the mid-1980s in the United States, and a few years later, in Canada. Today the term 'institutional abuse' can refer to sexual abuse alone, or to sexual, physical and emotional abuse. It may refer to residential or out-of-home care alone, or it may include both closed contexts (A3) and community-based (A2) settings. I will focus on a wider set of abuses (not just sexual) and on A3 contexts.[17]

My research on 19 major cases of institutional abuse of children in Australia and Canada shows that although victims (or their family members) did make complaints to people in authority, including the police or government officials, no legal action was taken. Their accounts of abuse were ignored or disbelieved, or investigations were dropped or did not result in charges being laid. It took, on average, nearly 40 years for an official response to be initiated, using a conservative measure (Daly, 2014b, pp. 101–106). Official responses occurred after pressure was placed on governments or churches by survivor advocacy groups and media stories, law suits against governments or churches and, at times, the charging or conviction of perpetrators.

Sexual abuse of boys by members of the Christian Brothers at Mount Cashel School, in St John's, Newfoundland (Canada) came to public attention in 1989. It launched one of the earliest judicial inquiries (1989–1991) to investigate the police and justice system handling of complaints of physical and sexual abuse against children in residential care.[18] Other Canadian cases followed in the 1990s. Several factors were responsible for the shift in sensibility that 'something must be done' to address institutional abuse of children. Among them was that the alleged abuse was *sexual*, 'a more disturbing form of abuse' (Corby et al., 2001, p. 83) than harsh physical regimes or corporal punishment, which officials had been aware of for over a century. I call this the 'sexual turn' in the institutional abuse story, and it was amplified by allegations that men were sexually abusing boys in their care. A second factor was adult survivors' first-hand accounts of institutional abuse, their 'public stories'. Davis (2005, p. 27) suggests that up to the 1970s, 'first-person accounts... outside a legal context were non-existent'. This changed when Florence Rush spoke at a feminist conference in 1971 of being sexually abused as a child. In the mid- to late 1980s, male adult survivors of institutional abuse began to come forward for the first time to tell their public stories.

Social and legal responses to historical institutional abuse differ from those in the standard rape scenario in A1 for several reasons. First, the victim is a child, often a vulnerable child, growing up in an institution or out-of-home care; and although an offender can be a specific person, it is also an organisation (church, government or charitable entity) that has a duty of care to the child. Second, the accounts of victimisation are not those of lone individuals; they are brought forward by the media and survivor advocacy groups, who tell a story of institutional victimisation that is experienced by a large number of people. Third, media and advocacy groups focus not only on abuses that occurred, but also church or state 'cover-ups' by authorities in deciding not to investigate or pursue cases, or policies and practices that harmed children or removed them from families without parental consent (Daly, 2014c). Thus, considerable political heat is felt at high echelons of church and state authority. Finally, although criminal prosecution of some individuals is possible and does occur, the social and legal responses that are most relevant to survivors are public inquiries, civil litigation, redress schemes, official apologies and commemorative and memory projects. This is because alleged offenders have since died and evidence of abuse from many years ago is difficult to gather. As importantly, survivor groups have more often sought (and continue to seek) forms of redress from government, religious and charitable organisations that do not rely solely on civil litigation. Redress schemes or packages include *ex gratia* payments, benefits, services, public apologies and memorialisation. Of the 19 cases in my sample, 14 had redress schemes or packages and two were finalised by major civil litigation settlements only. The remaining three are national Australian cases –

Stolen Generations, Child Migrants and *Forgotten Australians* – for which the government's response to date has been service provision (counselling), apologies and memorialisation (see Daly, 2014b, pp. 150–157 and Appendices 4 and 5).

A striking feature of victim-survivors of *historical* sexual abuse, in particular, those who come forward to public inquiries or government investigations, is the male share of cases. Drawing from Australian and Canadian investigations or inquiries, the female-to-male victim ratio was 2:1 (Berger, 1995, p. 13), 1:1 (Mullighan, 2008, p. xi) and 1:1.6 (Australian Royal Commission into Institutional Responses to Child Sexual Abuse, 2014, p. 285).[19] Put another way, males have comprised 33–62 per cent of those who have come forward to speak to officials. Dutch research on the prevalence of *contemporary* sexual victimisation of children in residential care in 2010 finds it was 2.5 times higher than in community-based settings, with a female-to-male sexual victimisation ratio in residential care of 2:1 (Daly, 2014b, pp. 55–56, 270). Compare these figures to the 2012 Australian Personal Safety Survey, for which the female-to-male ratio of sexual victimisation was 4.25:1 (Australian Institute of Family Studies, 2015). Thus, we see a shifting gendered face to sexual victimisation: predominantly female victims in contemporary and community-based (non-institutional) estimates, and an increasing male share in historical and institutional estimates.

At the same time, Joanna Penglase (2005, p. 145), who grew up in residential care in Australia, argues that 'sexual abuse is always highlighted as if it is the "worst" abuse... What gets lost is that children were violated in every sense in an institution, and being used sexually was just one of those violations'. She quotes a survivor, who had been in a Queensland farm home in the 1950s, as saying 'in a place so full of brutality, sexual abuse did not rank as highly as other forms of abuse' (p. 142). These and other adult survivors' memories of institutional life and their experiences of redress schemes (Daly, 2014b, chapters 3 and 7) lead me to think that social and legal responses to institutional abuse have placed too much emphasis on sexual abuse alone. Survivors' memories of abuse do not focus solely on specific abusive acts, but recall a 'dehumanizing institutional environment' of fear, non-care and bleakness (Penglase, 2005, p. 48). Optimally, then, justice should not simply be redress for physical or sexual acts, but rather for organisational regimes and social policies that had little or no interest in children's welfare or development. Survivors seeking justice for institutional abuse have done so (and continue to do so) as part of a collectivity; this may promote solidarity, support and a shared narrative of wrongs that survivors argue should be recognised and subject to redress. At the same time, survivor groups may suffer fatigue, demoralisation and division in moving their claims for redress forward. In the 14 cases with redress schemes, it took on average seven to eight years to achieve a tangible result of monetary recompense, once an official response began (Daly, 2014b, pp. 145–146). This is a long time to wait for justice.[20]

Conclusion

I have argued for the importance of understanding sexual violence and justice in diverse contexts of victimisation. When doing so, we see that one context dominates the social and legal landscape of thought and action. I have also argued for a research focus on a variety of justice mechanisms, not on 'types of justice': the latter is broad, often imprecise, and does a disservice to how justice works on the ground. My case studies of sibling sexual abuse and historical institutional abuse of children sought to illustrate why and how context matters. Compared with standard A1 contexts, each recasts images of victims, offenders and relationships of abuse; and the practices and possibilities for justice. My proposed way forward is to fully grasp the ubiquity, variability and ambiguity of sexual violence in political and empirical terms. Let's not be content with understanding sexual violence and justice solely in standard A1 contexts of victimisation. Let's not assume that what occurs in A1 can be generalised to other contexts. Let's develop a global and highly contextualised theoretical, research and policy agenda, one that pays attention to sexual victimisation that currently sits in the shadows or on the periphery, and one that moves self-consciously across diverse contexts of victimisation to identify similarities, differences and new justice forms.

Notes

1. According to Sy (2013), victims are as young as 15 weeks and as old as 98 years (see Evelynn Deuman and 'Anna' entries, respectively).
2. For example, the parties to a sexual activity do not think it is wrong, but legal authorities do. Sexual activity as paid work, service or barter occurs in diverse contexts, some of which are dangerous and coercive; others, empowering; and still others, in between.
3. Up to the mid-1980s, men's sexual abuse of boys in residential care was called 'homosexual abuse', but the terminology had changed to 'child sexual abuse' by the end of the 1980s (Daly, 2014b, pp. 93–94).

4. Other conventional mechanisms include victim impact statements, specialist courts and civil litigation.
5. Other innovative justice mechanisms include people's tribunals, documentary and street theatre, and art and activist projects in civil society.
6. Conventional criminal justice is typically (but wrongly) termed 'retributive' justice (see Daly, 2000, 2002).
7. There is, of course, more than justice (broadly defined) to consider in the aftermath of sexual victimisation. Other victim needs for safety, food and housing may be of more immediate importance.
8. Space limitations preclude my defining each term here; see Daly (2014a, 2014b).
9. This Matrix was first published in Daly (2014a).
10. Intra-familial victimisation can also be viewed as occurring in a symbolically closed community of 'the family' (an A4 context), a point that several colleagues have raised.
11. The South Australian data are of all youths (N = 385) charged with sexual offences (1995–2001); 59 were sibling sexual abuse cases. The US data are of over 13,000 sibling sexual abuse cases reported to the police (2000–2007).
12. Project research methods, cases and outcomes are detailed in Daly et al. (February 2007), Daly et al. (July 2007, 3rd revision) and Daly and Wade (2012).
13. Siblings include biological, foster and step-relations. An additional 24 cases involved cousins.
14. South Australia is one of three world jurisdictions in which the police and/or courts can refer youth sex offence cases to a conference as a routine practice; the others are Queensland and New Zealand.
15. Although considerable research exists on child sexual abuse and justice, the focus is on adult, not youth, offending.
16. As detailed in Tarczon and Quadara (2012), the Australian Bureau of Statistics (ABS) defines 'sexual abuse' as 'involving a child (under the age of 15) in sexual activity beyond their understanding or contrary to currently accepted community standards', whereas sexual assault is defined to include 'rape..., attempted rape, aggravated sexual assault..., indecent assault [and other related offences]' of those 15 and over. Thus, in addition to problems of ambiguity in classifying sexual behaviour between siblings (and especially for the offending sibling), a second reason for using 'sexual abuse' rather than 'sexual assault' (which includes rape) is the ability of a child victim to 'know' what is (or is not) harmful or wrong. A third reason is the ability of the ABS (or any other data-gathering organisation) to make accurate estimates of childhood sexual victimisation (that is, of those under 15) from sample surveys that ask adult respondents about such experiences.
17. Of the 19 cases, four centred on sexual abuse only.
18. The first judicial inquiry, carried out in 1984–1986, investigated sexual abuse of boys by lay male staff at Kincora Boys' Hostel, and abuse in eight other children's homes in Northern Ireland. The inquiry centred on allegations of 'homosexual offences', but of the nine hostels or homes examined, five housed both boys and girls (Hughes, 1986).
19. In an analysis of 1,476 private sessions between 7 May 2013 and 30 April 2014, the Australian Royal Commission (2014, p. 285) reports that two in

three survivors who came forward to speak in private sessions were male. Later on the same page, it reports that males comprised 61.7 per cent of survivors. Thus, the female:male ratio is 1:1.6.

20. In other contexts of collective victimisation, especially in Matrix cell C5, the wait for justice can be even longer. The wait for justice for survivors pursuing civil litigation is highly variable.

References

Australian Institute of Family Studies. (2015) 'Facts & Figures – Sexual Violence Research', *Personal Safety Survey*, 2012; Retrieved from http://www.aifs.gov.au/acssa/statistics.html

Australian Royal Commission. (2014) *Royal Commission into Institutional Responses to Child Sexual Abuse Interim Report* (Vol. 1, Appendix C: Private Session Information) (Canberra: Attorney General's Department).

Ballantine, M. (2012) 'Sibling Incest Dynamics: Therapeutic Themes and Clinical Challenges', *Clinical Social Work Journal*, 40, 56–65.

Berger, T. (1995) *Report of the Special Counsel Regarding Claims Arising out of Sexual Abuse at Jericho Hill School* (Vancouver: Ministry of the Attorney General).

Corby, B., Doig, A. and Roberts, V. (2001) *Public Inquiries into Abuse of Children in Residential Care* (London, UK: Jessica Kingsley Publishers).

Daly, K. (2000) 'Revisiting the Relationship between Retributive and Restorative Justice', in H. Strang and J. Braithwaite (eds.) *Restorative Justice: Philosophy to Practice* (Dartmouth: Ashgate), pp. 33–54.

Daly, K. (2002) 'Restorative Justice: The Real Story', *Punishment and Society*, 4(1), 55–79.

Daly, K. (2011) 'Conventional and Innovative Justice Responses to Sexual Violence', *ACSSA Issues* 12 (Melbourne, Australia: Australian Institute of Family Studies).

Daly, K. (2014a) 'Reconceptualizing Sexual Victimisation and Justice', in I. VanFraechem, A. Pemberton and F. Ndahinda (eds.) *Justice for Victims: Perspectives on Rights, Transition and Reconciliation* (London, UK: Routledge), pp. 378–395.

Daly, K. (2014b) *Redressing Institutional Abuse of Children* (Basingstoke: Palgrave Macmillan).

Daly, K. (2014c) 'Conceptualising Responses to Institutional Abuse of Children', *Current Issues in Criminal Justice*, 26(1), 5–30.

Daly, K. and Bouhours, B. (2010) 'Rape and Attrition in the Legal Process: A Comparative Analysis of Five Countries', *Crime and Justice: A Review of Research*, 39, 565–650 (Chicago: University of Chicago Press).

Daly, K., Bouhours, B. and Curtis-Fawley, S. (2007, February) *SAJJ-CJ Technical Report No. 4: In-Depth Study of Sexual Assault and Family Violence Cases* (Brisbane: School of Criminology and Criminal Justice, Griffith University).

Daly, K., Bouhours, B., Curtis-Fawley, S., Weber, L. and Schol, R. (2007, July) *SAJJ-CJ Technical Report No. 3 (3rd edition): Sexual Assault Archival Study (SAAS), an Archival Study of Sexual Offence Cases Disposed of in Youth Court and by Conference and Formal Caution* (Brisbane: School of Criminology and Criminal Justice, Griffith University).

Daly, K. and Wade, D. (2012) *SAJJ-CJ Technical Report No. 5: In-Depth Study of Sexual Assault and Family Violence Cases, Part II: Sibling Sexual Assault, Other Sexual Assault, and Youth-Parent Assault* (Brisbane: School of Criminology and Criminal Justice, Griffith University).

Daly, K. and Wade, D. (2014) 'Sibling Sexual Violence: Offending Patterns and Dynamics in Youth Justice Conferences', in A. Hayden, L. Gelsthorpe, V. Kingi and A. Morris (eds.) *A Restorative Approach to Family Violence: Changing Tack* (Surrey: Ashgate), pp. 185–195.

Davis, J. E. (2005) *Accounts of Innocence: Sexual Abuse, Trauma, and the Self* (Chicago: University of Chicago Press).

Herman, J. (2005) 'Justice from the Victim's Perspective', *Violence Against Women*, 11(5), 571–602.

Hughes, W. H. (with Patterson, W. J. and Whalley, H.) (1986) *Report of the Committee of Inquiry into Children's Homes and Hostels* (Belfast: Her Majesty's Stationery Office).

Koss, M. (2006) 'Restoring Rape Survivors: Justice, Advocacy, and A Call to Action', *Annals of the New York Academy of Sciences*, 1087, 206–234.

Krienert, J. and Walsh, J. (2011) 'Sibling Sexual Abuse: An Empirical Analysis of Offender, Victim, and Event Characteristics in National Incident-Based Reporting System (NIBRS) Data, 2000–2007', *Journal of Child Sexual Abuse*, 20(4), 353–372.

Mullighan, E. P. (2008) *Children in State Care Commission of Inquiry: Allegations of Sexual Abuse and Death from Criminal Conduct* (Adelaide: Office of the Commissioner).

Pemberton, A. and Reynaers, S. (2011) 'The Controversial Nature of Victim Participation: Therapeutic Benefits in Victim Impact Statements', in E. Erez, M. Kilching and J. Wemmers (eds.) *Therapeutic Jurisprudence and Victim Participation in Justice: International Perspectives* (Durham, NC: Carolina Academic Press), pp. 229–248.

Penglase, J. (2005) *Orphans of the Living: Growing up in 'Care' in Twentieth-Century Australia* (Fremantle: Curtain University Books).

Shaw, R. and Waldorf, L. (2010) (eds.) *Localizing Transitional Justice: Justice Interventions and Local Priorities after Mass Violence* (Stanford: Stanford University Press).

Stathopoulos, M. (2012) 'Sibling Sexual Abuse', *ACSSA Research Summary* (Melbourne, Australia: Australian Institute of Family Studies).

Sy, J. U. (2013) 'A Compilation of the Worst Rape Cases in the World by James U. Sy Jr.'; Retrieved from https://jamessyjr.wordpress.com/2013/02/13/a-compilation-of-the-worst-rape-cases-in-the-world-by-james-u-sy-jr/

Tarczon, C. and Quadara, A. (2012) 'The Nature and Extent of Sexual Assault and Abuse in Australia', *ACSSA Resource Sheet* (Melbourne, Australia: Australian Institute of Family Studies).

Weinstein, H. M., Fletcher, L. E., Vinck, P. and Pham, P. (2010) 'Stay the Hand of Justice: Whose Priorities Take Priority?', in R. Shaw and L. Waldorf (eds.) *Localizing Transitional Justice: Justice Interventions and Local Priorities After Mass Violence* (Stanford: Stanford University Press), pp. 26–48.

4

Reassessing the Place of Criminal Law Reform in the Struggle Against Sexual Violence

A Critique of the Critique of Carceral Feminism

Lise Gotell

Introduction

Feminist struggles against sexual violence have been identified as responsible for the development of a 'law and order' state form that constructs women as victims, while further criminalising and disempowering the marginalised. In this chapter, I consider the complex outcomes of sexual assault law reform in light of recent critiques of what critics have labelled 'carceral feminism' (Bernstein, 2007, 2010, 2012; Bumiller, 2008; Gottschalk, 2008; Halley, 2006; Reece, 2011). While a broad objective of this book is to think beyond rape law reform, this task is best accomplished by *thinking through law reform as a feminist strategy*. Against those who see feminist movements as complicit in the regressive politics of the law and order state, I offer a qualified defence of feminist strategies of law reform.

The first section of the chapter provides an overview of a contemporary backlash to anti-rape feminism and outlines the critique of carceral feminism. Next, focusing on Canadian campaigns, I demonstrate how second-wave feminists had a sophisticated analysis of criminalisation. While critics of carceral feminism contend that feminists wholeheartedly embraced criminalisation in their struggles to end sexual violence, the historical records show that activists appreciated the dangers of emphasising law reform and insisted on the importance of connecting legal and extralegal strategies. I argue for renewed attention to some of these older political and theoretical insights. In the third section, I challenge the claim that sexual assault law reform constituted an unqualified feminist victory. Focusing on the complex implications of an affirmative consent standard, I demonstrate how changes to the Canadian law have produced highly contradictory outcomes. In contrast to the instrumentalist conception of law that informs the critique of carceral feminism, I argue for an analytic approach to law reform that appreciates the complex outcomes of earlier struggles, as well as the uneven development of law. Finally, I highlight the sexual libertarianism and anti-statism inherent in the critique of carceral feminism. While acknowledging the dangers of feminist engagements in contemporary law and order politics, I contend that we cannot simply turn our backs on law. The absolute rejection of criminalisation strategies might well have the effect of re-privatising sexual violence, with the inevitable return of impunity for perpetrators.

Backlash and carceral feminism

Efforts to think through sexual assault law reform must take into consideration the contemporary context of backlash. In the past few years, counterclaims to anti-rape feminism have proliferated, reconstructing the story of feminist criminal law reform as regressive and presenting contemporary feminism as a force of stultifying political correctness. In newspaper columns and on popular news websites, the concept 'rape culture' has been identified as a feminist-produced moral panic (see, for example, Kitchens, 2014). Statistical evidence of rape's pervasiveness has come under fire, with right-wing commentators casting rape prevalence research as feminist junk science (see, for example, MacDonald, 2014). Recreating the narrow category of 'real rape' (violent stranger rape), rape is presented as being rare and, far from being condoned, is acknowledged as a horrific crime. Many of the 'rape culture as hysteria' analyses hone in on the issue of drinking and rape, insisting that the best way for women to prevent sexual violence is to avoid getting drunk (see, for example, Wente, 2013). Efforts to respond to the pervasiveness of sexual violence on university campuses have been condemned as abuses of due process (MacDonald, 2014).

This vocal resistance shares much with earlier manifestations of what some have called the anti-anti-rape backlash (Bevaqua, 2000, p. 181). In the 1990s, amidst feminist-inspired law reform inroads, post-feminists Camille Paglia (1992) and Katie Roiphe (1994) pushed back against feminist research showing the pervasiveness of sexual violence. They criticised a sexually correct form of feminism for convincing women to redefine 'bad sex' as rape, in the process, producing a manufactured crisis. These polemical claims were eagerly taken up in a surrounding culture anxious to avoid the troubling claims of anti-rape feminists (Gavey, 2005, pp. 63–68).

We should be mindful of the analytic problems of the metaphor of backlash. This concept presents a simplified view both of feminism and resistance to feminism, obscuring historical, social and cultural complexities (Chunn et al., 2007, p. 6). As Dorothy Chunn, Susan B. Boyd and Hester Lessard argue in their overview of debates about the concept of backlash, feminist movements for social change produce resistance and this is always a part of the political culture of liberal states. Resistance is not a phenomenon that emerges full blown at particular points. Nevertheless, the intensity of resistance is stronger during some periods (Chunn et al., p. 10; Gavey, 2005, p. 64). I wonder whether this is not one such moment, marked by multiple voices pushing back against anti-rape feminism. If the emergence of backlash is an indication of influence, the effects of anti-rape activism may be more significant than we have been willing to acknowledge.

There is a strong similarity between popular manifestations of the contemporary backlash and the scholarly critique of 'carceral' or 'governance' feminism. According to many critics, the women's movement has been deeply implicated in the rise of the punitive state, associated with the social disenfranchisement of the poor, and the disproportionate incarceration of racialised populations (Bernstein, 2007, 2010, 2013; Bumiller, 2008; Gottschalk, 2008). Feminist struggles against sexual violence, in particular, have been singled out as having facilitated carceral politics. Kristin Bumiller (2008, p. 84), for example, contends that 'neoliberalism appropriated the feminist movement against sexual violence' by emphasising criminal law reform as a central tactic for gaining recognition of the harm of sexual violence. As such, she states, feminists have been complicit in punitive agendas. Elizabeth Bernstein (2007, p. 143), one of the strongest voices against criminalisation campaigns, argues that activists have abandoned earlier concerns with social justice goals. In fact, Bernstein (2012, p. 236) defines carceral feminism as 'a cultural and political formation in which previous generations' justice and liberation strategies are recast in carceral terms'.

According to post-feminist legal scholar Janet Halley (Halley et al., 2006, p. 340), the outcome of this embrace of punishment is not only an alliance with conservative groups, but also a 'quite noticeable installation of feminists ... in actual legal-institutional power'. Halley's (2006, p. 21) concept of governance feminism, with its metaphor of feminists 'walk[ing] the halls of power', represents feminists as having achieved a kind of coup d'état, while at the same time being in denial about their own influence. Helen Reece (2011, p. 207), drawing on the governance feminism thesis, contends that this tendency to underestimate influence allows feminists to distance themselves from state discourses and policies that have helped to shape and thus encourage an 'amplification and intensification of the carceral message'. Reece approvingly cites my own work (Gotell, 1998, 2007) where I show how feminist agendas and Canadian state policy converged around a series of criminal law reforms in the 1990s; but she disagrees with my argument that 'government recognition of "violence" has been marked by the *appropriation* and *transformation* of feminist discourses' (Gotell cited in Reece, 2011, p. 239, emphasis added), rather than a direct outcome of feminist goals and influence.

In presenting feminism as caught in an intimate carceral embrace and yet perpetually in denial, scholars like Bernstein (2007, 2010, 2012), Bumiller (2008), Halley (2006) and Reece (2011) paint a distorted picture of struggles against sexual violence. I am interested in how critiques of the neoliberal law and order state have become increasingly tied to a repudiation of feminism. Not only do critics avoid interrogating historical records documenting feminist campaigns, they also depict engagements with criminal law as always regressive and misguided, thus ignoring contradictory outcomes. Here, my argument against the critique of carceral feminism is threefold. First, on an empirical level, these critics misrepresent feminist struggles against sexual violence. Second, critics rely upon a simplistic instrumentalist view of the state. Third, and normatively, the thrust of this critique is to prescribe an anti-carceral agenda as the only possible progressive position, leading inexorably toward the conclusion that sexual assault should be decriminalised.

Canadian feminist law reform campaigns

The depiction of feminism as complicit in punitive agendas obscures actual positions that were broader than criminal law reform and that acknowledged the perils of the carceral embrace. In the 1990s, gender violence briefly emerged on the political agenda as the Canadian federal government responded to the tragedy of the Montreal Massacre (Gotell, 1998, 2007). This deliberate act of misogynous terror precipitated a national debate about male violence. In this period, coinciding with the shift towards neoliberal governance, it was becoming difficult to make any gender-specific demands on state actors, and feminist voices were being delegitimised. Gendered victimisation became one of the last few legitimate gender-specific bases for claims to social entitlement, tied intimately to the development of the law and order state.

Sexual assault law reform was placed squarely on the political agenda when, in a stunning legal decision, the Supreme Court of Canada (SCC) struck down Canada's rape shield law as a violation of the accused's fair trial rights (in *R v. Seaboyer*, 1991, 2 SCR 577). The federal government's move to re-enact restrictions on sexual history evidence created a political opportunity for feminists to push for wider reforms. The post-*Seaboyer* reform context, alongside federal consultations on violence against women held between 1994 and 1997, precipitated sexual assault law reforms that occurred in Canada far earlier than in many other jurisdictions. Analysis of historical records, including transcriptions of consultations, minutes of parliamentary committees and position papers of feminist organisations, reveals that activists were not naive about the dangers of criminalisation, nor were they limited in their demands.

The agenda advanced by 1990s campaigns extended far beyond criminal law reform. In fact, activists used consultations on violence against women as a site for contesting the gendered implications of neoliberalism, including the hollowing out of the welfare state, the de-funding of feminist activism and intensified gender, race and class disadvantage. The National Action Committee on the Status of Women (NAC) document, *99 Federal Steps Toward an End to Violence Against Women* (Lakeman, 1993), laid out the agreed-upon agenda for women's groups participating in yearly Department of Justice consultations on gender violence. This document articulated a broad programme focused on the empowerment of women through equality-enhancing social policy and stable funding for women's centres and shelters. Explicitly challenging a narrow focus on legal responses, sexual violence was here framed as a systemic problem, rooted in gendered and racialised inequalities. 'Male violence', as *99 Federal Steps* declared, cannot be dealt with through a 'crime prevention model', as it is 'clearly an issue of the status of women' (Lakeman, 1993, p. 18). Moreover, '[r]acism must be acknowledged... as compounding the effects of sexist attacks' (Lakeman, 1993, p. 23).

Rather that capitulating to a law and order agenda, feminists articulated a strong critique of punitive politics. Activists castigated the justice system as racist and classist, condemning the 'the overrepresentation in the jails of aboriginal men, other men of colour and poor men' (Justice Canada, 1995, Julie Kubanek, DNA Project, p. 163). Aboriginal women participating in consultations called attention to how correctional budgets were being increased to fund the expansion of women's prisons where highly disproportionate numbers of aboriginal women were being incarcerated (Justice Canada, 1995; Marge Friedel, National Metis Women of Canada, p. 99). Law and order politics were criticised for increasing police budgets, at the same time as funding for women's organisations was being cut (Lakeman, 1993, p. 34). In terms that echo Bernstein (2012) and Halley (2006), activists issued harsh condemnations of the violence of prisons: 'The prison system brutalizes the few men it jails and sends them back into the community to attack more viciously' (Lakeman, 1993, p. 34).

Despite this overt critique of the law and order state, activists nevertheless argued that the routine discounting of violence against women and the mistreatment of complainants demanded improved criminal justice responses. As explained by Lee Lakeman (2004, p. 127), representative of the Canadian Association of Sexual Assault Centres (CASAC) and a central participant in these campaigns, 'it has never been the position of CASAC that violence against women should be considered by government... primarily as a matter of criminal justice'. Yet as Lakeman (2004, pp. 127–128) emphasised, responding to women's justice and safety needs must remain a core focus of anti-violence activism.

In feminist positions expressed during these reform processes, achieving harsh punishment for sex offenders was never a principal goal and was most often explicitly disavowed. As NAC emphasised in its submission to the Parliamentary Committee considering the 1992 law reforms: 'NAC is certainly not among those who believe that the way to justice is through tougher sentences for those who committed violence against women' (Canadian House of Commons, 1992, pp. 1–25). Feminists repeatedly stressed the importance of respecting fair trial rights, although within a framework that recognised women's constitutional rights to equality and justice processes free from discriminatory myths. Far from demanding long periods of incarceration, the question of sentencing was simply not articulated as a concern.

Bernstein (2012, p. 238) underlines how the symbol of the sex offender has been deployed as justification for the elaboration of the law and order state. Yet rather than focusing on the threat of the sex offender, Canadian campaigns instead called attention to partners and acquaintances as perpetrators of sexual violence. This was particularly evident in the positions that shaped the 1992 redefinition of consent. This law reform laid the foundation for an affirmative consent standard. Feminists hoped that the codification of a strict consent standard would challenge a heterosexual script in which male sexual aggression and female submission is normative (McIntyre, 2000).

There is an important distinction between the carceral demand for heightened conviction rates and the feminist aims of improving the legal story of rape and ensuring that complainants' participation in the criminal justice system does not compromise their dignity and autonomy (Larcombe, 2011). If one objective of Canadian feminist campaigns was to challenge the myth of 'real rape' by ensuring that legal definitions come to reflect the typical ways women experience sexual violence, another core aim was to improve the treatment of complainants. This was a time when defence lawyers were explicitly engaged in what they referred to as a 'whack the complainant' strategy (Schmitz, 1988, p. 22). Feminists pushed for restrictions that would prevent the discounting of complainants through myth-laden cross-examinations on sexual history and fishing expeditions into their private records. In these ways, activists were attempting to constrain the circulation of discriminatory myths in trials.

By the end of the decade, Canadian feminists could claim responsibility for fundamental changes to the Criminal Code provisions on sexual assault, with new evidentiary restrictions on sexual history (*Criminal Code*, 1985, s. 276), strict limitations on the disclosure of complainants' confidential records (s. 278.1) and most crucially, the codification of a strong framework for sexual consent. As a result of feminist pressures, a statutory definition of consent as 'the voluntary agreement to engage in the sexual activity in question' (s. 273(1)2) was embedded in the *Criminal Code*, transforming consent into 'something that a woman does and freely chooses to do, not something that men fanaticize or choose for her' (McIntyre, 2000, p. 76). The revised code also enumerated a non-exhaustive set of situations where no consent is presumed to exist, including when agreement is expressed by another person, when the complainant is 'incapable of consenting', when the accused abuses a position of power, trust or authority, and when the complainant expresses a lack of agreement to engage or continue to engage in the sexual activity (s. 273(1)3). According to Sheila McIntyre (2000, p. 76), a participant in these law reforms, this provision was intended to 'convert self-serving rape-myths and rationalizations proffered as honest, but mistaken beliefs in a woman's consent, into errors of law'. Finally, the defence of mistaken belief was limited by a new requirement that the accused must have taken 'reasonable steps' to ensure consent and by specifying that there can be no such defence when this belief arises through 'recklessness' or 'willful blindness' (*Criminal Code*, 1985, s.273(2)b).

The 'reasonable steps' provision was a Canadian innovation; it modified what had been a purely subjective *mens rea* standard by introducing a quasi-objective fault element. Popularly referred to as the 'no means no' amendment, the positive definition of consent as a voluntary agreement, as well as limitations on the defence of mistaken belief, had the effect of distinguishing consent from submission, challenging a version of normative heterosexuality founded on feminine acquiescence (Gotell, 2007).

The uneven effects of rape law reform

The elaboration of consent unfolds in a context in which feminism has been delegitimised through the entrenchment of the neoliberal state, accompanied by a renewed emphasis on the rational liberal individual, choice and individual responsibility (Gotell, 2007). Many of the feminist organisations that shaped the 1990s law reforms no longer exist, disenfranchised by funding cutbacks. Over the past two decades, the policy field formed around violence against women has been replaced by the degendered policy discourse of victims' rights (Gotell, 2007, p. 132). And while the incidence of sexual violence has remained depressingly constant (Johnson, 2012), it is increasingly discussed through the language of risk. Translated into risk discourse, sexual assault becomes, like so many 'accidents', something that the individual must try to avoid.

Proponents of the carceral feminism thesis overstate the influence of feminism on policy, particularly in a context in which it seems clear that feminists have so little power. Halley (2006, p. 22) claims that feminists have 'come to power' and that struggles for justice have moved from the street to the state. Bernstein (2007, p. 143) too insists that criminal law has become a feminist 'enforcement apparatus'. Both critics invoke an image of the state as consistently repressive and of feminist law reform as an authoritarian triumph. This depiction is both troubling and empirically flawed. Comparative research conclusively demonstrates that rape law reform has not been a success story, instead revealing a widespread justice gap characterised by low reporting and prosecution rates (Tempkin & Krahé, 2008, p. 208). Despite Canada's relatively strong legal framework (as demonstrated above), statistics underline the extent to which sexual violence remains unregulated, with conviction rates actually in decline since feminist law reform projects began (Daly & Bouhours, 2010). The most recent data show dramatically high rates of sexual violence, with 3.4 per cent of Canadian women experiencing sexual assault yearly (Perreault & Brennan, 2013), police reporting rates hovering at 10 per cent, high no-criming (unfounding) rates, low clearance rates and conviction rates that remain the lowest of any violent crime (Johnson, 2012). This flat attrition pyramid has caused Holly Johnson (2012, p. 634), Canada's leading empirical researcher on violence against women, to conclude that sexual assault law reform has not resulted in improvements in the criminal justice response to survivors.

While it remains important to contest the depiction of sexual assault law reform as a feminist victory, I worry that whenever we raise the question of criminalisation as a strategy, and perhaps especially if we call on the justice gap to respond to the distorted picture painted by the critics of carceral feminism, we remain trapped within a limited analytic framework. The question of feminist law reform becomes reduced to an evaluation of influence. This framing rests upon a concept of law as a unified instrument to be seized. Indeed, an instrumental view of law was soundly criticised by feminist legal theorists in the 1980s and 1990s. Drawing on Carol Smart's (1989) insights, which were widely embraced by feminist legal scholars, law was reconceived as a dis-unified field and as a site of struggle over gender. According to Smart, legal discourse constructs and reconstructs gendered subjects and contributes to common-sense perceptions of difference. As Smart (1995, pp. 154–156) argued, law develops unevenly and is simultaneously a site of change and an obstacle to change. Such an approach directs attention to conditions under which particular laws are more or less successful in initiating change. Applying Smart's insights about the uneven development of law to the question of rape law reform leads to a far more complex analysis of feminist impact than the carceral feminism thesis allows.

We must also pay attention to how sexual assault law plays a powerful role in discursively constructing and reconstructing normative heterosexuality. This approach allows us to move beyond seeing law either as a tool for the realisation of feminist goals or as inevitably reproducing forms of domination. Instead, feminists need to appreciate law as a site of discursive struggles, with contradictory implications. Sexual assault decisions do not simply fix the line between rape and normal heterosexuality. Empowered by Law's claim to 'Truth', judicial discourses prescribe normative heterosexuality and privileged forms of masculinity and femininity (Smart, 1989).

The past two decades have witnessed significant progress towards an affirmative consent standard in Canadian law (Gotell, 2008). From the statutory foundation established through the 1992 amendments, the starting point of sexual assault trials has shifted away from the assumption that women exist in a state of consent, towards the requirement that there be some positive evidence of agreement. In *R v. Ewanchuk* (1999, 1 SCR 330), the SCC articulated a standard for consent that approaches 'only yes means yes' by unanimously ruling there is no implied consent and by establishing that silence and ambiguity cannot be taken as indications of consent. The Court defined the *actus reus* of sexual assault as non-consensual sexual touching, where consent is determined from the subjective perspective of the complainant at the time of the sexual contact, finding that steps to re-establish agreement are needed after someone has withdrawn consent. Key appellate rulings have consolidated an 'only yes means yes' standard by giving teeth to the requirements that consent must be specific and voluntary (*R v. Stender*, 2005, 1 SCR 914), and by holding that consent-seeking must comprise positive steps to secure agreement (*R v. Malcolm,* 2000, 148 Man. R. (2d) 143; *R v. Cornejo,* 68 OR (3d) 117 (Ont. C.A. 2003)). In *R v. J.A.* (2011, 2 SCR 440), the SCC determined that there can be no advance consent to sexual contact that takes place during unconsciousness, emphasising that consent must be ongoing during each moment of a sexual encounter. This doctrinal shift towards a strict and temporally specific consent standard might be seen as evidence of law's instrumentality.

The elaboration of a subjective standard (for consent) and a positive/communicative standard (for belief in consent) means that a concept of sexual autonomy is given increased weight in Canadian sexual assault law. Words and/or actions signalling consent are needed and judges are placing more onus on those initiating sexual contact to secure agreement. As this occurs, the masculine gaze that has for so long defined the consent/coercion dichotomy is challenged. This is because a subjective standard for consent necessarily focuses legal attention on the meaning of the contact from the complainant's perspective. Despite these gains, it is important to acknowledge the inconsistent application of this standard by trial judges and also the contradictory and Janus-faced nature of consent itself. As Carol Patemen (1980) argues, consent is the specifically modern means of legitimising power relations. Even when framed through an 'only yes means yes' standard, consent is not a measure of whether a woman desires sex, but instead whether she agrees. Consent thus functions as a sign of subordination (that is, submission to another's power) and a means of its legitimation. Rather than challenging the ways in which gendered power frames sexual violence, a profoundly individualising and decontextualising rationality continues to define the analytical focus of the consent doctrine. This rationality echoes the way in which the systemic nature of sexual violence has been increasingly erased in a context of neoliberal governance. As judicial decisions have developed stricter legal standards for sexual consent, they have simultaneously promoted new forms of normative sexual subjectivity built upon the anticipation of sexual risk and the necessity of clear sexual communication (Gotell, 2007, pp. 144–153). Emphasis has been placed on discrete sexual transactions, consent-seeking actions and the moment of agreement. In this way, sexual violence is atomised; its manifestations are never collected, never considered in a context where sexual assault is a mechanism for sustaining gendered power relations. Judicial decisions have recognised sexual autonomy, but in a form that is consistent with individuated norms of criminal law. Normative sexual citizens are reconfigured as being like rational economic subjects, assuming responsibility for their actions and the risks that they take (Gotell, 2008).

The production of risk-managing subjects who diligently practice sexual safekeeping becomes privileged as a technique for managing the once social and political problem of sexual violence (Gotell, 2008). The legal discourse of affirmative consent produces good masculine sexual subjects, defined through the imperatives of consent-seeking and disciplined through the risk of criminalisation. Good feminine sexual subjects are, by contrast, reaction heroes, who anticipate the risks of sexual violence floating everywhere. Victim-blaming constructions emerge repeatedly when complainants fail to behave as responsible risk managers. Even as convictions are entered, complainants are often described as having 'questionable judgement', as being 'careless', as displaying 'youthful naiveté', as engaging in 'provocative and foolish behaviour' and are also criticised for failing to respond quickly and assertively in the face of sexual threats (Gotell, 2008, pp. 879–880). In one striking example of this revised form of victim-blaming, a trial judge, convicting two men of drugging and sexually assaulting a young woman whom they had met in an internet chat room, emphasised the reckless nature of the complainant's behaviour, stating that 'she allowed herself to get into the situation in the first place' (*R v. Saadatmandi*, 2008, BCSC 250 at para. 86; Benedet, 2010, pp. 440–441).

As other feminist critics have also argued, even as a positive and specific consent standard is confirmed by doctrine, many decisions continue to be infused by discriminatory assumptions that prevent legal recognition of unwanted sexual intrusions (Benedet & Grant, 2007; Sheehy, 2012). When sexual safekeeping is privileged, those who can be viewed as inhabiting spaces of risk or as living a so-called 'high risk lifestyle' are 'hyper-responsibilised' and discredited (Gotell, 2008). In *R v. Rhodes* ('Trial Decision' as cited in LEAF, 2010, at para. 9), for example, the accused was convicted of sexually assaulting a young indigenous woman at the side of a rural highway in the middle of the night. This assault occurred after an evening of drinking, and after the complainant and her friend went for a drive to a lake with the accused and another man. The judge believed the complainant's testimony that she was afraid, that she did not consent to being penetrated, that she had told the accused that it hurt and that she ran away through the bush, ending up hailing down cars while naked from the waist down. Despite these findings, the complainant was framed as a precipitating agent in these events – 'this was different from sexual assaults where there is no perceived invitation' ('Transcript of Proceedings on Sentencing' as cited in LEAF, 2010, at para. 32). By contrast, the accused was characterised as an inconsiderate 'Clumsy Don Juan' who misread the signals because 'sex was in the air' ('Sentencing' as cited in LEAF, 2010, paras 3, 33, 34). This is one of a number of tragic cases demonstrating how the culpability of men enacting sexual violence against aboriginal women is often minimised, while victims are held responsible for their own violation because they are engaged in 'risky' actions such as drinking, partying or getting into cars with strangers (Gotell, 2008, pp. 882–884; Razack, 2000). Filtered through norms of risk management, the power relations that produce vulnerabilities disappear. The decontexutalised logic of affirmative consent, and the manner in which choice and responsibility are highlighted, pose problems for many marginalised groups of women.

In addition, the focus in *R v. Ewanchuk* on what the complainant was thinking creates problems when she is not able to tell the court what was going on in her mind at the time of the sexual activity (Benedet & Grant, 2007). The sexual assault of unconscious complainants is a depressingly recurrent scenario in decisions recorded in Canadian legal databases (Benedet, 2010; Gotell, 2007; Sheehy, 2012). As Elizabeth Sheehy (2012, p. 45) has argued, there is a systemic problem of sexual assaults against women who are intoxicated, asleep or unconscious. Scholars have demonstrated how the doctrine of consent has been misapplied in cases of intoxication and, at least before the decision in *R v. J.A.*, in cases of unconsciousness (Benedet, 2010; Sheehy, 2012). When complainants cannot remember, it is difficult to provide evidence of their subjective experience of the sexual activity. Drinking and drug use defy the disciplinary imperatives of sexual safekeeping, often resulting in judicial victim-blaming. Yet, since *R v. Ewanchuk* (1999), and certainly since *R v. J.A.* (2011), there has been a higher likelihood of conviction in such cases (Benedet, 2010; Gotell, 2007). Janine Benedet (2010, pp. 44–52) has found that judges appear less willing to apply the claim of mistaken belief when a complainant is intoxicated, often finding that the duty to take reasonable steps is elevated. Proceeding with sex in such situations is often viewed as recklessness or wilful blindness. Judges have also been more likely to rule that complainants lacked capacity to consent, especially when the latter have been rendered intoxicated involuntarily (Benedet, 2010, p. 46).

Thinking *through* feminist law reform by interrogating the productive and disciplinary dimensions of legal power reveals a complex post-reform landscape largely obscured by the carceral feminist thesis. Reece (2013, p. 445), for her part, acknowledges that 'rape law reform has been a symbiosis of success and failure'. Yet here too the emphasis placed on 'success versus failure' as the fulcrum of analysis ignores how sexual assault decisions play a role in shifting and readjusting sexual subjectivities within the context of neoliberal governance. While I have emphasised that a temporally specific consent standard obscures power relations that constrain choice, it is also important to acknowledge how this standard has a potentially radical edge. As an outcome of doctrinal changes, sexual violence against 'non-paradigmatic victims', including complainants who are intoxicated and those affected by acquaintance rape, appears to be gaining legal recognition.

Decriminalisation?

The extent to which the affirmative consent standard has widened the legal understanding of sexual assault is not something that would be applauded by critics of carceral feminism. Instead, this redrawing of the boundary between sexual violence and normative heterosexuality beyond the stereotype of 'real rape' would likely be seen as exemplifying the repressive impact of feminist campaigns against sexual violence. Critics like Bernstein (2012) and Halley (2006) seem particularly worried about the criminalisation of what has been seen to be normative masculine sexual behaviour. Bernstein criticises the emergence of 'feminist family values' in campaigns against sex trafficking and prostitution. Enforced through criminalisation, 'feminist family values' seek to domesticate male sexuality and to repress a recreational sexual ethic with the effect of bolstering heterosexual domesticity (Bernstein, 2012, pp. 246–250). Halley is even more overt in her attack on what she sees as the sexually repressive implications of governance feminism. While Halley is concerned with how governance feminism constructs women as victims and fails to respect their sexual agency, she seems much more worried about the impacts of anti-rape campaigning for men's sexuality. For Halley (2006, p. 65), it is unregulated sexual pleasure and masculine men that are most threatened by feminist calls for the legal regulation of sexual harm. This is a post-feminist form of anti-statism, in which state regulation of sexual harm is condemned as 'schoolmarmish', against which the transgressive pleasures of an unregulated sexual marketplace are celebrated (McCluskey, 2009). As McCluskey (2009, p. 133) has pointed out, governance feminism is analogous to the metaphor of the nanny state within libertarian discourses.

For critics of carceral feminism, the question of what to do about perpetrators of sexual violence gets brushed aside. Much of Bernstein's (2007, 2010, 2012) analysis is based on the specific example of movements against sex trafficking and prostitution, and she explicitly advocates decriminalisation. But even though she makes wider claims about feminist campaigns against sexual violence, a strategic approach to the problem of sexual assault is left unarticulated. When an anti-carceral position is put forward as the only possible progressive stance, and when anti-rape feminists are condemned for their complicity in the law and order state, decriminalisation is implied and sometimes explicitly embraced. The endorsement of a rigid anti-carceral stance treats the question of criminalisation as an all-or-nothing affair. The contradictory implications of feminist law reform are ignored, along with the possibilities of progressive engagements with criminal law.

In Canada, the prospects for further feminist law reforms of the kind enacted in the 1990s have closed. Since the election of the Harper Conservatives in 2006, the gender-neutral rhetoric of victims' rights has been deployed to legitimise a harsh 'tough on crime' agenda that has included: mandatory minimum sentences; the abolition of conditional sentencing (non-carceral) for serious crimes, including sexual assault; and the end of statutory (early) release policies encouraging offenders to participate in rehabilitation programming (Mallea, 2010). While sexual assault law reforms were enacted in the 1990s in an explicit effort to combat 'violence against women', the current government's crime agenda is instead about using incarceration to promote 'safety'. This agenda has accelerated the politics of punishment in Canada, with rising rates of incarceration and the increased use of imprisonment to manage marginalised populations. Canada's federal prison population has increased by more than 7 per cent since 2006, with all new net growth accounted for by increases in the number of aboriginal and racialised inmates (Office of the Correctional Investigator, 2013).

Within this context, it is important for feminists to publicly disengage from the politics of punishment and to rearticulate the same critiques of the law and order state that accompanied 1990s law reform campaigns. As Wendy Larcombe (2011) and Claire McGlynn (2011) have both argued, feminists need to ensure that the demand for justice is not equated with securing harsh punishment and imprisonment. Larcombe contends that we should stop measuring success through rape conviction rates, not only because the goal of punishment is inconsistent with feminist aims, but also because efforts to increase convictions tend to reinforce a narrow prosecutorial focus on violent, stranger rape. She recommends that rape law should instead be measured against survivor-centred outcomes, including by the extent to which the law reflects women's experiences of sexual assault, while not disempowering or increasing the vulnerability of complainants. Given the importance of respect, acknowledgement and voice as core elements of justice from the standpoint of survivors, McGlynn (2011, p. 826) insists that feminist activism move beyond punishment to encompass broader notions of justice, including an expansive approach to restorative justice. Significantly, feminist scholars recommending a reconceptualisation of rape justice avoid sliding into the kind of sexual libertarianism that underpins the critique of carceral feminism. While McGlynn (2011, p. 841) insists that our energies be redirected from conventional criminal justice to alternative justice measures, she does not suggest abdicating the terrain of criminal law. Indeed, as Larcombe (2011, p. 43) warns, continued feminist engagement with rape law is necessary 'to ensure that the ground gained by feminist-inspired reforms over the past 30 years is not now ceded to non-feminist measures'.

While criminal law reform has had contradictory effects, the absolute rejection of criminalisation strategies would only intensify the silence around sexual violence as a systemic problem, re-privatising sexual assault and risking the return of impunity for acts of sexual violence. Critical analysis of criminal law must be combined with renewed attention to diverse extralegal strategies that would re-politicise the problem of sexual assault and offer alternative responses. While I agree with McGlynn (2011) that we need to widen the focus beyond conventional criminalisation responses, I wonder whether it would also be productive to think about how we might strategically redeploy the legal standard for affirmative consent outside law. Other chapters in this book confront alternative justice measures that could recognise the harms of sexual violence and offer strategies for perpetrator accountability (see Daly, Chapter 3; Flynn, Chapter 6; Godden, Chapter 7; and Henry, Chapter 12). What are the mechanisms for ensuring that sexual violence is dealt with through such measures? Acknowledged violations of a voluntary, communicative and contemporaneous understanding of consent could provide a set of criteria for triggering restorative justice or community justice processes. Just as important, this conception of consent has the potential to challenge those discourses positioning women as individually responsible for rape avoidance that are evident both in law (as already discussed), and indeed within public accounts of rape typical of a backlash to anti-rape feminism (see, for example, Yoffe, 2013). Rape avoidance in a context of neoliberal governance relies on self-management and divides women on the basis of adherence to constraining safety rules. Yet through the requirement of active agreement in the moment, an affirmative consent standard also offers the possibility of liberating women from the disciplinary rules of sexual safekeeping. If what one does before a sexual assault becomes irrelevant to the 'moment', then the rules that have enforced women's conformity to sexual safety norms ('don't drink too much', 'don't go out alone', 'don't...') no longer have legitimacy. Feminist deployments of specific consent can legitimise defiance of the rules of sexual safekeeping.

Conclusion

Feminists concerned about the deficiency of legal responses to sexual violence have good reasons for exploring the potential of rape justice beyond law. To completely abandon criminal law, however, would result in the further deregulation of sexual violence. In the flattened narrative spun by the critics of criminalisation, 'carceral' feminism is folded into the law and order state, constructed as inherently regressive and positioned as something to be liberated from. By telling a more complex and empirically grounded story of Canadian feminist law reform campaigns, I have demonstrated how the carceral feminism thesis produces a caricature of what were complex and critical feminist engagements with the state. As an important outcome of Canadian feminist law reform, the affirmative consent standard has had highly contradictory implications, at once decontextualising sexual violence while also providing a discursive platform for a radical challenge to the victim-blaming and disciplinary norms of rape avoidance. We need to maintain an approach to law that is capable of revealing its complexities, if only because contradictions can be exploited for progressive feminist ends. Feminists have pursued law reform strategies to gain recognition of the harms caused by sexual assault, not to punish and incarcerate perpetrators. The discourse of affirmative consent, strategically redeployed in the contemporary context of backlash, holds the potential to disrupt the re-responsibilisation of women and cultivate social responsibility for sexual violence.

References

Benedet, J. (2010) 'The Sexual Assault of Intoxicated Women', *Canadian Journal of Women and the Law*, 22, 435–462.

Benedet, J. and Grant, I. (2007) 'Hearing the Sexual Assault Complaints of Women with Mental Disabilities: Consent, Capacity and Mistaken Belief', *McGill Law Journal*, 52, 243–289.

Bernstein, E. (2007) 'The Sexual Politics of the "New Abolitionism" ', *Differences*, 18(3), 128–151.

Bernstein, E. (2010) 'Militarized Humanitarianism Meets Carceral Feminism: The Politics of Sex, Rights and Freedom in Contemporary Antitrafficking Campiagns', *Signs*, 62(1), 45–71.

Bernstein, E. (2012) 'Carceral Politics as Gender Justice: Neoliberal Circuits of Crime, Sex, and Rights', *Theory and Society*, 41(1), 233–259.

Bevaqua, M. (2000) *Rape on the Public Agenda: Feminism and the Politics of Sexual Assault* (Boston, MA: Northeastern University Press).

Bumiller, K. (2008) *In an Abusive State: How Neoliberalism Appropriated the Feminist Movement Against Sexual Violence* (Durham, NC: Duke University Press).

Canadian House of Commons (1992) *Legislative Committee on Bill C-49: An Act to Amend the Criminal Code Sexual Assault, Minutes and Proceedings* (Ottawa: Queen's Printer).

Chunn, D., Boyd, S. B. and Lessard, H. (2007) 'Feminism, Law, and Social Change: An Overview', in D. Chunn, S. B. Boyd and H. Lessard (eds.) *Reaction and Resistance: Feminism, Law, and Social Change* (Vancouver: University of British Columbia Press), pp. 1–28.

Daly, K. and Bouhours, B. (2010) 'Rape and Attrition in the Legal Process: A Comparative Analysis of Five Countries', *Crime and Justice*, 39(1), 565–650.

Gavey, N. (2005) *Just Sex?: The Cultural Scaffolding of Rape* (London, UK: Routledge).

Gotell, L. (1998) 'A Critical Look at State Discourse on "Violence Against Women": Some Implications for Feminist Politics and Women's Citizenship', in M. Tremblay and C. Andrew (eds.) *Women and Political Representation in Canada* (Ottawa: University of Ottawa Press), pp. 39–72.

Gotell, L. (2007) 'The Discursive Disappearance of Sexualized Violence: Feminist Law Reform, Judicial Resistance and Neo-liberal Sexual Citizenship', in D. E. Chunn, S. B. Boyd and H. Lessard (eds.) *Feminism, Law and Social*

Change: (Re)action and Resistance (Vancouver: University of British Columbia Press), pp. 127–163.

Gotell, L. (2008) 'Rethinking Affirmative Consent in Canadian Law: Neoliberal Sexual Subjects and Risky Women', *Akron Law Review*, 41, 865–898.

Gottschalk, M. (2008) 'Hiding in Plain Sight: American Politics and the Carceral State', *Annual Review of Political Science*, 11, 235–260.

Halley, J. (2006) *Spit Decisions: How and Why to Take a Break from Feminism* (Princeton, NJ: Princeton University Press).

Halley, J., Kotiswaran, P., Shamir, H. and Thomas, C. (2006) 'From the International to the Local in Feminist Legal Responses to Rape, Prostitution/Sex Work, and Sex Trafficking: Four Studies in Contemporary Governance', *Harvard Journal of Law and Gender*, 29, 335–423.

Johnson, H. (2012) 'Limits of a Criminal Justice Response: Trends in Police and Court Processing of Sexual Assault', in E. Sheehy (ed.) *Sexual Assault in Canada: Law, Legal Practice and Women's Activism* (Ottawa: University of Ottawa Press), pp. 613–634.

Kitchens, C. (2014) 'It's Time to End Rape Culture', *Time Magazine*, 20 May 2014.

Lakeman, L. (1993) *99 Federal Steps to End Violence Against Women* (Toronto: National Action Committee).

Lakeman, L. (2004) *Canada's Promises to Keep: The Charter and Violence Against Women* (Vancouver: Canadian Association of Sexual Assault Centres).

Larcombe, W. (2011) 'Falling Rape Conviction Rates: (Some) Feminist Aims and Measures for Rape Law', *Feminist Legal Studies*, 19, 27–45.

LEAF (2010) Motion Brief of the Proposed Intervener in *R. v. Rhodes*, Manitoba Court of Appeal (Court file number AR 11-30-07535).

MacDonald, H. (2014) 'This Obama Administration's Deserving Victims', *National Review Online*; Retrieved from http://www.nationalreview.com/article/377492/obama-administrations-deserving-victims-heather-mac-donald/page/0/1

Mallea, P. (2010) *The Fear Factor: Stephen Harper's 'Tough on Crime' Agenda* (Ottawa: Canadian Centre for Policy Alternatives).

McCluskey, M. T. (2009) 'How Queer Theory Makes Neoliberalism Sexy', in M. A. Fineman (ed.) *Feminist and Queer Legal Theory: Intimate Encounters, Uncomfortable Conversations*, e-book (Burlington: Ashgate).

McGlynn, C. (2011) 'Feminism, Rape, and the Search for Justice', *Oxford Journal of Legal Studies*, 34(3), 825–842.

McIntyre, S. (2000) 'Tracking and Resisting Backlash Against Equality Gains in Sexual Offence Law', *Canadian Woman Studies*, 20(3), 72–83.

Office of the Correctional Investigator (2013) *40th Annual Report to Parliament*, Government of Canada; Retrieved from http://www.oci-bec.gc.ca/cnt/comm/presentations/presentationsAR-RA1213info-eng.aspx

Paglia, C. (1992) *Sex, Art and American Culture* (New York: Random House).

Pateman, C. (1980) 'Women and Consent', *Political Theory*, 8, 149–168.

Perreault, S. and Brennan, S. (2013) *Criminal Victimization in Canada 2009* (Ottawa: Statistics Canada); Retrieved from http://www.statcan.gc.ca/pub/85-002-x/2010002/article/11340-eng.htm

Razack, S. (2000) 'Gendered Racial Violence and Spatialized Justice: The Murder of Pamela George', *Canadian Journal of Law and Society*, 15, 91–130.

Reece, H. (2011) '"Unpalatable Messages"? Feminist Analysis of United Kingdom Legislative Discourse on Stalking 1996–1997', *Feminist Legal Studies*, 19(3), 205–230.

Reece, H. (2013) 'Rape Myths: Is Elite Opinion Right and Popular Opinion Wrong', *Oxford Journal of Legal Studies*, 33(3), 445–473.
Roiphe, K. (1994) *The Morning After: Sex, Fear, and Feminism* (Boston, MA: Little Brown).
Schmitz, C. (1988) '"Whack" Sexual Assault Complainant at Preliminary Inquiry', *Lawyers Weekly*, 27 May, 22.
Sheehy, E. (2012) 'Judges and the Reasonable Steps Requirement: The Judicial Stance on Perpetration Against Unconscious Women', in E. Sheehy (ed.) *Sexual Assault in Canada: Law, Legal Practice and Women's Activism* (Ottawa: University of Ottawa Press), pp. 483–540.
Smart, C. (1989) *Feminism and the Power of Law* (London, UK: Routledge).
Smart, C. (1995) *Law, Crime and Sexuality* (London, UK: Sage).
Tempkin, J. and Krahé, B. (2008) *Sexual Assault and the Justice Gap: A Question of Attitude* (Oxford: Hart Publishing).
Wente, M. (2013) 'When Booze Culture and Rape Culture Meet', *Globe and Mail*, 22 October 2013.
Yoffe, E. (2013) 'College Women Stop Getting Drunk', *Slate*, 15 October 2013.

5
When Yes Actually Means Yes
Confusing Messages and Criminalising Consent

James A. Roffee

Introduction

There is little question that unwanted – that is, non-consensual – sexual activities have rightly been the focus of much public concern, academic debate and criminal justice system response. A primary concern for regulators in choosing to use criminal law is the protection of those who are subjected to unwanted sexual activity. However, regulators have also enacted criminal prohibitions against a range of other sexual activities that *are* consensual and not unwanted by the individuals involved. Although a number of common law jurisdictions have sought a clear and coherent rationale for the selection and categorisation of acts to be contained more generally within the criminal law, there has been little success to date in creating a coherent body of law. As such, the regulation of sex, in particular, through the criminal law, is done in an ad hoc and crude manner.

This chapter focuses on the incoherent regulation of consent in sexual activities and highlights the confusion caused by the messages communicated through law that have serious implications for responding to unwanted sexual activity. Consent is a key concept in the contemporary regulation of sex and often the focus of much attention. This chapter will discuss some present difficulties in the operationalisation of the concept of consent in sexual offences and calls for strengthening both the meaning and use of consent as a model in the regulation of sexual activity. It is argued that regulators must avoid confusing the messages relating to consensual and non-consensual behaviour. The use and then selective ignorance of the concept of consent in law is problematic for the legal system, victims, offenders and the public at large. Regulators' selective interest and muddled use of consent in law to control sexual activity has serious implications for the achievement of justice for victims of rape and unwanted penetrative and other serious and offensive sexual activity. The incoherent and murky use of consent has allowed for consensual sexual acts to be recast as criminally abusive. It has also created space for calls for the expansion of the concept of rape to represent seemingly consensual acts, which, although offensive, do not match common understandings of the most serious criminal sexual acts. However, consent has not always been a core concern of law. For example, historically the law on sexual offences reflected patriarchal structures concerning the position of women as chaste property, violable only by their husbands, which meant that a woman's agreement to any sexual act was not a concern of law. The regulation of sex within Western democracies has seen significant change in the past century, including shifts in the legal status of women in society, the decriminalisation of a number of sexual offences including adultery, fornication, sodomy and buggery, and the enactment of new offences including the criminalisation of some forms of extreme and child pornography, child grooming, sex trafficking and the purchase of some sexual services.

This chapter begins by placing the regulation of sexual behaviour in context and recognising the need to ensure that responses to sexual activity are not only theoretically sound, but also practically workable. This is followed by a section on the appropriation of consent into law. Examples are used to highlight the multiple mixed messages provided when consent is used in law, including where consent is deemed to be impossible in some circumstances (where children are present), and where consent is ignored with regard to other sexual activities (sodomy and buggery, as a shorthand for homosexuality). Other examples include where consensual sexual activity (sadomasochistic acts and between some family members) continues to see over-regulation through the conflation and reinterpretation in law with 'abuse' or 'violence', using an overly simplistic consent/non-consent binary. Before concluding, the final section argues that if consent is to remain central to the definition of rape, there remains the difficult task of drawing lines around what vitiates consent. This will allow pressing contemporary issues such as sex with fraud, potential mistake or sex by deception to receive an appropriate and more effective regulatory response.

Regulation of sexual behaviour

The norms of society are reflected in the laws it enacts. As such, neither society nor the law stand independent of each other. Moore (1973, p. 719) noted that 'the law' is a short term for a 'very complex aggregation of principles, norms, ideas, rules, practices, and the activities of agencies... and enforcement'. Changes in societal understandings of appropriate sexual conduct have been reflected and codified in law. As these understandings change, a society responds by ensuring that the law is reflective of social and cultural understandings of wrongdoings in a sexual context. Engle-Merry (1988) has argued that the legal system stands in a relation of superior power to other systems of regulation as the ultimate source of coercive power. Accordingly, appropriate legal responses are necessary not merely for providing protection to those who may be subject to such behaviour, but also in providing a socially educative function (Attorney General's Department of New South Wales, 2005, p. 34; Australia, Model Criminal Code Officers Committee, 1999, p. 35). The labels attached to incidents of wrongdoing are also crucial. Actors seeking to combat rape and other unwanted sexual activity, including the state and non-governmental organisations, as well as members of the public, look to the law and legislation as the rules to regulate behaviour. Perkins and Boyce (1982, p. 5) suggest than 'an incidental but very important function of the criminal law is to teach the difference between right and wrong'. Many scholars have argued that law provides both identity and boundaries for political society, as well as simultaneously expressing and structuring social life. Thus, it is law that makes society possible (Cotterrell, 2006; Fitzpatrick, 1995). Such law must therefore be moulded to allow for responses that acknowledge the true nature of the incident being addressed.

Academics and commentators have argued that the current regulation of sex and sexuality through the criminal law requires radical reconceptualisation (Langdridge, 2006) and of particular concern is the law's use of consent. Langdridge (2006, p. 277) has argued that consent 'is a particularly problematic concept', and widely respected academics have advocated abandoning consent altogether (see Tadros, 2006). Tadros (2006) has argued that even if consent is central to the most appropriate theoretical investigation into the scope of the law of rape, its malleable and ambiguous nature distracts legal actors from addressing the true issue of whether the survivor's autonomy was respected. Theoretically, feminist academics have heavily critiqued the use of consent in an individualistic and liberal state, some further suggesting that patriarchy results in consensual sex being a myth for women who do not have the freedom of choice (MacKinnon, 1987; see also Pateman, 1988). Chandra-Shekeran (1997) has persuasively argued that the partial application of consent (in the laws' categorisation of, and response to, heterosexual and homosexual sexual encounters) casts a very large shadow of doubt over its use as a functional category within the realm of sexualised violence. She suggests we should therefore recognise a continuum of violence through which sexual acts can be understood and responded to through the use of the law.

Current structures for dispute resolution are a long way from being able to handle criminal events using radically different approaches. Our inability to appropriately conceptualise and coherently regulate sexual behaviour continues to lead to a number of pressing contemporary concerns. With the recognition that the criminal law should be used to delineate behaviour that is truly criminal and not merely socially undesirable, many hours have been spent rethinking how to operationalise consent. These calls for greater protection for those subjected to unwanted sexual activity are often muted by the omnipresent concerns about the unnecessary expansion of the state (see also Gotell, Chapter 4). Transcending the philosophical debates about the use of criminal law to ensure that practical and workable solutions are available to respond to contemporary problems is no easy task. The remainder of this chapter presents some current concerns and potential avenues for change in the use of consent to address serious unwanted sexual conduct.

The legalisation of consent

Regulators have appropriated consent into law in a number of different areas, including contract, property offences, offences against the person, medical law and sexual offences. In the criminal law, consent is used by legislators to delineate between behaviour which, although potentially socially undesirable, the community is willing to tolerate and that which should be prohibited as criminal. In the medico-legal sphere, it is used through the concept of informed consent relating to risks involved in medical treatment (Berg et al., 2001; Leino-Kilpi et al., 2003; White & Ashley, 2012). It also acts as a defence in a number of potential offences against a person, including in injurious sporting and recreational activities (Farrugia, 1996). Brett (1998) suggests that consent in the area of sexual activity is quite different from consent in medical treatment. Brett argues that the emphasis placed on the survivor's subjective attitude towards the sexual act in question forms the basis of the decision, as opposed to an objective understanding when dealing with medical patients. Thomas (2000) notes that the concept is central to defining sexual offending and that all sexual activities are expected to be consensual. It is morally axiomatic to suggest that individuals should be free agents able to decide when, where and with whom they engage in sexual activity. In the cases where one party in a sexual activity has not consented, we begin to move into the realm of sexual offences.

Across common law jurisdictions there exist multiple definitions and a plethora of different offences criminalising unwanted sexual conduct. Some of these non-consensual incidents include where consent is obtained by force, through fear or fraud, mistake, threats, abuse of power or other pressures. Dingwall (2002, p. 32) notes that while a defendant's actions can be understood on a continuum of conduct, in legal terms, consent is an 'absolute concept'. Our attention should therefore turn, and serious consideration be given to, its use to delineate between the 'stark... dichotomy' of those who are to be considered rapists and those who are not *in law*. His concern is undoubtedly a legitimate one; that there is a need for a position that is philosophically justifiable and that also satisfies the demands for legal certainty, and provides protection for those at risk from forms of non-violent sexual coercion.

With the understanding that the law is an instrument of public policy, academics and lawyers call for a consistent approach to consent and thus expect the concept to have similar, if not identical, definition and application across the multiple areas of regulation. Inconsistent approaches have been inherently problematic and there have been calls for an extension of consent in sexual offences to match understandings of consent in property offences (Elliott & De Than, 2007). However, even if we are unable to achieve consistency between areas of law – for example, between civil and criminal law – or even between different areas of criminal law – such as property offences and sexual offences – it should be of the utmost importance that we achieve consistency within the same area of regulation.

Attempts to provide consistency in the regulation of sex have progressed through the development of a number of overarching 'meta-principles'. These include sexual autonomy (Schulhofer, 1992),[1] sexual integrity (see Lacey, 1998) as well as sexual violation and sexual possession (Rubenfeld, 2013). In 2003, England and Wales attempted to use a number of general principles in a wholesale reform of the body of law regulating sexual activity. The two key guiding principles included the requirement that the judgement of what is right and wrong should be based on an assessment of the harm done to the individual and secondly, that the criminal law should not intrude unnecessarily into the private lives of adults. Other guiding principles were found in the terms of reference and included fairness and non-discrimination, acting in accordance with human rights instruments, and development of laws that provide appropriate punishment, protection and clarity, and coherence. The legislative outcome was progressive and a vast improvement from the previous arbitrary and discriminatory set of offences. However, as I have argued elsewhere (Roffee, 2014b), the concept of sexual autonomy and in particular, the consensual nature of sexual activity was used to justify, rather than inform, the outcome which became law in England and Wales. Unfortunately, the selective and ad hoc use of consent did not lead to a coherent regulation of sexual offences. Instead, consent was rhetorically used to regulate socially disapproved yet undoubtedly consensual sexual acts. For example, although it was recognised in pre-legislative reports (and by ministers in Parliament) that it would be inappropriate to use the criminal law to respond to instances of consensual and non-coercive sibling sexual activity, such activity was included within the term 'incest'. Thus, the decision to adopt provisions to tackle the problem of 'incest' (commonly understood as familial adult–child sexual abuse) enabled the reconstructed law to be used to respond to consensual sibling activity in a similar manner to non-consensual and abusive conduct (Roffee, 2014b).

As occurred in this British 2003 legislative reform example, consent was appropriated and operationalised through a binary coding. Two polemic categories of sexual activity are possible: the consensual, which is equated to the wanted and the acceptable; and the antithesis, the non-consensual, the unwanted and the unacceptable. The law turns acts that exist on a continuum into acts that can (and will, in the eyes of the law) be neatly assigned into one of the binary categorised groupings to be operationalised in the courts. The regulators' irreverence for the true nature of consent and its existence on a spectrum has serious implications for victim-survivors of rape and in particular, individuals who practice non-traditional sexual scripts.

The law requires a clear line of distinction between consensual behaviours and non-consensual behaviours; it does not cope well with shades of grey. For example, the law struggles to deal appropriately with consensual adult sibling relations and sadomasochistic sexual activity. However, outside of law, there is recognition that this binary does not reflect the true nature of sexual acts. Rejecting a binary understanding of sexual activity, Kelly (1987, p. 54) places sexual acts on a continuum 'moving from choice to pressure to coercion to force'. For example, some young women might not necessarily physically resist or say 'no' when they do not want to have sex, for reasons which vary from feeling pressured, whether directly or indirectly, to acquiescence (Powell, 2007, p. 24).[2] Moreover, it is possible to envisage situations where a partner engages in sexual compliance, in the absence of any duress, without wanting to partake in such sexual activity. Impett and Peplau (2003), for example, found that 'sexual capitulation' occurred, amongst other reasons, to impress peers, gain partner approval and promote intimacy between sexual actors. Distinguishing between 'pressured' or 'compliant' sex, and in what circumstances any of these experiences might be understood as 'rape', is not in practice straightforward. When adopting a binary approach, the law requires a jury to assign each of these incidents with a consensual or non-consensual label. In law, such a label does not always appropriately reflect the nature of the incident and how the participants experienced and understood it.

Understanding the deficiencies in our current operationalisation and regulation of the concept of consent and any disjuncture in this from social reality is key to understanding how and where we can take action to better regulate unwanted sexual activity. Unfortunately, many common law jurisdictions have failed to adequately and consistently approach consent within sexual offences. The next section looks at a number of hard cases: situations where individuals consent to the sexual activity in question, but the state intervenes, signifying disapproval of the sexual activity between two autonomous actors and thereby labelling the activity criminal. Regulators have indicated in a number of situations that they regard the existence of consent as immaterial, and although consent exists between the parties, they nonetheless treat the act as criminal. These overlapping groupings can broadly be categorised as situations where consent is deemed by the state to be impossible, ignored or is reinterpreted. The following sections will present a number of situations where although the parties say 'yes' to the sexual activity, the state says 'no', and acts to criminalise and censor such conduct.

Young people consenting to sexual activity

The law has prevented young people and children from giving consent to sexual activities on the basis that they are unable to comprehend fully what they would be consenting to. As such, they are found to lack sufficient competence to consent to sexual activity, and any consent is deemed impossible (see Daly, Chapter 3). It is generally accepted that young people should receive the protection of the law, even if this is through the rough and rather arbitrary determination of capacity on the basis of age. Complexities arise, however, through a lack of consistency across jurisdictions both within and across national boundaries, as well as differences in perceived capacity to consent on the basis of sex, sexual orientation and particular sexual activity taking place. This problem is not solely one related to the criminal law, but more broadly to the treatment of young people by legislators through the use of law.

It is, therefore, a matter of public policy that a standard age is selected, and sexual activity between any person and the minor is not permitted. Although there are a number of commentators who argue that such legislation impacts on the rights of the child, there has been recognition that some states have enacted overly broad laws to protect children from potential abuse (Perry, 2009). Thus, while in practice a young person in Victoria (Australia) may be fully aware about the consequences of the activity to which they are consenting, if they are under 16 years of age, the law deems them unable to consent to such activity (depending on the age of the other person engaging in the sexual activity). As such, in addition to any potential moral basis, the desire to communicate a clear and consistent message results in age-based regulations being regarded as necessary for the protection of minors.

'Homosexual' sexual acts

The law has traditionally been irreverent to sexual activities between gay men, although many states were uninterested in criminal law regulation of female-to-female sexual activity. Until very recently in a number of common law countries, homosexual men have not been able to legally have sexual relations with each other. In a number of jurisdictions, sexual activity (often termed, amongst other things, sodomy, buggery and gross indecency) was criminalised regardless of whether or not consent was present. Although applicable to heterosexuals, these prohibitions had a disproportionate impact on gay citizens.

In addition to criminalising the specific sexual acts, discrimination against gays and lesbians occurred in a number of other ways. For example, once the specific act was no longer criminalised, differential ages of consent for sexual activity (as compared with heterosexual sexual acts) were argued to be necessary in order to protect younger men from the predatory acts and corrupting ways of older gay men. In Tasmania (Australia), decriminalisation of sex between adult men did not occur until 1997 in response to an anti-discrimination challenge in the High Court of Australia. In Queensland (Australia), there still exists a crime of unlawful sodomy under section 208 of the *Criminal Code 1899* (Qld), which among other things, criminalises consensual anal intercourse (and attempts) involving any person who is under 18. Although a number of Australian states decriminalised homosexual acts, differential age categories (for homosexual/heterosexual sexual activity) remained in Western Australia until 2002, and in New South Wales and the Northern Territory until 2003.

Prior to 1967 in England and Wales, sexual activity between two men was criminal. However, section 1 of the *Sexual Offences Act 1967* (Eng) set the age of consent at 21 years for males. Before this time, the consensual nature of sexual activity between the parties was ignored and the acts criminalised. Indeed it was the social disapproval of such behaviour that formed the basis for the criminalisation and enforcement of the laws against such acts. These arbitrary morally based regulations were applied in an inconsistent manner and added to the patchwork of incoherent rules regulating sexual activity.

Sex between family members: 'Incest'

Consent has also been deemed to be irrelevant to a whole range of sexual activity between family members. However, the fact that 'incest' provisions apply to both consensual and non-consensual activity has drawn criticism (England and Wales, Home Office, 2000; Heath, 2005; Roffee, 2012; Victoria Department of Justice, Criminal Law Review, 2013). There is a line of thought that suggests incest is seen as less serious than rape and that it may be a disincentive for an abused family member to report an incident for fear of prosecution themselves (Heath, 2005). The *Criminal Law Review* in Victoria (Australia) recently suggested that 'the very existence of the offence contributes to a perception that child victims/survivors are complicit in some way in incestuous sexual abuse' (Victoria Department of Justice, 2013, p. xi). Commonly known as incest, although better labelled as 'familial sexual activity', this behaviour encompasses a wide array of activities, including penile–vaginal, –oral and –anal penetration (Roffee, 2012). I have argued elsewhere that consent was used in an amorphous way in England and Wales during the preparation of the latest criminal provisions prohibiting consensual familial sexual activity (Roffee, 2014a, 2014b). The labelling of consensual sexual activity between adult family members – in the absence of grooming, pressure or coercion – as *non-consensual* facilitated the passage of an act that failed to adhere to the principles of non-discrimination and sexual autonomy that the state sought to uphold (Roffee, 2014a, 2014b). A number of sophisticated rhetorical and semantic techniques were used to liken consensual sexual activity between adult siblings to abusive conduct. This ultimately facilitated the continued criminalisation of sexual activity that did not meet the meta-principles of sexual autonomy and non-discrimination, and arguably while legislation remains enacted, it continues to breach international human rights treaties including Article 8 *The Right to Respect for Private and Family Life* and Article 14 *Prohibition of Discrimination in the European Convention on Human Rights* (Roffee, 2014a).

Sadomasochistic sexual activity

The contemporary regulation of sadomasochistic sexual conduct is likewise an area of great controversy. It has been argued that the law disregards the sexual nature of the acts in sadomasochistic sexual encounters and instead focuses on what it interprets as violent and dangerous non-normative behaviour (Richters et al., 2008). There have been a number of high-profile cases that have received much critical attention. The famous British case, *R v. Brown* ([1994] 1 AC 212), involved the investigation of 43 men, with 15 taken to trial for a whole host of offences relating to:

> beatings of buttocks, legs, cocks and balls with leather straps, canes, nettles etc. Hot wax being dripped onto genitals, torso, legs, etc. Play piercings of tits, scrotums, cock knobs, shafts, and foreskins. Genital application of heat (hair driers) and cold (ice cubes)... scrotal stretching and pinning out with needles etc. Nipple and cock branding...
>
> (White, 2006, p. 169)

The judge in the case prevented the parties from relying on the defence of consent. Chandra-Shekeran's (1997) analysis persuasively articulates the power in legal discourse to both produce and vilify those engaging in the sexual activities in this case. She detailed how violence was used as a descriptor for the acts, thus preventing the use of consent as a defence against the criminal charges. Academics and commentators have argued that this was a notoriously problematic decision resulting from nothing more than the judge's consultation with his conceptions of appropriate sexual behaviour and morality.

This case became the basis for subsequent cases marginalising others' sexual expression within the criminal law and deciding there was public interest in disallowing individuals to engage in such sexual activities (Furlong, 1991). Although claiming not to be moralising in their analysis, others such as Hanna (2000, p. 270) dismiss encounters involving bondage, discipline, sadism and masochism (BDSM) as dehumanising, and promote the use of the law to create a 'civilized masculinity'.

Unlike other activities involving bodily injury, including boxing and body piercing, the consensual nature of the BDSM activities is disregarded and has not yet been deemed to be in the public interest. This unsatisfactory situation remains in a number of common law countries where the law remains over-inclusive in regulating such consensual activity.

Indeed, there remains strong reluctance to criminalise sports that result in serious bodily harm. Instead, regulators prefer codes of self-regulation on the basis of a perceived personal and social benefit from allowing individuals to engage in dangerous and risky activities (Corkery, 2011). Researchers (Förstl et al., 2010) have suggested there are serious health complications arising from boxing and that these have been largely outside the scope of any critical analysis – although the level of risk is disputed (Loosemore, Knowles & Whyte, 2007; Walsh, 1994). Regulators also continue to allow body piercing on the basis of public interest, despite many studies indicating that body piercing is a risk factor for several infectious diseases including viral hepatitis (Hayes & Harkness, 2001; Tweeten & Rickman, 1998). The unwillingness to regulate these activities is not seen in relation to sadomasochistic acts, with reasoning around bodily harm less than effectively disguising the seemingly moralistic basis for regulation of BDSM activities.

Responding to potential mistake or sex by deception

In recent times, there has been a flurry of attention concerning situations where a 'victim has consented to sexual activity after the defendant has deceived her or him in some way' (Herring, 2002, p. 182). These include the heavily debated Israeli case of Sabbur Kashur – an Arab man convicted of rape. The basis of the conviction was that he pretended he was Jewish, when he had sex with a Jewish woman, who ostensibly consented to intercourse. The Israeli Court found the lie to be sufficient to negate consent and thus the act was regarded as rape (BBC, 2010). Gross (2007, p. 220) suggests that 'what might be called "seemingly consensual sex" has become one of the most written about crimes of our time'.

While prima facie deceptive behaviour may seem odious and thus socially undesirable, we should be equally concerned with the potential for excessive use of the criminal law to regulate or respond to such activities. Some pro-expansionists (in relation to criminal law) such as Herring (2002) have utilised meta-principles such as sexual autonomy to expand what we know to be rape. His argument is based on the morally axiomatic, though arguably factually far-fetched, statement that 'sexual relationships involve intimacy and trust and therefore heightened obligations of fiduciary nature' (Herring, 2002, p. 193). While we might agree that 'we would expect higher standards of truth from a lover than from a sales person or politician!' (Herring, 2002, p. 193), to Herring, any breach of sexual autonomy can be equated with a lack of true consent, and in the current legal formation of rape law, lack of consent makes the act rape. Herring fails to acknowledge that this utopian ideal is an application of morality as law to a large number of sexual acts where the actors do not hold the same idealistic views. His argument fails to appreciate that while there are some negative consequences with sexual deception, for many, sexual encounters may be understood as an exchange process (Marelich & Graham, 2013; Marelich et al., 2008). This exchange may happen for a number of reasons, not all of which require criminal sanction.

Equally, Herring's vehement belief that *any* deception invalidates consent, and should therefore be equally criminally defined as rape, is arguably at odds with the spectrum of possible deceptions that might vary considerably in terms of their maliciousness and resulting harm. For instance, being infected with HIV following a deceptive statement from one of the parties to a sexual act can be seen as being objectively more harmful than learning that the person with whom you believed you had consented to sexual intercourse is not in reality an airline pilot, but a schoolteacher. Contrary to Herring's moralistic position, emerging research suggests that lying and deception are an integral part of human sexual encounters (see Eyre, Read & Millstein, 1997; Haselton et al., 2005; Rowatt, Cunningham & Druen, 1998, 1999; Tooke & Camire, 1991). Responding to all deceptive penetrative activities through the use of rape law both diminishes the seriousness of some incidents – including those with multiple assailants, kidnapping and use of violence – and potentially places an overemphasis on the subjectivity of the incident's severity to the victim-survivor of the deceptive incident. Thus, alternative justice measures outside of criminal rape laws may be more appropriate for responding to such unwanted conduct (see, for example Daly, Chapter 3; Flynn, Chapter 6; and Godden, Chapter 7).

Rape is a heinous crime. It has been recognised as such and has attracted significant punishment. However to expand (as has been the case in Israel) our understanding of rape to include contact between, for example, X and Y, when Y agrees to penetration but has been deceived as to X's religious affiliation, is to weaken the concept of rape. Schulhofer (1998) suggests there exists 'verbal confusion' surrounding 'rape', its use in law and the dissonance of legal and general conceptions. To label X a rapist after Y consented would further distance public understandings of rape from legal ones.

Some have reconceptualised the law of rape without the concept of consent and have instead focused solely on the defendant's conduct and state of mind (Dripps, 1992), or with a focus on the 'injury' caused to the victim (Rush, 2011). Dripps has suggested that 'non-consent' is merely a label for actions that the state deems illegitimate or immoral. McGregor (1996) argues that such an account remains inadequate because there is no theory behind Dripps' (1992) perspective of what is illegitimate and thus what should be deemed as criminal. Rubenfeld (2013) has sought to respond to the inconsistent and unsatisfactory formulation of rape law and its treatment of sex by deception through a radical reappraisal. He makes use of another meta-principle (being self-possession) to articulate when an act should be deemed criminal; although this too has been subject to significant criticism (see Dougherty, 2013; Falk, 2013; Ramachandran, 2013; Tuerkheimer, 2013).

If consent remains central to the definition of rape, there remains the difficult task of drawing lines around what vitiates consent. By taking an all-encompassing view of the factors that invalidate consent, the law risks losing public acceptance and respect. The proponents of expanding the offence of rape to include sex by deception fail to justify why there should not be another separate offence. There is no bar to the creation of other sexual offences that identify deception as having occurred. A consensual act, although with an error or mistake by one of the parties as to the purpose or a contingent fact, should not be reread in order to make consent ineffective, concomitantly transforming the act into rape. Many academics and policymakers are concerned with ensuring that the wrong is appropriately dealt with by law. Yet this desire for legal resolution, hastily supported by many, bolsters calls for easy and immediate responses like extending the scope of the offence of rape. This fast fix is at the expense of sufficient thought being given to addressing 'the wrong' inherent within the incident. There is increasing recognition that the labelling of actions, particularly in relation to a number of highly stigmatic offences, has frequently been unproductive and in clinical settings has been shown to cause increased offender resistance rather than behaviour change (Mann & Rollnick, 1996). While the deceptive behaviour of X potentially meets the requirement of seriousness to merit a legal response, it should be heavily questioned whether it ought to be conceptualised as rape.

To suggest that there are gradations of seriousness in relation to sexual offences is highly controversial. Nonetheless, many jurisdictions have laws against sexual offences that are graded on the basis of the legislature's perception of the seriousness and harm present. President Obama made headlines in 2012 (see Moore, 2012) responding to Republican Todd Akins' comments on 'legitimate rape' by stating that categories of rape are inappropriate. Outside of the rhetorically charged political statements, there is space for an objective recognition that some offences are more serious than others, but this should never deny the subjective impact of the incident on a victim-survivor. Todd's use of the word 'legitimate' was highly offensive. However, this should not prevent any thoughtful attempt to distinguish degrees of seriousness or harm for use as the basis of the state response. The failure to distinguish between activities with differing levels of seriousness or harm could result in the expansion of this legal category of rape to include all sexual wrongs. Indeed, a number of jurisdictions have recognised differences in the commission of offences in law through the overt identification in the name of the offence and the component parts distinguishing the act on the basis of the use of a weapon, infliction of serious personal injury, number of offenders and use of force or against the will of the other.[3] Those concerned with appropriately addressing the wrong committed, as well as the rule of law, should be offended at wide and encompassing 'catch-all' legislative provisions that do not distinguish between the nature and seriousness of the offending behaviour.

There is no suggestion here that the law should not continue to be strengthened in order to provide a more coherent and appropriate response to unwanted sexual activity. Indeed, the expansion of legal definitions of rape has been widely welcomed to match broader understandings of serious unwanted sexual acts beyond forceful penile–vaginal intercourse. We must remember that any conceptualisation can never be anything more than an inexact categorisation of an incident grouped alongside events deemed to be similar in nature or severity. The solution to our terminological problems could come from an expansive reconceptualisation of all sexual offences to more accurately identify the alleged wrongdoing. Such offences could mirror US-style provisions identifying 'degrees' of seriousness in offending and the presence of aggravating factors including penetration secured with the use of weapons; penetration secured by physical abuse; penetration secured by mental abuse or under duress; and penetration secured through abuse of a position of trust, by drugs or alcohol, or by impersonation. While such categorisation and gradation are not directly designed to respond to the victim's needs, they allow for state mechanisms of penal sanction and redress to react to the differing categories of seriousness or harm. The lack of consistency in responses should not be surprising as different actors, both within and across differing jurisdictions, attempt to respond to the complex and varied needs of the multiple interest groups. These actors, institutional, non-governmental and individuals, all impact the legislative process in order to further their differing agendas and prevent the implementation of any truly coherent approach to the enactment of criminal sanctions against unwanted sexual activity.

Conclusion

More thought must be given to the implications of the ways in which regulators seek to manage social behaviour, particularly through the use of the criminal law. Falk (2013) argues that we should think more robustly about what meaningful consent and sexual autonomy require. She suggests that while turning our attention to respond to and reconcile sex by deception cases with principles of sexual autonomy, we should ensure we do not take backward steps: for example, by defining rape as focusing on force. It is hard to disagree. Although there is work still to be done, much progress in rape law reform has been made. In particular, the use of consent in law sends signals to the wider community. However, much of the work achieved through the law in educating people both young and old will undoubtedly be lost when the messages are confused. Regulators, therefore, need to work to communicate clearer and more coherent messages than is currently the case. Clear messages as to the types of conduct that are acceptable and unacceptable in sexual encounters remain crucial in helping to mitigate a number of risks surrounding sexual activity. We cannot expect all sexual interactions to be clear and free from doubt; indeed many argue that mystery and spontaneity are at the heart of sexual encounters. Nevertheless, the state plays a central role in identifying and communicating what behaviour is and is not acceptable, and in enforcing the rules that secure personal, bodily and sexual autonomy for all parties to a given sexual activity.

We must pause to reconceptualise our proposed solutions to identified failings in law and craft a more nuanced approach to state-sanctioned responses to ensure appropriate redress for the wrong done. Current approaches towards regulating sexual activity continue to show the influences of their past historical, social and cultural norms. As demonstrated in this chapter, consent has been used in a number of different ways. In some cases, consent has been deemed to be impossible (where children are present), and ignored with regard to other sexual activities (sodomy and buggery, as a shorthand for homosexuality). In other areas, consensual sexual activity (sadomasochistic acts and between some family members) continues to see over-regulation through the conflation and reinterpretation in law with 'abuse' or 'violence' using an overly simplistic consent/non-consent binary. In particular, presenting a consistent and appropriate response to sexual activity with deception is challenging. Expanding consent to an extent that would allow for later rewriting of the parties' consent, and resulting labelling of one of the parties a rapist, is disingenuous and offensive to those who are victim-survivors of rape.

The crude and ad hoc use of consent creates confusion. It is not only problematic in leading to potential injustices for the parties involved, but it also incorrectly conceptualises 'the wrong' of rape, which at its core is the violation of one's sexual autonomy. Those responsible for bridging the gap between the social and legal should continue to foreground the impacts of their changes on the actors involved, and be reminded that justice extends beyond the realm of the criminal law.

Notes

1. See further Schulhofer (1998).
2. While many Western nations have sought to move away from a legal requirement of force for a successful prosecution, there is still a need in some jurisdictions for physical, or at least verbal, resistance to indicate a lack of consent. Some jurisdictions also direct juries that silence should not be equated with consent and thus, by implication, *something* is required to indicate the presence of consent. This 'affirmative consent' standard is required in both England and Wales and Canada. The US-based 'Only Yes Means Yes' campaign has been seeking the implementation of an 'active-consent model' whereby every individual must give active consent to sexual activity, and anything other than active consent is rape. Deliberately onerous on both parties, the active-consent model requires parties to establish the existence of consent and has been proposed as a partial solution to the problem of determining the presence of consent and consequent lack of successful prosecutions for rape. In September 2014, the California legislature added a section to the Education Code, mandating that colleges have an 'active-consent policy for sexual activities' in order to be eligible to receive state funds in the form of student financial assistance. Although not a criminal law response, and not enforceable against potential offenders, the law signals the importance of actively communicating and receiving communication of the consent of both parties to sexual acts.
3. See, for example, the distinctions made in North Carolina General Statute, Article 7A Rape and other sex offenses §14–27.2 First-degree rape, §14–27.3 Rape of a child; adult offender and §14–27.4 Second-degree rape §14–27.7

Intercourse and sexual offenses with certain victims; consent no defense §14–27.7A Statutory rape or sexual offense of a person who is 13, 14 or 15 years old. Other examples include Washington State Legislature, Revised Code of Washington (RCW) Title 9A Washington Criminal Code 9A.44 Sex Offenses Rape in the first 9A.44.040, second 9A.44.050 and third degree 9A.44.060.

References

Attorney General's Department of New South Wales, Criminal Justice Sexual Offences Taskforce (2005) *Responding to Sexual Assault: The Way Forward* (Sydney: Oxford Publishing).

Australia, Model Criminal Code Officers Committee (1999) *Model Criminal Code Chapter 5 Sexual Offences Against the Person* (Canberra: Standing Committee of the Attorney's General).

BBC (2010) 'Israeli Arab Who "Raped" a Woman Says Verdict "Racist"', *BBC News Online News Middle East*; Retrieved at http://www.bbc.co.uk/news/world-middle-east-10717186

Berg, J. W., Appelbaum, P. S., Lidz, C. W. and Parker, L. S. (2001) *Informed Consent: Legal Theory and Clinical Practice* (New York: Oxford University Press).

Brett, N. (1998) 'Sexual Offenses and Consent', *Canadian Journal of Law and Jurisprudence*, 11(1), 69–88.

Chandra-Shekeran, S. (1997) 'Theorising the Limits of the Sadomasochistic Homosexual Identity in R. v. Brown', *Melbourne Univerity Law Review*, 21, 584–600.

Corkery, J. (2011) 'Dangerous Sports and Obvious Risks-Anyone for Cricket?' *Sports Law eJournal*, (2).

Cotterrell, R. (2006) *Law, Culture and Society: Legal Ideas in the Mirror of Social Theory* (Aldershot: Ashgate).

Dingwall, G. (2002) 'Addressing the Boundaries of Consent in Rape', *King's College Law Journal*, 13, 31–52.

Dougherty, T. (2013) 'No Way Around Consent: A Reply to Rubenfeld on "Rape-by-Deception"', *The Yale Law Journal Online*, 123, 321–389.

Dripps, D. A. (1992) 'Beyond Rape: An Essay on the Difference Between the Presence of Force and the Absence of Consent', *Columbia Law Review*, 92(7), 1780–1809.

Elliott, C. and De Than, C. (2007) 'The Case for a Rational Reconstruction of Consent in Criminal Law', *The Modern Law Review*, 70(2), 225–249.

England and Wales, Home Office. (2000) *Setting the Boundaries: Reforming the Law on Sexual Offences*, Vol I (London, UK: Home Office Communication Directorate).

Engle-Merry, S. (1988) 'Legal Pluralism', *Law and Society Review*, 22(5), 869–896.

Eyre, S. L., Read, N. W. and Millstein, S. G. (1997) 'Adolescent Sexual Strategies', *Journal of Adolescent Health*, 20(4), 286–293.

Falk, P. J. (2013) 'Not Logic, but Experience: Drawing on Lessons from the Real World in Thinking about the Riddle of Rape-by-Fraud', *The Yale Law Journal Online*, 123, 353–389.

Farrugia, P. J. (1996) 'Consent Defence: Sports Violence, Sadomasochism, and the Criminal Law', *Auckland University Law Review*, 8, 472–502.

Fitzpatrick, P. (1995) 'Being Social in Socio-legal Studies', *Journal of Law and Society*, 22, 105–112.

Förstl, H., Haass, C., Hemmer, B., Meyer, B. and Halle, M. (2010) 'Boxing – Acute Complications and Late Sequelae: From Concussion to Dementia', *Deutsches Ärzteblatt International*, 107(47), 835–839.

Furlong, A. (1991) *Sado-masochism and the Law: Consent Versus Paternalism* Legal Notes No. 12 (London: Libertarian Alliance).

Gross, H. (2007) 'Rape, Moralism and Human rights', *Criminal Law Review*, March, 220–227.

Hanna, C. (2000) 'Sex is Not a Sport: Consent and Violence in Criminal Law', *Boston College Law Review*, 42, 239–290.

Haselton, M. G., Buss, D. M., Oubaid, V. and Angleitner, A. (2005) 'Sex, Lies, and Strategic Interference: The Psychology of Deception Between the Sexes', *Personality and Social Psychology Bulletin*, 31(1), 3–23.

Hayes, M. O. and Harkness, G. A. (2001) 'Body Piercing as a Risk Factor for Viral Hepatitis: An Integrative Research Review', *American Journal of Infection Control*, 29(4), 271–274.

Heath, M. (2005) 'The Law and Sexual Offences Against Adults in Australia', *ACSSA Issues*, (Vol. 4) (Melbourne, Australia: Australian Centre for the Study of Sexual Assault); Retrieved from http://www.aifs.gov.au/acssa/pubs/issue/i4.html

Herring, J. (2002) 'Does Yes Mean Yes – The Criminal Law and Mistaken Consent to Sexual Activity', *Singapore Law Review*, 22, 181–201.

Herring, J. (2005) 'Mistaken Sex', *Criminal Law Review*, July, 511–524.

Impett, E. A. and Peplau, L. A. (2003) 'Sexual Compliance: Gender, Motivational and Relationship Perspectives', *The Journal of Sex Research*, 40(1), 87–100.

Kelly, L. (1987) 'The Continuum of Sexual Violence', in J. Hanmer and M. Maynard (eds.) *Women, Violence and Social Control* (Atlantic Highlands, NJ: Humanities Press International), 46–60.

Lacey, N. (1998) 'Unspeakable Subjects, Impossible Rights: Sexuality, Integrity and Criminal Law', *Canadian Journal of Law and Jurisprudence*, 11, 47–68.

Langdridge, D. (2006) 'Voices from the Margins: Sadomasochism and Sexual Citizenship', *Citizenship Studies*, 10(4), 373–389.

Leino-Kilpi, H., Välimäki, M., Dassen, T., Gasull, M., Lemonidou, C., Scott, P. A. and Kaljonen, A. (2003) 'Perceptions of Autonomy, Privacy and Informed Consent in the Care of Elderly People in Five European Countries: Comparison and Implications for the Future', *Nursing Ethics*, 10(1), 58–66.

Loosemore, M., Knowles, C. H. and Whyte, G. P. (2007) 'Amateur Boxing and Risk of Chronic Traumatic Brain Injury: Systematic Review of Observational Studies', *British Medical Journal*, 335, 809–818.

MacKinnon, C. A. (1987) *Feminism Unmodified: Discourses on Life and Law* (Cambridge: Harvard University Press).

Mann, R. E. and Rollnick, S. (1996) 'Motivational Interviewing with a Sex Offender Who Believed He Was Innocent', *Behavioural and Cognitive Psychotherapy*, 24(2), 127–134.

Marelich, W. D. and Graham, J. L. (2013) 'Social Exchange and Social/Physical Topography of One-Night Stands in College-Age Students', *Electronic Journal of Human Sexuality*, 16; Retrieved from http://www.ejhs.org/volume16/onenight.html

Marelich, W. D., Lundquist, J., Painter, K. and Mechanic, M. B. (2008) 'Sexual Deception as a Social-Exchange Process: Development of a Behavior-Based Sexual Deception Scale', *The Journal of Sex Research*, 45(1), 27–35.
McGregor, J. (1996) 'Why When She Says No She Doesn't Mean Maybe and Doesn't Mean Yes: A Critical Reconstruction of Consent, Sex, and the Law', *Legal Theory*, 2(03), 175–208.
Moore, L. (2012) 'Rep. Todd Akin – "Legitimate Rape" Statement and Retraction', *The New York Times*, 20 August, A13.
Moore, S. F. (1973) 'Law and Social Change: The Semi-autonomous Social Field as an Appropriate Subject of Study', *Law & Society Review*, 7(4), 719–746.
Pateman, C. (1988) *The Sexual Contract* (Stanford: Stanford University Press).
Perkins, R. M. and Boyce, R. N. (1982) *Criminal Law* (Mineola: Foundation Press).
Perry, A. D. (2009) 'Unlucky Section 13: Sexual Activity Between Children and the Sexual Offences Act 2003', *King's Law Journal*, 20(2), 327–337.
Powell, A. (2007) 'Youth "At Risk"?: Young People, Sexual Health and Consent', *Youth Studies Australia*, 26(4), 21–28.
Ramachandran, G. (2013) 'Delineating the Heinous: Rape, Sex, and Self-Possession', *The Yale Law Journal Online*, 123, 371–388.
Richters, J., De Visser, R. O., Rissel, C. E., Grulich, A. E. and Smith, A. M. A. (2008) 'Demographic and Psychosocial Features of Participants in Bondage and Discipline, "Sadomasochism" or Dominance and Submission (BDSM): Data from a National Survey', *The Journal of Sexual Medicine*, 5(7), 1660–1668.
Roffee, J. (2012) 'Incest: The Exception to a Principled Scottish Sex Law', *Juridical Review*, 2012(2), 91–110.
Roffee, J. A. (2014a) 'No Consensus on Incest? Criminalisation and Compatibility with the European Convention on Human Rights', *Human Rights Law Review*, 14(3), 541–572.
Roffee, J. A. (2014b) 'The Synthetic Necessary Truth Behind New Labour's Criminalisation of Incest', *Social & Legal Studies*, 23(1), 113–130.
Rowatt, W. C., Cunninghan, M. R. and Druen, P. B. (1998) 'Deception to Get a Date', *Personality and Social Psychology Bulletin*, 24(11), 1228–1242.
Rowatt, W. C., Cunningham, M. R. and Druen, P. B. (1999) 'Lying to Get a Date: The Effect of Facial Physical Attractiveness on the Willingness to Deceive Prospective Dating Partners', *Journal of Social and Personal Relationships*, 16(2), 209–223.
Rubenfeld, J. (2013) 'Riddle of Rape-by-Deception and the Myth of Sexual Autonomy', *The Yale Law Journal Online*, 122, 1372–1443.
Rush, P. D. (2011) 'Jurisdictions of Sexual Assault: Reforming the Texts and Testimony of Rape in Australia', *Feminist Legal Studies*, 19(1), 47–73.
Schulhofer, S. J. (1992) 'Taking Sexual Autonomy Seriously: Rape Law and Beyond', *Law and Philosophy*, 11(1–2), 35–94.
Schulhofer, S. J. (1998) *Unwanted Sex: The Culture of Intimidation and the Failure of Law* (Cambridge: Harvard University Press).
Tadros, V. (2006) 'Rape Without Consent', *Oxford Journal of Legal Studies*, 26(3), 515–543.
Thomas, T. (2000) *Sex Crime: Sex Offending and Society* (Devon: Willan Publishing).
Tooke, W. and Camire, L. (1991) 'Patterns of Deception in Intersexual and Intrasexual Mating Strategies', *Ethology and Sociobiology*, 12(5), 345–364.

Tuerkheimer, D. (2013) 'Sex Without Consent', *The Yale Law Journal Online*, 123, 335–352.

Tweeten, S. S. M. and Rickman, L. S. (1998) 'Infectious Complications of Body Piercing', *Clinical Infectious Diseases*, 26(3), 735–740.

Victoria, Department of Justice, Criminal Law Review (2013) *Review of Sexual Offences Consultation Paper* (Melbourne, Australia: Department of Justice).

Walsh, K. M. (1994) 'Boxing: Regulating a Health Hazard', *Journal of Contemporary Health Law and Policy*, 11, 63–84.

White, C. (2006) 'The Spanner Trials and the Changing Law on Sadomasochism in the UK', *Journal of Homosexuality*, 50(2–3), 167–187.

White, S. M. and Ashley, M. (2012) 'Consent', *Anaesthesia & Intensive Care Medicine*, 13(4), 141–144.

6
Sexual Violence and Innovative Responses to Justice
Interrupting the 'Recognisable' Narrative

Asher Flynn

Introduction

Within law, the desired outcome is purportedly obtaining justice. Yet on a global scale, the law has consistently failed in providing justice, empowerment, status or control to sexual violence victims, while simultaneously failing to adequately consider the complexities and individuality of sexual violence experiences. A key problem for the law in responding to these failings has historically been the dominant cultural, political and social narratives around what constitutes 'real rape', what is consent and who fits into the normative sexual victim and offender labels. However, as the capacity for conventional legal processes to achieve or provide 'justice' in cases of sexual violence has been increasingly critiqued, and attention has shifted towards better integration of victims' needs in legal proceedings, these same failings have facilitated opportunities for the interruption of the recognisable narratives of rape, justice and the lived, versus stereotyped, experiences of women. In response, we have witnessed a range of initiatives – official and unofficial; within and beyond the criminal law – explored and implemented, with the aim of providing alternative forms of justice for sexual violence victims.

This chapter examines some of the dominant discourses around sexual violence that have historically framed the recognisable rape narrative, before considering how innovative responses seeking to address failings in the law and its processes have emerged to challenge these governing assumptions. A brief outline of victims' justice needs is also provided to demonstrate how an increased focus on these needs has shifted understandings of what constitutes justice. This chapter explores these issues in the context of two initiatives operating within and beyond the realm of law: first, the use of specialist courts and prosecution units, and second, restorative justice.

This chapter engages with primary and secondary sources, and draws briefly from the findings of my three-year study (2007–2009) of plea-negotiations in Victoria (Australia), in which 51 prosecutors were observed engaging in plea-negotiation practices over several months, and 67 interviews were conducted with prosecutors, defence counsel, judicial officers and policy advisors (Flynn, 2010). For the purposes of this chapter, only observations and interviews with prosecutors, primarily those working within the specialist sexual offences unit, are discussed. Pseudonyms are used to protect the identity of participants.

The recognisable rape narrative

According to Foucault (1980, p. 194), our social and cultural lives are ordered through discourses that produce and reproduce knowledge and understanding about particular events, based on hierarchies of social norms. The discourses around sexual violence are no exception to this. Take, for example, the persistent victim-blaming attitudes that assign responsibility to the victim not only for the assault but for also failing to effectively use strategies to prevent it from occurring. This is perhaps most prevalent in relation to rape risk prevention narratives which, although operating under the guise of 'prevention', focus social understanding and knowledge on addressing the 'risky' behaviours of women (see Powell & Henry, 2014). Rape prevention campaign materials, often displaying images of unconscious or distressed young women, include captions such as: 'Know Your Limits… One in three reported rapes happen when the victim has been drinking' (Evans, 2014); 'Don't let a night full of promise, turn into a night full of regret: Don't leave yourself more vulnerable to regretful sex or even rape. Drink sensibly' (Dolan, 2012); and '02:19am – She didn't want to do it but she couldn't say no: see what could happen when your friends drink too much' (Edwards, 2011). The strong messages outlined in these and many other 'prevention' campaigns produces both spoken and unspoken problematic narratives of rape and blame. These reinforce a 'real rape' narrative, which perpetuates dangerous myths about women's responsibility for incidents of sexual violence which can infiltrate courtroom proceedings and juror decision-making. Further to this, they reflect and contribute to a broader narrative and social understanding that forces the responsibility onto women to decrease their risk of victimisation, for example, by not drinking alcohol (see Gotell, Chapter 4; see also Ellison & Munro, 2009; Finch & Munro, 2005; Grubb & Turner, 2012; Powell et al., 2013).

The production and reproduction of knowledge and social understanding of sexual violence is also evident in punitive crime control policies and the taken-for-granted assumption of what 'justice' means for rape victims. As Gotell argues (Chapter 4), feminist campaigns that have advocated greater recognition of sexual violence and harm have incorrectly been associated by post-feminists and others with a 'retributive ethos', and a tough law and order agenda. This view has infiltrated the recognisable rape narrative, whereby sexual violence (or more correctly, sexual violence fitting a 'real rape' narrative) is viewed as a most abominable and severe form of crime where justice can only be secured through punitive punishment. In this context, a complicit, but dominant view is accepted that justice for 'real rape' victims equates to retribution and little room is left to consider the viability of alternate forms of securing justice.

The reason we allow such views to colour and dominate our perceptions of sexual violence is because in society, the overwhelming tendency is to take the meaning of things to be pre-inscribed, to be recognisable – which in itself tends toward the reproduction of particular social relations (Flynn et al., 2015). This reproduction – for example, the repeated inclination to warn women against engaging in certain 'risky' behaviours – relies upon the world appearing as a series of recognisable things, events, experiences and so forth (Deleuze, 1994, pp. 139–141). Thus too often the complexity of rape is reduced to the simplest narrative, which allows us to *recognise* rape as a clearly inscribed type of event that holds the woman accountable for the act itself, and/or for not preventing it from occurring. The dominant narratives we tell about what rape is – a stranger assault, violent, the result of risky activities by women – lead us as a matter of course to assume that women are in some way responsible for preventing their own assaults, and that justice will be achieved by a criminal trial, conviction and carceral punishment of 'real rape' offenders.

Our need to recognise events in a particular narrative (the 'real rape' scenario), and the power of discourse in shaping responses to sexual violence (carceral punishment, risk prevention strategies) is further demonstrated in the many news articles and online blogs that reinforce rape avoidance. See for example, '7 Ways to Protect Yourself Against Rape', appearing in *Marie Claire* magazine (Kelly, 2011), and 'The Best Rape Prevention: Tell College Women to Stop Getting So Wasted'

(Yoffee, 2013). It is also evident in 'innovative' products designed to 'empower' women to 'protect' themselves against rape, such as the development of 'rape-resistant' underwear that can 'be worn comfortably while still being able to frustrate an assault' (AR Wear, 2015); and 'rape prevention nail polish', which changes colour when it detects the presence of date-rape drugs (Their slogan: 'the first fashion company empowering women to prevent sexual assault') (Smith, 2014).

As these examples demonstrate, sexual violence has historically been treated as a recognisable event, as something Deleuze (1994) would say fits the 'image of thought'. And where recognition is primary, there is little or no experimentation outside the dominant narrative; in this case, outside developing strategies for women to 'protect' themselves against potential threats or acts of sexual violence, or for justice responses beyond the realm of law. However as conventional legal systems continue to be increasingly publicly criticised for failing to deliver justice for sexual violence victims – see for example, 'Criminal Justice System Failing Most Rape Victims' appearing in *The Age* newspaper (Silvester, 2013) and 'Suicides Show How Justice System Fails Rape Victims', appearing in *The Conversation* (Cook, 2014) – an opportunity has been provided for a break in the recognisable narrative. This has simultaneously been fuelled by victims' voices becoming a more integral component in policy development, whereby greater attention is given to the complex and individual needs of victims; needs which, as described in the next section, require responses that often fall outside conventional legal processes.

Interrupting the recognisable rape narrative

Pali and Madsen (2011, p. 59) suggest that sexual violence victims need:

> [t]heir suffering to be recognised and validated by the one who has caused it. They want an apology, or justification. They want what happened to them not to happen to anyone else. They want to get on with their lives, to live no longer in 'his' shadow. They want to feel free and safe again. They want to add another narrative to the story of the assault and restore their dignity.

Julich and colleagues (2010, pp. 20–21) further explain that when describing what justice would entail, sexual violence victims typically identify needing:

> [t]o have their stories heard...in a safe forum based on equality; acknowledgment of the difference between right and wrong; for the

offender to take responsibility and demonstrate accountability; and an experience of victimisation validated by offenders, bystanders and outsiders.

Research examining the experiences of sexual violence victims within conventional criminal justice processes consistently finds that the court system does not provide a complete mechanism to address these often complex, individualised needs. Indeed, Herman (2005, p. 574) suggests that when victims' needs are considered in light of how conventional legal processes operate, the needs and the operation of the justice system are in effect, 'diametrically opposed'. The failings of the legal system as a mechanism to secure justice are further evidenced by the persistent low reporting, attrition and conviction rates globally. In Australia, for example, it is estimated that just one in six victims will report their assault to the police, and of these, between 15 and 20 per cent will result in charges being laid. From here, the rates drop even further with only 3.5 per cent of these matters likely to proceed to trial and result in conviction (ABS, 1996, 2006; Daly, 2011; Heenan & Murray, 2004; Mouzos & Makkai, 2004). These figures are mirrored internationally. In England, the Ministry of Justice (2013, p. 6) estimates around 15 per cent of women report their victimisation to police. In the US, estimates of rape reporting range from 8 to 40 per cent, with only two of every ten reported rapes proceeding to prosecution and just 13 per cent of these resulting in a conviction (Daly & Bouhours, 2010; Herman, 2005; Koss, 2014; RAINN, 2014).

In light of these problems, there has been a breadth of reforms to sexual violence laws globally, including (but not limited to): extending definitions of rape; limiting the cross-examination of a victim's sexual history; criminalising marital rape; and increased police training, to name just a few (CIJ, 2014, p. 11). And while there existed some 'optimism' that reforms to the criminal law would 'change the landscape of police and criminal justice responses, make the system more efficient (e.g. lead to higher convictions), and enhance positive experiences for victims' (Daly, 2011, p. 3), such hopes have not fully eventuated. As Stubbs (2003, p. 23) explains, legal reforms have 'symbolic value', but their effectiveness in securing justice for victims or offering a way to empower or recognise the lived experiences of victims is limited, in large part because of 'resilience of cultural mythologies about women and sexuality'; in other words, the recognisable rape narrative. Daly and Curtis-Frawley (2006, p. 230) similarly maintain that 'despite decades of legal reform, the police and courts continue to fail victims... [and] existing law and procedure, coupled with social attitudes about gender and sexual violence, thwart just outcomes for victims'. Accordingly, it has been argued that:

> [F]ormal criminal justice has had its chance... and has not proved effective for these sorts of crimes... It is reasonable to ask, therefore, whether there is something fundamental in criminal law that limits its potential to achieve justice and safety for women.
>
> (Hudson, 2002, p. 263)

Significantly, as implicit in the quote above, the inability of conventional legal processes to respond to victims' needs or provide substantive justice has paved a pathway for the discussion, exploration and integration of innovative, alternative responses to the significant social problem of sexual violence. This can be seen in the various attempts both within and beyond the conventional legal system to interrupt the recognisable rape narrative with discourses which acknowledge that victims don't have uniform views or experiences, that not all rapes are the same and that more complex, multilayered and original approaches are required to respond to and prevent sexual violence. See, for example, the White House Public Service Announcements developed in 2014, in which US politicians and celebrities discuss sexual assault and consent:

> We have a big problem and we need your help... It's called sexual assault and it has to stop... If she doesn't consent or she can't consent, it's rape. It's assault. It's a crime... If I saw it happening, I would speak up. If I saw it happening, I would never blame her, I'd help her... It's up to all of us to put a stop to sexual assault, and it starts with you.
>
> (Excerpt from *One is Too Many*, 2014)

The *Don't Be That Guy* Campaign in Edmonton, Canada, initiated in 2010 provides another example of this interruption beyond the law, whereby advertisements featuring the slogan 'sex without consent = sexual assault. Don't be that guy', are accompanied by statements like: 'Just because she isn't saying no... doesn't mean she's saying yes' and 'Just because you help her home... doesn't mean you get to help yourself' (Butterfield, 2012).

In this climate, sexual violence has the potential to be responded to both within and beyond conventional legal processes, as though sexual violence is what Deleuze (1994) calls, 'an encounter'; that is, something un-coded; something which doesn't fit one specific narrative and which requires a response of invention and experimentation. An example of this shift in the treatment of sexual violence more towards an 'encounter' that requires an appreciation of the complexities of sexual violence experiences within the realm of law is the development of more responsive methods to prosecute sexual violence. This can be seen in the creation of specialist courts tasked with hearing only sexual violence cases, and the establishment of specialist prosecution divisions that utilise a multi-agency approach to prosecuting sexual violence, working with police units, sexual assault counsellors, witness assistance programmes and forensic/health specialists. In the next section, I examine the potentials and limitations that these mechanisms have for subverting the recognisable rape narrative, particularly in regards to challenging the treatment of victims within the prosecution process.

Specialist courts and prosecution units

Specialist sexual offence courts were introduced in South Africa in 1993, initially through the creation of the Wynberg Sexual Offences Court in Cape Town. The courts were introduced with three primary purposes: (1) to reduce secondary victimisation by improving the general treatment of victims in the prosecution process; (2) to establish a co-ordinated and integrated approach between agencies; and (3) to improve reporting and conviction rates (Cossins, 2010, p. 294; Ministerial Advisory Task Team, 2013, p. 18; Walker & Louw, 2005, p. 232). In 2002, the courts began operating under a specified model, which required each court to have two specialist prosecutors with at least three years' experience in criminal litigation; experienced judicial officers assigned to the court for at least six months; victim assistance services to prepare and support victims; victim-friendly environments, including separate waiting rooms, private consultation areas and CCTV facilitates; and on-hand counselling services (Cossins, 2010, p. 295; Ministerial Advisory Task Team, 2013, pp. 21–22). At their peak in 2005, Walker and Louw (2005, p. 235) posit that approximately 700 sexual violence cases were heard in these courts.

While the creation of specialist courts appears to demonstrate a strong commitment to recognising and responding to the harms and complexities of sexual violence, evaluations of the South African courts reported mixed outcomes. Some of the key concerns revolved around victims not having sufficient access to services or follow-up care, and experiencing long delays before their cases were heard (Walker & Louw, 2005). Walker and Louw (2005) also reported a failure of the courts' service teams to properly communicate case outcomes to victims, and judicial officers failing to protect victims from intimidation by offenders and defence counsel. Significantly however, a key achievement of the courts was a reported increase in victim satisfaction, regardless of the case outcome. Based on surveys with 44 victims (39 women, 5 men) who had progressed through the courts, Walker and Louw (2005, p. 240) found only 10 per cent of victims were dissatisfied with the process, with the remainder reporting feeling satisfied (36 per cent), more than satisfied (32 per cent) or totally satisfied (22 per cent). These findings are significantly higher than those identified in research examining sexual assault victims' experiences with mainstream court processes (Daly & Curtis-Frawley, 2006).

Another perceived achievement of the courts was an increase in convictions rates, which was identified as signifying a positive shift in broader societal attitudes towards victims and the range of activities that can constitute rape (Ministerial Advisory Task Team, 2013, p. 24). Between January 2002 and November 2003, an audit of all South African regional courts revealed rape convictions sitting at 42 per cent, compared with 62 per cent in the specialist courts (Ministerial Advisory Task Team, 2013, p. 24). Similarly, in 2007, the Baragwanath Thuthuzela Care Centre had three sexual offence courts operating with a conviction rate of 78 per cent. If we (perhaps contentiously) accept that increasing conviction rates can be equated with an increase in social acceptance and understanding of the complexities and multifaceted ways in which sexual offending can play out, then the potential of the specialist courts to shape social and juror understanding of sexual violence as something that doesn't fit the recognisable rape narrative can also be demonstrated by what occurred following the closure of many of the courts, where there was a significant decline in convictions rates. By the end of 2005, 74 specialist courts were operating across South Africa (Ministerial Advisory Task Team, 2013, p. 23); however, due to concerns about the funding prioritisation of specialist courts (arguably at the expense of mainstream courts) and the increasing backlog of cases waiting to be tried, by 2012 only nine specialist courts remained in operation (Ministerial Advisory Task Team, 2013, p. 24). In 2008, following the closure of the sexual specialist courts in the Baragwanath Thuthuzela Care Centre, the conviction rate for sexual offences dropped by 10 per cent (to 68 per cent) (Ministerial Advisory Task Team, 2013, p. 24). Between 2009 and 2012, this rate fluctuated between 45 and 67 per cent (Ministerial Advisory Task Team, 2013, p. 25). The changes in conviction rates, combined with the data showing increased victim satisfaction with the court process regardless of the case outcome, demonstrates the potential for specialist courts to provide a more responsive and improved mechanism within the law for adjudicating sexual offences. Indeed, following a review conducted in 2013, the South African government has committed to re-establishing 22 new sexual offence courts given their potential collective benefit to the community in recognising the harms of sexual violence (Manyathi-Jele, 2013).

In Victoria (Australia), while not a specialist court as such, the Sexual Offences List ('List') operating in the court system and the specialist sexual offences unit operating within the Office of Public Prosecutions (OPP) were simultaneously established to recognise the complexities of sexual violence and to differentiate these prosecutions from mainstream legal processes. The aim of the List is to use experts to help compensate for the often complex nature of sexual assault trials, due largely to the complexities of rape laws, and to reduce delays in sexual assault pre-trial proceedings and trials, which in turn reduces the stress and trauma of victims waiting for cases to proceed. This is achieved by having matters heard only by judicial officers who are specifically trained in sexual violence cases, and the imposition of time restrictions, including the requirement that the committal (a pre-trial hearing that determines whether an accused should stand trial) be heard within three months of an accused's arraignment, and that trials be held within three months of the committal. If no committal is held (the accused can waive their right to this pre-trial hearing), then the trial must commence within three months of the arraignment (*Criminal Procedure Act 2009* (Vic) ss. 126 (1)(a), 212).

The specialist sexual offences unit (hereafter, 'unit') brings together specialised criminal justice agencies in handling investigations and prosecutions of sexual offences (Daly, 2011, p. 11). One of the main motivations in the unit's creation was to improve public confidence in the prosecution of sexual offences and improve victim experiences with the prosecution process (Flynn, 2010). By improving public confidence, the unit also sought to increase public reporting of sexual offences. The unit comprises publicly funded prosecutors who have recognised expertise in handling sexual offence cases and working with sexual assault victims, thereby providing a mechanism for increased understanding of the differing lived experiences of victims and creating an environment that better recognises that there is no one form of rape; no structured narrative. A multidisciplinary focus is applied, whereby prosecutors work closely with Victoria Police and witness assistance services to improve victim experiences throughout the entire legal process. Unlike other prosecution divisions, in which prosecutors and solicitors are located in different parts of the building (and even on different floors), the workspaces of the unit's prosecutors and solicitors are shared. According to John – a prosecutor in my study – this enables the unit to 'create a consistent, team approach to crimes involving sexual offences'. The unit also aims to minimise the trauma experienced by victims as a result of delays in court proceedings, by having a primary focus on early resolution (Flynn, 2010). As John explained, this focus emerged because:

> There are a number of [guilty] pleas in sex cases; however, a lot of these don't eventuate until the trial day or close to it. These create a huge ordeal, trauma and stress upon the victim, preparing them for a trial and then getting a last-minute offer [to plead guilty]. The unit will therefore hopefully eliminate this drawn-out procedure, with its early resolution approach.

To assist in achieving these ideals, the unit has an early resolution manager (ERM) who undertakes a preliminary assessment of each case to evaluate its strengths and weaknesses, and any issues that could potentially be resolved. As another prosecutor, Claire, explained:

> The ERM is supposed to read files very early, pretty much after the arraignment hearing, contact the defence, contact the [police] informant and find out what everyone's thinking in terms of possible resolutions... Once the ERM has detailed what they think is appropriate in terms of how the case proceeds, if the solicitor allocated to the case supports this, then they check with the prosecutor, and then the defence and victims can be contacted to discuss the possibility of a negotiated guilty plea and to get their opinions [on this].

The two main benefits of this approach, as identified by those working in the unit, are its ability to provide consistency in prosecutorial approaches to sexual offences and victims, which allows for 'fewer points of contact for victims' (Claire), and its ability to focus the attention of all parties on the possibility of early resolution. These potential benefits were also identified by prosecutors working outside the unit, who recognised the potential for 'specialised structures and groups to become the norm in all sections of the OPP, especially those divisions that deal with victims and where early resolution is, as a result, so beneficial' (Sam). While there are debates as to the benefits of an early-resolution outcome, as opposed to a victim having 'their day in court' (Flynn, 2012), a common need consistently identified by victims is the desire to be kept informed at all stages of the case's progression through the criminal justice process (Shapland, Willmore & Duff, 1985; Strang & Sherman, 2003). When such information is provided – as is the approach utilised in the unit – it has been recognised that victims feel an increased level of satisfaction and are more likely to have at least some of their justice needs met, which goes some way towards improving sexual violence victims' experiences and treatment within court proceedings.

There are contrasting concerns around the messages specialist courts and prosecution units send to the community. On the one hand, Finn (2011, p. 102) argues that separating sexual offences from the mainstream process may result in them being considered less serious – not worthy of the 'real' court treatment – or it may have the opposite effect of privileging sexual assault victims above victims of other crimes. On the other hand, it is argued that separating these offences reiterates the seriousness of sexual violence, which may have an impact on public attitudes and possibly increase reporting rates. The unique approach to prosecuting sexual offences in Victoria, with its focus on early resolution and upholding victims' rights, demonstrates a clear shift in prosecutors' traditional perceptions and approaches to sexual offence victims, and towards the potentially beneficial role of negotiated guilty pleas. This was reflected in an evaluation which found the unit had improved support levels for victims both before and during the court process (Success Works, 2011, p. ii). Additionally, the use of specialist courts and prosecution units represents a legitimate effort to interrupt the recognisable rape narrative by reflecting an internal recognition within the law that not all sexual assaults fit into a clear, concise experience, and there are more complex, multilayered considerations that must be applied to prosecuting these crimes. This is achieved in both a collective and specific form; collectively, by showing the community that sexual violence is recognised as a significant social issue that requires a specialised response (courts and prosecution teams); and specifically, by providing a more sensitive way for prosecutions to proceed where victims' needs and rights are considered, and rapes are not treated as one 'recognisable' event. Importantly, specialist prosecution divisions and courts represent a shift in the treatment of sexual violence offending, demonstrating 'a realisation by courts and legislators that social problems may require social, rather than [just] legal solutions' (Freiberg, 2001, p. 9).

Furthermore, they reflect a shift in understandings of sexual offence prosecutions to require expertise in responding to victims' needs and the often technical nature of rape laws (Ministerial Advisory Task Team, 2013, p. 25).

Restorative justice

Changes in our understanding and acceptance of the variability of rape and the justice needs of victims in different relational and other contexts have also seen challenges to the recognisable narrative of how justice is best served (see Daly, Chapter 3; Gotell, Chapter 4; and Godden, Chapter 7); that is, that justice may not always be secured through conventional legal processes. As such, there have been explorations of various alternative and innovative responses to sexual violence which recognise the complexities and individuality of sexual violence experiences and the differing justice needs of victims. In this way, the accepted 'logic' of the narrative around sexual violence has been interrupted to allow for experimentation with approaches that move beyond and in conjunction with the conventional realm of law (see Godden, Chapter 7, where this shift is further demonstrated in the context of the civil justice system which, she argues, has some potential to better recognise and respond to women's lived experiences of rape, than that of the criminal justice system).

One clear example where an innovative response to rape has emerged from interrupting the recognisable narratives of justice, sexual violence and victims' needs is the use of restorative justice (RJ) processes. RJ is a blanket term that describes a range of practices focused on repairing the harm resulting from crime by involving the main parties to the dispute, most notably, by giving the victim and offender key roles in the process and the outcome (Daly, 2000, p. 167). The concept loosely emerged out of Christie's (1977) examination of the ways in which the state had 'stolen' conflicts from the victim and offender, which had the twofold effect of shutting the victim out of the process and removing the opportunity for an offender to truly express remorse or be forgiven. RJ is based on a philosophy that offending needs an appropriate response that doesn't necessarily involve conventional legal methods, procedures or outcomes, and that justice should be flexible enough to respond to the particular demands, personal needs and potential for individualised action in each case; a philosophy that very much reflects the multilayered dynamics of sexual violence experiences.

Daly (2006, p. 335) summarises RJ practices as having four core elements:

> First, a person has admitted responsibility for offending, either explicitly or implicitly ... RJ does not adjudicate or mediate facts, but is part of the post-adjudication (or penalty) phase of the criminal process. Secondly, an offender typically (but not always) has a face-to-face meeting with a victim (or a representative for a victim) ... along with other supporters or relevant community members. Thirdly, it is an informal process that relies on the knowledge and decision-making capacities of lay actors, but it is linked to and constrained by established criminal justice practices ... Fourthly, the aims of RJ are to hold offenders accountable for their behaviour and to make up for what they did.

In this way, RJ is an innovative mechanism to respond to shifting understandings of what justice means for sexual violence victims, and to recognise the harms caused in an official process that is not possible through conventional, adversarial prosecutions.

Project Restore is a holistic example of a RJ practice created to respond to the perceived shortcomings of the prosecution process, and to interrupt the recognisable narratives of carceral justice and sexual violence within and beyond the realm of law. Operating in New Zealand, *Project Restore* is framed on the US *RESTORE* programme, which has been evaluated as: 'feasible ... conducted safely, achiev[ing] acceptable levels of satisfaction, and attain[ing] many of [its] envisioned outcomes' (Koss 2014, p. 1655). *Project Restore* works in conjunction with the law by accepting referrals from the court system where the offender has entered a formal guilty plea. However, it also operates beyond the law, accepting referrals from the community and self-referrals from the victim or offender. Community referrals and self-referrals can involve acts of sexual violence that have not been reported to the police, but the offender must be prepared to admit the behaviour.

In their analysis of *Project Restore*, Julich and colleagues (2010, pp. 25–26) observed 29 referrals: including 10 from the community, 16 pre-sentencing and 3 post-sentencing. All cases were assessed according to set eligibility criteria based on: the ability and readiness of the offender to demonstrate accountability; the offender's capacity to be assessed for and enter into treatment (if recommended); the preparedness of the victim to engage in the process without coercion; and the victim's willingness to share their story (Julich et al., 2010, p. 27).

Not unsurprisingly, Julich and colleagues (2010, p. 19) also found that running cases depended on practical and resource factors, such as staff workload and time constraints. Of the 29 referrals, 4 offenders and 11 victims declined to participate, and only 9 resulted in completed conferences – 3 of which were community referrals. The researchers identified the disparity between referrals and conferences as resulting in part because of the discretionary involvement of the parties, and in part due to the 'rigorous processes by which each case is assessed... [as being] safe or appropriate' (Julich et al., 2010, pp. 25–26).

The key aim of *Project Restore* is to provide victims with 'an experience of a sense of justice, [to] support offenders to understand the impacts of their behaviour and to facilitate the development of an action plan' (Julich et al., 2011, p. 223); a significant shift from the procedures and outcomes of conventional legal processes. The programme follows established practice guidelines, but permits unique processes to be developed for individual cases. It adopts a similar framework to other RJ group conference models, but also includes: a facilitator with an in-depth understanding of sexual violence dynamics; two community specialists (a qualified counsellor with specific expertise in sexual violence and a qualified therapist working with individuals who sexually offend); and clinical psychologists who provide professional supervision and joint team leadership, but have no contact with the stakeholders (Julich et al., 2011, p. 223). By incorporating expertise, stringent eligibility and assessment criteria, and focusing on the individual needs and circumstances of each case, *Project Restore* offers an alternative way to respond to sexual violence that seeks to reduce the stigma, trauma and stress associated with the conventional prosecution process, and which better recognises the individual and often complex needs of both victims and offenders in responding to the lived experiences of, and harms caused by, sexual violence.

It is beyond the scope of this chapter to examine the debates around RJ as a response to sexual violence in any detail (for this, see CIJ, 2014; Cossins, 2008; Daly, 2002, 2006, 2011; Hudson, 2002; Koss, 2010; Shapland et al., 2011; Stubbs, 2003, 2010). However, a brief summary of some perceived limitations include that: RJ risks decriminalising sexual violence and being seen as a less serious way to deal with sexual offending; there is a public benefit and interest in prosecuting and punishing sexual violence through a conventional criminal justice system, and a danger that RJ practices will remove gendered violence from public view; there is a limited ability to monitor compliance with outcomes; RJ focuses on the penalty stage, rather than offering any advances in how we can better respond to the victim's role in conventional prosecutions; victims may not want to confront their offender; there is the possibility that power imbalances may be replicated; and focusing on forgiveness 'may be antithetical to helping a victim's suffering' (Daly & Stubbs, 2006, p. 19). Cossins (2008, p. 270) also argues that RJ permits a distinction between an offender having to admit guilt but not necessarily take full responsibility for the offence, and thus victims may still experience attributions of blame.

In contrast, and again in summary form, some perceived benefits of RJ practices include: giving victims a voice and a key participatory role; providing victims and their experiences with validation; creating a more flexible and communicative environment in which victims can express themselves without the constraints applied to witness testimony; the victim's credibility is not a core issue of proceedings; it encourages offenders to admit and acknowledge the offence; victims are not subject to cross-examination; it offers a tailored, individual process; and it can reduce a victim's sense of powerlessness, by giving them ownership of the case and having a decision made by the parties involved, not a judge, jury, prosecutor or police member. In her analysis of 118 conferences, 226 court cases and 41 formal cautions of youth sexual offenders in South Australia, Daly (2006, p. 352) also found that RJ can offer a more efficient, speedier resolution for victims:

> Court cases took twice as long to finalise as conference cases, they shifted jurisdiction more often, and victims would have had to attend court an average of six times to learn the outcome of their case. If they appeared in court on the day of finalisation, nearly half would find that the case was dismissed or withdrawn.

While there are some concerns regarding the use of RJ in responding to sexual violence, as Larson (2014, p. 36) explains, 'what is certain is that where RJ is done well, it goes beyond what traditional responses can achieve and as a result, the potential impact upon individuals, communities and society is substantial'. This view is similarly supported in a Centre for Innovative Justice report:

> When too few victims of sexual assault have options in the criminal justice process, or the prospect of any real justice outcomes; and when evidence suggests that restorative justice conferencing meets victims' justice needs to a greater extent than the conventional criminal justice system, it is difficult to justify any further reluctance to embrace reform.
>
> (CIJ, 2014, p. 36)

RJ is a clear example of how we have come to view both sexual violence and what justice means for victims, in ways that sit outside the dominant carceral justice and 'real rape' narratives. RJ treats sexual violence as an 'encounter': as something un-coded which doesn't fit one specific narrative, and which requires a response of invention and experimentation. It achieves this by responding to sexual violence and victims' justice needs on a more individualised basis, and through challenging responses to, and assumptions of, rape, justice and the lived experiences of sexual violence victims at both a collective and specific level. Specifically, it achieves this by offering individualised ways to respond to the harms and needs of those directly involved; and collectively, it provides a legitimate formalised option to understand, discuss and repair the harms caused by sexual violence, outside the constraints of a trial, where the language and constrictions of the law can work towards the promotion and acceptance of a 'real rape' narrative. In moving forward with RJ as a response to sexual violence harms, it is important that the recognisable narrative is not focused on whether it should be done, but on the most effective ways to implement these processes so they can operate both within and beyond the conventional justice system (Koss, 2014, pp. 1655–1656).

Conclusion

The failings of conventional legal processes have prompted the development of innovative, alternative forms and processes of justice for sexual violence victims – both within and beyond the context of law. These alternative mechanisms allow for the conventional narratives of rape and of justice for sexual violence victims to be interrupted in ways that promote greater understanding of the complexities and individualities of this significant social problem. Examples of this can be seen in the creation of specialist units and courts with expertise in sexual violence matters, through to RJ practices that give the victim a voice in the process and outcome of their case. We have also witnessed this interruption in campaigns that attempt to shift the focus away from warning women to take precautions to avoid and prevent the threat or acts of sexual violence, towards educating and instructing males as the potential offenders of sexual violence to take responsibility for their own conduct. These innovations – while still gaining momentum and operating within a society that problematically can readily accept rape myths – demonstrate the ways in which we can seek to interrupt the accepted 'logic' (or more precisely, 'illogic') of the narratives that permeate social understandings and knowledge of sexual violence.

As this chapter (and many others throughout this book) has argued, sexual violence is not a recognisable event, in the Deleuzian (1994) understanding of this term. Sexual violence is un-coded. It doesn't fit into one specific narrative. And it requires responses that allow for innovation and experimentation both within and beyond the conventional realm of law. While the examples discussed above provide some insight into how these narratives are being disrupted, and shed some light on the potential benefits that can arise from this, there remains a significant path to pave.

References

ABS [Australian Bureau of Statistics] (1996) *Personal Safety Survey* (Canberra: Australian Government Publishing Service).

ABS [Australian Bureau of Statistics] (2006) *Personal Safety Survey* (Canberra: Australian Government Publishing Service).

AR Wear (2014) 'AR Wear Website'; Retrieved from https://www.indiegogo.com/projects/ar-wear-confidence-protection-that-can-be-worn

Butterfield, M. (2012) 'Edmonton Sexual Assault Awareness Campaign, "Don't Be That Guy" So Effective City Relaunches with New Posters', *Huffington Post*, 12 January.

Christie, N. (1977) 'Conflict as Property', *British Journal of Criminology*, 18(1), 1–15.

CIJ [Centre for Innovative Justice] (2014) *Innovative Justice Responses to Sexual Offending: Pathways to Better Outcomes for Victims, Offenders and the Community* (Victoria, Australia: Centre for Innovative Justice, RMIT).

Cook, K. (2014) 'Suicides Show How Justice System Fails Rape Victims', *The Conversation*, 28 February.

Cossins, A. (2008) 'Restorative Justice and Child Sex Offences: The Theory and the Practice', *British Journal of Criminology*, 4(3), 359–378.

Cossins, A. (2010) *Alternative Models for Prosecuting Child Sex Offences in Australia* (Sydney: National Child Sexual Assault Reform Committee, University of New South Wales).

Daly, K. (2000) 'Revisiting the Relationship Between Retributive and Restorative Justice', in H. Strang and J. Braithwaite (eds.) *Restorative Justice: Philosophy to Practice* (Aldershot: Ashgate/Dartmouth), pp. 33–54.

Daly, K. (2002) 'Sexual Assault and Restorative Justice', in H. Strang and J. Braithwaite (eds.) *Restorative Justice and Family Violence* (Cambridge: Cambridge University Press), pp. 62–88.

Daly, K. (2006) 'Restorative Justice and Sexual Assault: An Archival Study of Court and Conference Cases', *British Journal of Criminology*, 46(2), 334–356.

Daly, K. (2011) *Conventional and Innovative Responses to Sexual Violence*, ACSSA Issues, no. 12 (Melbourne, Australia: Australian Centre for the Study of Sexual Assault).

Daly, K. and Bouhours, B. (2010) 'Rape and Attrition in the Legal Process: A Comparative Analysis of Five Countries', *Crime and Justice: An Annual Review of Research*, 39, 485–565.

Daly, K. and Curtis-Frawley, S. (2006) 'Justice for Victims of Sexual Assault: Court or Conference?', in K. Heimer and C. Kruttschnitt (eds.) *Gender and Crime: Patterns of Victimization and Offending* (New York: New York University Press), pp. 230–265.

Daly, K. and Stubbs, J. (2006) 'Feminist Engagement with Restorative Justice', *Theoretical Criminology*, 10(1), 9–28.

Deleuze, G. (1994) *Difference and Repetition* (New York: Columbia University Press).

Dolan, A. (2012) 'Fury as Police Anti-drinking Campaign Suggests Drunk Women Are to Blame', *Daily Mail*, 3 August.

Edwards, J. (2011) 'Pennsylvania's Blame the Rape Victim Ad Follows a Long History of Lousy Campaigns', *Business Insider*, 10 December.

Ellison, L. and Munro, V. (2009) 'Of "Normal Sex" and "Real Rape": Exploring the Use of Socio-sexual Scripts in (Mock) Jury Deliberation', *Social & Legal Studies*, 18(3), 291–312.

Evans, S. (2014) 'Outrage Over Government's Alcohol Awareness Poster That Shifts Blame onto Rape Victims If They Drink Too Much', *Daily Mail*, 27 July.

Finch, E. and Munro, V. (2005) 'Juror Stereotypes and Blame Attribution in Rape Cases Involving Intoxicants: The Findings of a Pilot Study', *British Journal of Criminology*, 45, 25–38.

Finn, J. (2011) 'Decision-Making and Decision Makers in Sexual Offence Trials: Options for Specialist Sexual Offence Courts, Tribunals of Fact and the Giving of Reasons', *Canterbury Law Review*, 17, 96–119.

Flynn, A. (2010) *Secret Deals and Bargained Justice: Lifting the Veil of Secrecy Surrounding Plea Bargaining in Victoria*, PhD thesis, Monash University.

Flynn, A. (2012) 'Bargaining with Justice: Victims, Plea Bargaining and the *Victims Charter Act 2006* (Vic)', *Monash University Law Review*, 32, 73–96.

Flynn, A., Halsey, M, and Lee, M. (2015, *forthcoming*) 'Emblematic Violence and Aetiological Cul-De-Sacs: On the Discourse of "One Punch" (Non) Fatalities', *British Journal of Criminology*, first published online 21 May, 2015.

Foucault, M. (1980) 'The Confession of the Flesh 1977 Interview', in C. Gordon (ed.) *Power/Knowledge: Selected Interviews and Other Writings* (New York: Pantheon Books), pp. 194–228.

Freiberg, A. (2001) 'Problem-Orientated Courts: Innovative Solutions to Intractable Problems', Melbourne: AIJA Conference, 21–23 July 2001; Retrieved from: http://www.aija.org.au/Mag01/Freiberg.pdf

Grubb, A. and Turner, E. (2012) 'Attribution of Blame in Rape Cases: A Review of the Impact of Rape Myth Acceptance, Gender Role Conformity and Substance Use on Victim Blaming', *Aggression and Violent Behavior*, 17, 443–452.

Heenan, M. and Murray, S. (2004) *Study of Reported Rapes in Victoria 2000–2003* (Melbourne, Australia: Statewide Steering Committee to Reduce Sexual Assault).

Herman, J. (2005) 'Justice from the Victim's Perspective', *Violence Against Women*, 11(5), 571–602.

Hudson, B. (2002) 'Restorative Justice and Gendered Violence: Diversion or Effective Justice?' *British Journal of Criminology*, 42(3), 616–634.

Julich, S., Buttle, J., Cummins, C. and Freeborn, E. (2010) *Project Restore: An Exploratory Study of Restorative Justice and Sexual Violence*; Retrieved from: https://www.academia.edu/274691/Project_Restore_An_Exploratory_Study_of_Restorative_Justice_and_Sexual_Violence

Julich, S., McGregor, K., Annan, J., Landon, F., McCarrison, D. and McPhillips, K. (2011) 'Yes There Is Another Way', *Canterbury Law Review*, 17, 222–228.

Kelly, M. (2011) '7 Ways to Protect Yourself from Rape', *Marie Claire*, 10 March.

Koss, M. (2010) 'Restorative Justice for Acquaintance Rape and Misdemeanor Sex Crimes', in J. Ptacek (ed.) *Restorative Justice and Violence Against Women* (New York: Oxford University Press), pp. 218–238.

Koss, M. (2014) 'The RESTORE Program of Restorative Justice for Sex Crimes: Vision, Process and Outcomes', *Journal of Interpersonal Violence*, 29(9), 1623–1660.

Larson, J. (2014) 'Restorative Justice in the Australian Criminal Justice System', *Australian Institute of Criminology: Research and Public Policy Series*, no. 127, Australian Institute of Criminology, Canberra.

Manyathi-Jele, N. (2013) 'Sexual Offences Courts to be Re-established', *DeRebus*; Retrieved from: http://www.saflii.org/za/journals/DEREBUS/2013/163.html

Ministerial Advisory Task Team (2013) *Report on the Re-establishment of Sexual Offences Courts in South Africa* (South Africa: Justice and Constitutional Development Department).

Ministry of Justice (2013) *An Overview of Sexual Offending in England and Wales* (London, UK: Ministry of Justice, Home Office and the Office for National Statistics).

Mouzos, J. and Makkai, T. (2004) *Australian Component of the International Violence Against Women Survey (IVAWS)* (Canberra: Australian Institute of Criminology).

Pali, B. and Madsen, K. (2011) 'Dangerous Liaisons? A Feminist and Restorative Justice Approach to Sexual Assault', *Temida*, 14(1), 49–65.

Powell, A. and Henry, N. (2014) 'Framing Sexual Violence Prevention: What Does it Mean to Challenge a Rape Culture?', in N. Henry and A. Powell (eds.) *Preventing Sexual Violence: Interdisciplinary Approaches to Overcoming a Rape Culture* (Basingstoke: Palgrave Macmillan), pp. 1–21.

Powell, A., Henry, N., Flynn, A. and Henderson, E. (2013) 'Meanings of Sex and Consent: The Persistence of Rape Myths in Victoria Rape Law', *Griffith University Law Review*, 22(2), 456–480.

RAINN [Rape, Abuse, Incest National Network] (2014) *RAINN Statistics*; Retrieved from: https://www.rainn.org/statistics

Shapland, J., Robinson, G. and Sorsby, A. (2011) *Restorative Justice in Practice: Evaluating What Works for Victims and Offenders* (London, UK: Routledge).

Shapland, J., Willmore, J. and Duff, P. (1985) *Victims in the Criminal Justice System* (Aldershot: Gower).

Silvester, J. (2013) 'Criminal Justice System Failing Most Rape Victims', *The Age*, 3 August.

Smith, L. (2014) 'Anti-date Rape Undercover Nail Polish Changes Colour When Drinks Are Spiked with Rohypnol and GHB', *International Business Times*, 26 August.

Strang, H. and Sherman, L. (2003) 'Repairing the Harm: Victims and Restorative Justice', *Utah Law Review*, 1, 15–42.

Stubbs, J. (2003) 'Sexual Assault, Criminal Justice, and Law and Order', *Women Against Violence*, 14, 14–26.

Success Works (2011) *Sexual Assault Reform Strategy – Final Evaluation Report* (Melbourne, Australia: Department of Justice).
Walker, S. and Louw, D. (2005) 'The Court for Sexual Offences: Perceptions of the Victims of Sexual Offences', *International Journal of Law and Psychiatry*, 28, 231–245.
White House Public Service Announcement (2014) *One is Too Many*; Retrieved from: http://www.youtube.com/watch?v=xLdElcv5qqc
Yoffee, E. (2013) 'College Women: Stop Getting Drunk', *Slate*, 15 October 2013.

7

Retribution, Redress and the Harms of Rape

The Role of Tort Law

Nikki Godden-Rasul

Introduction

Increasing the prosecution and punishment of sexual offenders has been a prominent goal of policymakers over the last few decades, corresponding with heightened public awareness of sexual violence and feminist activism directed at rape law reform. However, the criminal law is not the only legal route that rape victim-survivors[1] have taken to secure justice. In recent years, there has been an increase in tortious claims against high-profile – often wealthy – individuals and institutions within which sexual abuse has been overlooked and tolerated. Illustrating both these kinds of case in the United Kingdom are the civil claims brought against the estate of Jimmy Savile, TV presenter and personality who abused adults and children, and against the BBC and NHS, which provided the conditions and opportunities for Savile to perpetrate his abuse unreported for over 50 years (BBC News, 2013). However, it is not only high-profile or wealthy defendants who have been sued in tort law for sexual violence, including rape.[2]

It is not difficult to find a ground for liability in tort law for redress. For instance, the trespass to the person torts – battery, assault and false imprisonment – encompass the crime of rape and other forms of non-consensual sexual contact. The tort of battery in particular, which is intentional and unlawful direct contact with a person (in this context meaning non-consensual), has long been known to encompass unwanted sexual contact.[3] Nevertheless, civil claims for rape remain relatively rare in the UK. It is likely that the practical limitations of the tort system, such as potentially high costs, prevent victim-survivors from pursuing such cases. But if the civil law were a viable option of redress it might be pursued by more victim-survivors, who may find it offers a sense of justice beyond the realm of traditional criminal justice.

For the legal system to provide justice for victim-survivors, it must recognise and respond to what is harmful about rape, reflecting women's lived experiences. If, as has historically been the case, it fails to do so, it maintains the gender injustices that are created and reinforced through sexual violence. In comparison with the criminal law, which focuses on punishing wrongdoers and administering retribution, tort law turns to compensating harms caused by wrongdoers. Thus, tort law may provide a different perspective from which to interrogate the harms of rape, the law's response and victim-survivors' hopes for justice. This chapter therefore centres on tort law and the harms of rape. I begin by outlining the advantages and disadvantages of using tort law as a response to rape, before turning to analyse the ways in which the harms of rape have been theorised by feminist scholars, and how the harm of rape has been conceptualised and responded to in the criminal law. Here I argue that the form of justice offered through the criminal justice system, in short, *recognition* of rape as a violation victim-survivors' autonomy (see Henry et al., Chapter 1) and carceral *punishment* of offenders (see Gotell, Chapter 4), may serve to marginalise or obscure the material harms that victim-survivors can suffer. In light of the limitations of criminal justice, the last section will examine the way in which the harms of rape are conceptualised in tort law, and how the harms of rape are responded to in judicial assessments of the damages to be awarded when a successful case has been made by the claimant. It will be argued that these cases illustrate the diversity of harms which rape victim-survivors can suffer, and their need for some form of *redress* as a matter of justice.

Tort claims for rape

Despite a clear cause of action founded in trespass to the person, civil claims for rape are uncommon in the UK. Similar to a woman's decision not to report rape to the police, some victim-survivors may be deterred from disclosing rape to lawyers and others for fear of being disbelieved, blamed and treated with hostility; because of the stress of the legal process; or because it is their partner or ex-partner who raped them. Moreover, a civil claim – for those who are aware of the option – is often not possible for practical purposes. For instance, in addition to the time and stress of pursing a tort case, it can be potentially costly, and for many victim-survivors there will be no lucrative defendant and therefore no prospect of compensation. This is highlighted by the litigation against John Worboys. Thirteen women brought a civil suit against Worboys, who opportunistically used his occupation as a taxi driver, and the taxi cab as the location, to intoxicate and sexually abuse his victims. As it was unlikely that the claimants would receive the full amount of compensation from Worboys, they also claimed the company that insured his taxi should be held liable. The High Court of Justice of England and Wales held that the claimants' injuries did not result from 'the use of a vehicle on the road' which insurance policies cover, as specified in the Road Traffic Act (1998 s. 145(3); *AXN and Others v. Worboys and Others* [2012] EWHC, 1730). As a result of the costs of the failed litigation, the net amount the claimants recovered by way of settlement from Worboys was £10,000 each.[4] This settlement is a far cry from the damages awarded in other relatively recent civil claims for rape, for which the general and aggravated damages have been around £75,000 (*Parrington v. Marriott* (1999) Unreported, Court of Appeal, 19 February 1999; *Lawson v. Glaves-Smith, Executor for the Estate of Dawes* [2006] EWHC 2865 (QB)). Nevertheless, the practical limitations of the system, as it currently operates, does not mean there is no value in tort law as a response to rape (Godden, 2011).

Tort law can provide compensation for harms caused to the victim-survivor, sometimes directly from the perpetrator, in line with corrective justice. In the civil legal system, the victim-survivor is a party to the proceedings, plays an active role in pursuing a suit against the perpetrator, and may have more control and choice throughout the process. Consequently, West (1992) suggests it may be empowering for victim-survivors. Feldthusen (1993) likewise argues that in exercising choice and power over the defendant through the process, the claimant may experience a sense of 'therapeutic justice'. In addition, a claimant may have a greater chance of securing civil liability than criminal liability. First, the standard of proof is lower than that of the criminal justice system – in the civil law, cases must be proved on the balance of probabilities rather than beyond reasonable doubt.[5] Second, in the civil system, it is likely that a reasonable belief in consent will not negate civil liability (and, as I have argued elsewhere, should not negate civil liability; Godden, 2011, pp. 163–167), whereas in the criminal justice system in England and Wales, such a belief relieves a person of criminal responsibility for a number of sexual offences, including rape (Sexual Offences Act 2003 s. 1(1)(c)).

It is important to note that tort law does not provide the perfect means to respond to rape. In addition to accessibility and financial limitations, there are some other drawbacks. For example, it may be argued that tort law allows men to 'buy' non-consensual sexual activity if they can have sex without a woman's consent, and pay for the privilege (albeit through compensation) after the event. Concerns may be raised over tort law's status as 'civil' and 'private' law. This could be seen to undermine feminist efforts to have a criminal definition for rape that reflects women's lived experiences of it, and which provides public condemnation and punishment by the state. Indeed, tort law may be seen as removing responsibility from the state to respond to rape, as it relies on victim-survivors pursuing cases. More generally, it is not surprising that some feminists are sceptical of tort law in general, given its gendered foundations and history (for an overview, see Conaghan, 2003). However, as Chamallas and Wriggins (2010) and Conaghan (2003, pp. 182–187) argue, tort law is not simply 'private' law, as, like all law, it contributes to constituting social reality, is distributive in nature and effects, and thus has the potential to be harnessed to address gendered harms. In light of these points, in the discussion below, I focus on one particular dimension of tort law; the way in which it redresses and conceptualises the harms of rape, which informs ideas as to how the law can provide a better sense of justice for victim-survivors.

Changing conceptions of rape: Harm, politics and law

Since the 1970s, feminist scholarship has revealed the extent of men's violence against women, and theorised the causes and harms of rape based on women's lived experiences. In broad terms, feminist scholars have focused on two dimensions of conceptualising the harms of rape. One dimension is what will be referred to as the 'core' harm of rape – that is, the harm which feminists have tried to conceptualise as the unifying feature of all rapes, which distinguishes rape from other harms. Typically, these discussions of the 'core harm' form the basis for criminal law reform proposals, so that the crime of rape better reflects and redresses the problem. The other dimension is what will be called the 'consequential' harms of rape. These are the different ways in which sexual violence can impact survivors' lives and those they are close to, and the economic and public health consequences of sexual violence. To some extent, these two dimensions of harm have been separated in legal research and policymaking. This analysis seeks to trouble this separation, and, to do so, the basis for the separation will be analysed through a brief historical account of the relationship between the core and consequential harms of rape in feminist theory, activism and law reform.

Historically, rape was understood as damaging a woman's social standing; for example, her capacity to marry 'well', which primarily harmed her husband or father. In addition, among other things, the risk of pregnancy constituted a threat to the family lineage and inheritance. The core harm was thus conceived of in terms of social and economic standing or value to the woman's (male) family. As such, the consequential harms were primarily considered to be pregnancy, physical injury to the woman and economic losses which may have had an impact on the father or husband (Bourke, 2012, p. 40). However, in the mid- to late twentieth century, feminist research began uncovering the extent and nature of sexual violence and rape came to be understood as harmful to women both individually and as a group (for example, see Brownmiller, 1975; MacKinnon, 1989). This changed conceptions of the core and consequential harms, which became based on women's rights and women's experiences. The core harm of the act came to be located in the violation of a woman – for example, in the violation of her sexual autonomy (Estrich, 1986), the violation of her sexual integrity (Lacey, 1998) and the disruption of her sense of self and denial of a female subjectivity (du Toit, 2009). Feminist campaigns for law reform, based on theories developed from women's lived experiences – primarily the conception of rape as the violation of sexual autonomy-led to a change in the legal definition of rape. The shift, from a focus on sex procured by physical force or fraud, to sex without consent, was able to accommodate more nuanced forms of coercion and deception (Cowan, 2007, p. 53).

During the same period, practitioners and scholars identified a causal link between sexual violence/abuse and psychological trauma (for example, Burgess & Holmstrom, 1974; Herman, 1997; Sutherland & Scherl, 1970), and effects of sexual violence on the physical and sexual health of victim-survivors (Golding, 1994) and their day-to-day lives (Koss, 1993). Empirical research on the impact of sexual violence relates to the theoretical claims as to the core harm of rape. As Herman (1997, p. 51) explains, traumatic events such as rape 'shatter the construction of the self that is formed and sustained in relation to others'. Feminists founded charitable organisations and support services to respond to the effects of sexual violence. They also argued for changes in criminal justice procedures and policies to recognise the psychological impact rape may have on victim-survivors. Thus, theorising the harm of rape and its consequences gained feminists political ground to influence change in law and policy, particularly in the criminal law and justice system.

Despite these progressive reconceptualisations, the breadth and diversity of consequential harms have been marginalised in the process, and victim-survivors are often left with no redress for these within the criminal justice system (for a wider discussion as to the consequences of criminal law and retribution in the context of rape, see Martin, 1998). Bourke (2012) makes this point in comparing historical responses to rape within the contemporary criminal paradigm. She explains that when rape was primarily understood as a harm to a woman and her family's social standing, it was a crime, but the tort of seduction – specifically designed to address this problem – provided financial and moral reparation to the head of the family (Bourke, 2012, p. 46). However, as feminists gained political ground leading to increased criminalisation of and punishments for harmful sexual behaviour, the material or consequential impacts of rape, and redress such as financial restitution, compensation or reparation, were eschewed (Bourke, 2012, p. 46). Moreover, in addition to marginalising some of the harms victim-survivors may experience, the criminal law has thus far failed to live up to its promise of protecting actual and potential victim-survivors through the legal recognition and punishment of rape. Consequently, the trend in feminist scholarship has shifted towards highlighting the need for prevention and dignified treatment of victim-survivors (see, for example, Kelly et al., 2005, pp. 87–88; Larcombe, 2011; Stern, 2010). Nevertheless, 'society has found it hard to resist the siren call of punishment' (McGlynn et al., 2012, p. 239).

This is not to say that the consequential harms of rape and compensation have been completely ignored by policymakers. As mentioned above, changes in criminal justice procedure have been introduced in response to heightened awareness of the potential psychological impacts of rape. Indeed, the link between trauma and rape is strong, such that Gavey and Schmidt's (2011) empirical study and analysis of the secondary literature indicates that scholars, policymakers and the public assume that rape inevitably has serious psychological consequences. However, they argue that this assumption is problematic, as social and legal responses often fail to account for the diversity of experiences and harms of rape. Furthermore, responses to the consequential harms of rape have typically been constructed as 'individual' problems which can be 'treated' through mental health programmes, with 'risk-avoidance' strategies for the victim-survivor to minimise the harm and prevent future rapes (Bumiller, 2008). Such responses, Bumiller (2008) argues, distort the social and gendered dimensions of rape, its aftermath and recovery.

It is also worth noting here that restitution and compensation have been introduced into the criminal justice system to recognise, to some extent, the particular harms the offender has caused the victim-survivor. For example, victim-survivors can apply to the Criminal Injuries Compensation Authority (for England, Scotland and Wales) for compensation to be awarded under the Criminal Injuries Compensation Scheme 2012, regardless of whether there has been a criminal prosecution and conviction. Awards granted through this scheme are based on a standardised tariff system with set awards for different types of sexual assaults which vary depending on the circumstances (for example, the award will be higher if there is a 'severe mental illness' than if there is a 'moderate mental illness' caused by the assault; Criminal Injuries Compensation Scheme, 2012, p. 69). However, the awards are not compensatory – that is, they are not intended to reflect and respond to the full amount of harm caused – and are instead tokenistic in nature. As such, the particular harms the victim-survivor suffers are not redressed. Another example is the use of impact statements in which victims detail the way the crime has affected them at the sentencing stage. While this opportunity may be important for the victim-survivor to convey the harms of the offence, there is no corresponding recognition of, response to, or redress for the harms voiced by the victim-survivor.

In summary, the focus on censuring the core harm of rape through criminal law has to some extent marginalised and eclipsed the diversity of consequential harms of rape in the legal system. While it cannot provide redress for the majority of rape victim-survivors, at least as currently conceived and structured, the lens of tort law can reveal the wider public and social effects a system of redress may have (see discussion above). It can indicate the significance of redressing the particular harms victim-survivors suffer, thus acknowledging the diversity of rape experiences.

The harms of rape and tort law

Before turning to the judicial recognition and redress provided through tort law for the wide range of harms experienced as a result of rape, it is first important to consider the way in which tort law conceives of the core harm of rape. The core harm is framed very similarly in tort law as it is in criminal law: as a violation of a person's bodily integrity and autonomy, which is captured in the trespass to the person torts, most obviously battery. As such, debates in relation to the merits and limitations of the criminal conception of the core harm, and its reliance on notions such as consent, similarly apply in the tort law context. It is not the place here to expand on those discussions. Nor is it to question whether battery is beneficial or problematic because it lacks the label 'rape', with the latter's powerful connotations and sexual and gendered dimensions (for a discussion, see Godden, 2011, pp. 162–163). Rather, the first point here is simply that there is basis for liability in tort law. The second point is that in tort law, the core harm is not necessarily the primary focus but rather it is compensating the particular harms caused by wrongdoing. This is unlike criminal law where the core harm is central to the purposes of fair labelling and proportionate punishment. As such, tort law may shed light on the diversity of harms victim-survivors may suffer and provide redress. To consider this possibility, the emphasis here is on remedies.

In *Lawson v. Glaves-Smith, Executor for the Estate of Dawes,* Mr Justice Eady found that the claimant, Ms Lawson, was falsely imprisoned, forcefully intoxicated and sexually assaulted on numerous occasions in Mr Dawes' properties on the island of Alderney. In considering the level of damages to be awarded, he determined – after reviewing conflicting evidence from expert witnesses – that Ms Lawson 'suffered disabling trauma and psychological symptoms as a direct result of what happened in Alderney' (para. 120). Similarly, in *Griffiths v. Williams,* Rose LJ accepted that the claimant was depressed as a result of being raped by her landlord and, at the time of the trial four years afterwards, she was still engaged in counselling ((1995) *The Times,* 24 November 1995). After she was raped twice and sexually harassed over an 18-month period by her former manager, another claimant successfully sued, it being accepted that she had experienced 'shame and humiliation, pain', depression and post-traumatic stress disorder (PTSD) (*Parrington v Marriott*). At the time of these cases, the earliest in 1995, the potential psychological impact of rape and other forms of sexual violence had become well known.

These cases highlight the prevalence of PTSD in victim-survivors of sexual violence. Indeed, childhood sexual abuse, rape and intimate partner violence have been found to be the most common causes of PTSD in women (United Nations, 2006, p. 164), and other common psychological consequences, such as guilt, shame, fear, anxiety and depression (Shaw and Campbell, 2011, p. 119). In contrast, with early civil claims for rape, such as *W v. Meah* and *D v. Meah* in 1986, damages were only awarded for the physical injuries caused by the rapes, sexual assault and physical abuse of the victim-survivors ([1986] 1 All ER 935, Woolf J at para. 942), amounting to £6750 and £10,250, respectively.

Wasco (2003) argues that feminists must be careful not to overemphasise or centralise diagnoses such as PTSD or trauma, as these do not capture the many different effects of sexual violence for women, particularly in patriarchal societies, to which more attention should be paid. Among other consequences, she says, sexual and other health problems associated with rape can be overlooked (Wasco, 2003, p. 314). For example, victim-survivors may experience sexually transmitted infections, unwanted pregnancy, abortion, sexual dysfunction and/or aversion and diseases or illnesses such as diabetes or chronic pelvic pain (Golding, 1994). In some of the reported cases in which a civil claim has been brought for rape, the wider impacts of the act on victim-survivors' lives were documented. It seems, for example, that the attempted rapes and sexual assaults to which Dawes subjected Ms Lawson contributed to her subsequent use of intoxicating substances (*Lawson v. Glaves-Smith, Executor for the Estate of Dawes*, para. 117) – a recognised consequence for some victim-survivors (Koss, 1993). Ms Lawson also had difficulties forming and maintaining relationships (*Lawson v. Glaves-Smith, Executor for the Estate of Dawes*, paras. 114–127). Similarly, D, who was sexually assaulted at knifepoint by Meah, struggled in social situations and lost any trust in men (*D v. Meah*, Woolf J at para. 940), and W, another of Meah's victim-survivors, said the assault contributed to the breakdown of her marriage (*W v. Meah*, Woolf J at para. 937). Also, Ms Griffiths, who was assaulted by her landlord, did not like men coming near her after the rapes and sexual harassment and had experienced repeated nightmares (*Griffiths v. Williams*, Rose LJ).

Given the potential physical, psychological and social impacts of rape, it is likely that victim-survivors will also suffer financially, for example through loss of earnings if she has had an extended period of absence from work or leaves her employment entirely. This indeed was the case for Ms Lawson, who prior to the events at Alderney, owned and ran a very successful hair salon and was considered a rising talent in her trade, but was subsequently unable to work or manage, and eventually lost her business. Her losses were calculated at £161,000 (*Lawson v. Glaves Smith, Executor for the Estate of Dawes*, Eady J). These examples indicate a judicial recognition through tort law of the diversity of experiences of the harms of rape and the different impact it may have on victim-survivors. In addition, there is redress provided in relation to these harms, which is not possible through victim–impact statements or tariff-set compensation awards from the Criminal Injuries Compensation Authority, as discussed above.

Furthermore, the gendered nature of the harms of rape has been recognised, to some extent, in the tort cases. That Ms Lawson, Ms Griffiths and D had difficulty trusting or forming relationships with others, and with men in particular, can be interpreted as illustrating the impact on gender relations more generally, with rape contributing to and reinforcing women's oppression. Moreover, fractured relationships may indicate that rape can damage a woman's sense of self; that it is a violation of personhood if the self is developed and constructed in relation to and via engagement with others (Herman, 1997). Indeed, in *Lawson v. Glaves-Smith, Executor for the Estate of Dawes*, Eady J described Ms Lawson as having undergone a 'personality change' due to the sexual assault and false imprisonment by Dawes (para. 28). Interestingly, in a few tort cases involving rape for which transcripts or reports are readily available, reference has been made to the harmful nature of the civil processes when deciding the level of damages, indicating that claimants in civil cases may be interrogated in such a way and to such an extent that they feel as though they themselves are on trial, as though they have done wrong or that the rape is their fault; a point which is commonly made in relation to criminal sexual offences trials (Temkin, 2002). In the civil case *Griffiths v. Williams*, for example, both Millett LJ and Thorpe LJ made the point that the nature of the trial and the way in which defence counsel attacked the claimant's character and credibility contributed to the £50,000 in damages being awarded. While any claimant may find civil procedures stressful, there are particular, gendered issues in trials concerning a sexual assault which may increase the stress for the claimant in such a case. This was recognised in *Lawson v. Glaves-Smith, Executor for the Estate of Dawes* in which Ms Lawson was awarded £12,000 in damages for lost earnings following the civil suit against her abuser because, Justice Eady suggested, the process would have been stressful and Lawson would need time to recuperate (para. 129). As such, in these civil judgements, the ways in which the legal system can contribute to and shape victim-survivors' experiences of harm is not only recognised, but also compensated for. There is an acknowledgment that there is a legal wrong that should be redressed as a matter of justice. Despite these advantages, it is problematic that it is not the state, as embodied in legal institutions, which is being held responsible for the harm, but the defendant. Moreover, as Seidman and Vickers (2005, pp. 471–473) argue in the context of the criminal justice system, the civil legal process should not increase the harm victim-survivors experience, but operate to reduce and address it.

One question raised from this discussion is of the level of damages awarded, as low levels of compensation may serve to undermine the harms caused. The level of damages may be a concern because, as Graycar (2012) has noted, typically the levels and categories of damages developed by judges place a higher value on men's experiences, undermining or excluding the harms which often pervade the lives of women. In early tort claims for rape – in the 1980s and early 1990s – judges mischaracterised the harm, focusing on the physical violation and injuries of claimants with total awards in the region of £6000 to £12,500 each (*Makanjuola v. Commissioner of Police for the Metropolis and Another* (1989) *The Times*, 8 August 1989; *Moores v. Green* (1990) *The Guardian*, 13 September 1990; *W v. Meah; D v. Meah*). Since that time, the range of damages awarded have increased as the nature and extent of harms for rape victim-survivors has become more widely known (for further detail, see Godden, 2012, pp. 171–173). For example, judges have awarded and sanctioned general and aggravated damages in the region of £55,000 (*Parrington v. Marriott*) and £78,500 (plus inflation) (*Lawson v. Glaves-Smith, Executor for the Estate of Dawes*) for the violation of rape. Total damages in these cases were approximately £73,000 and £259,000, respectively; the difference consisting primarily of compensation for loss of earnings. Despite this, Adjin-Tettey (2012) argues that gendered assessments of damages in Canadian tort cases for sexual violence and abuse illustrate that tangible harms are privileged over remedies for the intangible, although the latter often feature prominently in the biographies of victim-survivors. In most of the tort claims brought for rape in England and Wales that are reported, the categorisation and levels of damages are not completely clear and often lack basic detail. Thus it may be that many aspects of the harm inflicted are not properly redressed through the compensation awarded. Nevertheless, the potential for judges to recognise and redress the diversity of harms is significant. Moreover, the civil judgments highlight many of the harmful material and financial consequences which are not commonly redressed in other areas of law.

Conclusion: Redressing the harms of rape

Redress for the harms of rape has often been eschewed in rape law and policy, which generally centres on the criminal law, criminal justice system and retributive punishment. However, redress, in the form of compensation for example, may be a matter of justice for some victim-survivors. For others, it may also, or alternatively, be a means to other ends, contributing to victim-survivors being able to move forward in their lives (Sheehy, 2004). Attending to and providing redress for the consequential harms of rape, and each victim-survivor's particular experience, is not currently within the remit of the criminal justice system. In the criminal law, the response to wrongdoing is punishment, with retribution being provided primarily in relation to the core harm of rape. While changing the legal definition of rape so that it better reflects women's lived experiences and drawing on the symbolic power of the criminal law has been – and still is – a significant part of the feminist movement, feminists have not failed to identify the limitations of the criminal justice system (see, for example, McGlynn & Munro, 2010).

In this chapter I have discussed a particular limitation of the criminal law; that is, the ways in which the diversity of harms from rape are obscured and marginalised, with the possibilities for redress for these harms eclipsed by a focus on punishment. Although some form of compensation has been argued for (for example, as provided via the Criminal Injuries Compensation Scheme), the tokenistic awards of the criminal system do not offer any serious engagement with the particular ways in which a victim-survivor of rape has been affected. The civil justice system, on the other hand, is supposed to provide the opportunity for victim-survivors to receive redress for the harms they have suffered because of another's wrongdoing. Indeed, where tort cases have been pursued the different ways in which rape has affected the claimants' lives have to some extent been recognised and responded to. However, first, as Adjin-Tettey (2012) argues, the traditional tortious categorisation and level of damages in this area need to be addressed so awards can better reflect and respond to the different kinds of harms of sexual violence. Importantly, this relates to 'intangible' harms, which judges have been slow to recognise. And second, although the civil justice system may be intended to exist outside of and complement the criminal justice system, in practice it is an option that is unavailable to the majority of victim-survivors, due often to an impecunious defendant or the potentially high costs of a civil suit. As such, for most, recognition and redress for the diversity of harms victim-survivors may suffer is out of reach.

Nevertheless, as I have argued here, viewing the harms of rape through the lens of tort law serves to highlight harms that the majority of victim-survivors may bear where a tort claim is not an option. Instead, victim-survivors must rely on their own resources, those of their families, of charitable organisations, state welfare and victim support services. Such support is not guaranteed; services are not conclusively provided by right and are often not available. These services are typically viewed as purely 'therapeutic' additions to the criminal justice system (Stern, 2010, p. 101). As such, these mechanisms are not typically provided as a matter of justice for rape victim-survivors. Recognising and redressing, as far as possible, the different ways in which rape can impact the lives of victim-survivors must constitute part of rape justice, and not merely be seen as incidental to it.

Acknowledgements

I would like to thank Harriot Rockey and Annie Topping for their valuable research assistance provided for this chapter. Thanks also to Aoife O'Donoghue and Kathryn Hollingsworth for productive conversations on this topic and to the editors for their helpful comments.

Notes

1. The term 'victim-survivor' will be used throughout this chapter to 'retain the empowerment conveyed by the word *survivor* and the outrage implied by the word *victim*' (emphasis in original) (Koss, 2010, p. 219).
2. For example, *W v. Meah; D v. Meah* [1986] 1 All ER 935; *Parrington v. Marriott* (1999) Unreported, Court of Appeal, 19 February 1999; *Lawson v. Glaves-Smith, Executor for the Estate of Dawes* (2006) EWHC 2865.
3. Lord Denning in *R v. Chief Constable of Devon and Cornwall, ex parte CEGB* [1982] QB 458, p. 471; with reference to Heuston (1977, p. 120).
4. The settlement is referred to in the defendant's submissions listed at para 43, *DSD, NBV v. The Commissioner of Police for the Metropolis* [2014] EWHC 2493 (QB), in which the court assessed the level of damages after the claimants successfully argued that Article 3 European Convention on Human Rights and the Human Rights Act 1998 had been breached by the police force in their negligent investigation of complaints of rape and sexual assault by Worboys; *DSD, NBV v. The Commissioner of Police for the Metropolis* [2014] EWHC 436 (QB).
5. In some civil cases in which the subject matter has been deemed 'serious', or has amounted to a crime, a higher standard of proof has been required. In these cases, however, the proof does not need to be as high as beyond reasonable doubt, which is required for criminal liability (see, for example, see *Bater v. Bater* [1950] 2 All ER 458, Lord Denning at 37; *Re H and others (Minors) (Sexual Abuse: Standard of Proof)* [1996] AC 563 (HL), Lord Nicholls at 586 (Lord Nicholls)). For a discussion in the context of rape, see Godden (2011, pp. 167–170).

References

Adjin-Tettey, E. (2012) 'Sexual Wrongdoing: Do the Remedies Reflect the Wrong?', in J. Richardson and E. Rackley (eds.) *Feminist Perspectives on Tort Law* (Abingdon: Routledge), pp. 179–204.

BBC News (2013) 'Jimmy Savile Estate and BBC Sued Over Alleged Abuse', 13 February 2013.

Bourke, J. (2012) 'Sexual Violence, Bodily Pain, and Trauma: A History', *Theory, Culture and Society*, 29(3), 25–51.

Brownmiller, S. (1975) *Against Our Will: Men, Women and Rape* (London: Penguin).

Bumiller, K. (2008) *In An Abusive State: How Neoliberalism Appropriated the Feminist Movement Against Sexual Violence* (Durham, NC: Duke University Press).

Burgess, A. W. and Holmstrom, L. L. (1974) 'Rape Trauma Syndrome', *American Journal of Psychiatry*, 131, 981–986.

Chamallas, M. and Wriggins, J. (2010) *The Measure of Injury: Race, Gender and Tort Law* (New York: New York University Press).

Conaghan, J. (2003) 'Tort Law and Feminist Critique', *Current Legal Problems*, 56, 175–209.

Cowan, S. (2007) 'Freedom and Capacity to Make a Choice', in V. E. Munro and C. Stychin (eds.) *Sexuality and the Law: Feminist Engagements* (Abingdon: Routledge-Cavendish), pp. 51–71.

du Toit, L. (2009) *A Philosophical Investigation of Rape: The Making and Unmaking of the Feminine Self* (New York: Routledge).

Estrich, S. (1986) 'Rape', *Yale Law Journal*, 95, 1087–1194.

Feldthusen, B. (1993) 'The Civil Action for Sexual Battery: Therapeutic Jurisprudence', *Ottawa Law Review*, 25, 203–234.

Gavey, N. and Schmidt, J. (2011) ' "Trauma of Rape" Discourse: A Double-Edged Template for Everyday Understandings of the Impact of Rape?', *Violence Against Women*, 17(4), 433–456.

Godden, N. (2011) 'Claims in Tort for Rape: A Valuable Remedy or Damaging Strategy?', *King's Law Journal*, 22, 157–182.

Godden, N. (2012) 'Tort Claims for Rape: More Trials, Fewer Tribulations?', in J. Richardson and E. Rackley (eds.) *Feminist Perspectives on Tort Law* (Abingdon: Routledge), pp. 163–178.

Golding, J. M. (1994) 'Sexual Assault History and Physical Health in Randomly Selected Los Angeles Women', *Health Psychology*, 13, 130–138.

Graycar, R. (2012) 'Damaging Stereotypes: The Return of Hoovering as a Hobby', in J. Richardson and E. Rackley (eds.) *Feminist Perspectives on Tort Law* (Abingdon: Routledge).

Herman, J. L. (1997) *Trauma and Recovery* (New York: Basic Books), pp. 205–226.

Heuston, R. (1977) *Salmond on Torts*, 17th ed. (London: Sweet and Maxwell).

Kelly, L., Lovett, J. and Regan, L. (2005) *A Gap or a Chasm? Attrition in Reported Rape Cases* (London: Home Office).

Koss, M. P. (1993) 'Rape: Scope, Impact, Interventions, and Public Policy Responses', *American Psychologist*, 48, 1062–1069.

Koss, M. P. (2010) 'Restorative Justice for Acquaintance Rape and Misdemeanor Sex Crimes', in J. Ptacek (ed.) *Restorative Justice and Violence Against Women* (Oxford: Oxford University Press), pp. 218–238.

Lacey, N. (1998) 'Unspeakable Subjects, Impossible Rights: Sexuality, Integrity and Criminal Law', *Canadian Journal of Law and Jurisprudence*, 11(1), 47–68.

Larcombe, W. (2011) 'Falling Rape Convition Rates: (Some) Feminist Aims and Measures for Rape Law', *Feminist Legal Studies*, 19, 27–45.

MacKinnon, C. (1989) *Toward a Feminist Theory of the State* (Cambridge: Harvard University Press).

Martin, D. (1998) 'Retribution Revisited: A Reconsideration of Feminist Criminal Law Reform Strategies', *Osgoode Hall Law Journal*, 36, 151–188.

McGlynn, C., Westmarland, N. and Godden, N. (2012) '"I Just Wanted Him to Hear Me": Sexual Violence and the Possibilities of Restorative Justice', *Journal of Law and Society*, 39, 213–240.
Ministry of Justice (2012) *The Criminal Injuries Compensation Scheme 2012* (London: The Stationery Office).
Seidman, I. and Vickers, S. (2005) 'An Agenda for the Next Thirty Years of Rape Law Reform', *Suffolk University Law Review*, 38, 467–492.
Shaw, J. and Campbell, R. (2011) 'Rape Crisis Centres: Serving Survivors and Their Communities', in T. Bryant-Davis (ed.) *Surviving Sexual Violence: A Guide to Recovery and Empowerment* (Plymouth: Rowman and Littlefield), pp. 112–128.
Sheehy, E. (2004) 'Compensation for Women who have been Raped', in J. V. Roberts and R. M. Mohr (eds.) *Confronting Sexual Assault: A Decade of Legal and Social Change* (Toronto: Toronto University Press), pp. 205–240.
Stern, Baroness V. (2010) *The Stern Review – An Independent Review into How Rape Complaints Are Handled by Public Authorities in England and Wales* (London: Home Office).
Sutherland, S. and Scherl, D. J. (1970) 'Patterns of Response among Victims of Rape', *American Journal of Orthopsychiatry*, 40(3), 503–511.
Temkin, J. (2002) *Rape and the Legal Process*, 2nd ed. (Oxford: Oxford University Press).
United Nations (2006) *In-Depth Study on All Forms of Violence Against Women; Report of the Secretary-General* (Geneva: United Nations, General Assembly).
Wasco, S. M. (2003) 'Conceptualizing the Harm Done by Rape Applications of Trauma Theory to Experiences of Sexual Assault', *Trauma, Violence and Abuse*, 4, 309–322.
West, N. (1992) 'Rape in the Criminal Law and the Victim's Tort Alternative: A Feminist Analysis', *University of Toronto Faculty Law Review*, 50, 96–130.

8
The European Court of Human Rights as a Mechanism of Justice for Rape Victims
Contributions and Limitations

Ivana Radačić

Introduction

Sexual violence, as a form of gender-based violence,[1] violates, impairs and nullifies women's human rights. It is also an impediment to securing a full range of human rights and freedoms of any individual and hence has far-reaching negative consequences for all societies (UNGA, 2006). Despite this, state responses often fail to appropriately condemn sexual violence and provide effective remedies to victims/survivors.[2] Criminal proceedings are often traumatising for the victims, who not only are called on to provide a detailed account of the assault, but whose character and behaviours are often scrutinised with reference to gender stereotypes and 'real rape' mythology. Three stereotypes regarding women's sexual behaviour are particularly widespread: that women enjoy being sexually possessed regardless of the circumstances; that they lie about being raped; and that they are responsible for their victimisation (see Edwards et al., 2011; Radačić, 2014a; Tempkin & Krahé, 2008). Based on these stereotypes, 'real rape' is defined as a violent attack on an unsuspecting and 'respectable' victim, who resists to her utmost. The application of such gender stereotypes often means that victims, rather than defendants, are placed at the centre of the trial.

International human rights law provides an avenue for redressing the ways in which state authorities treat rape victims. Its mechanisms provide victims with a sense of justice when domestic remedies have failed. International human rights law also has important symbolic and normative powers. Defining rape as a serious human rights abuse has secured 'woman' within the definition of 'human', with which human rights discourse is engaged, while the imposition of a wide range of obligations on states has initiated reforms of rape laws and practices in different domestic jurisdictions.

However, international human rights law also has its limitations. Some concern relates to the procedures of international law (which largely exclude the victims), as well as the problems of the (non-)execution of international standards. There are also more substantive issues. One example is the problematic application of the public/private divide in the interpretation of rights (see Romany, 1994), which has created hierarchies of rape and rape victims. Another is the reluctance of the international – particularly judicial – bodies to address gendered cultural norms (on the debate on women's rights and culture see, for example, Rao, 1995), and the often narrow understanding of relevance in examining individual complaints (for the critique of the legal notion of relevance see Bartlett, 1990), due to which international human rights law has not used its full potential in challenging gender stereotypes and rape myths.

This chapter discusses the contributions and limitations of one international human rights law mechanisms, considered to be the most effective in securing justice for rape victims – the European Court of Human Rights ('the Court'). It also examines how rape has been conceptualised and what obligations have been imposed on the states in its jurisprudence of the European Court of Human Rights ('the Court'). I first briefly introduce the Court and its case law on rape. I then analyse different categories of cases: a case concerning a refusal to institute criminal proceedings for non-voluntary sexual intercourse; cases concerning ineffective prosecution of rape by state agents; cases concerning ineffective prosecution of 'date rape'; cases concerning ineffective prosecution of rape where the application of force was established; and a case concerning a delayed conviction to a short prison term for 'gang rape'. After examining these cases, I discuss the Court's potential and limits in securing justice for rape victims, and end with conclusions.

The Court's case law on rape

Since 1 November 1998, the Court is the only implementing organ of the European Convention on Human Rights.[3] It is still the only international human rights court to which individuals can directly petition. Its jurisprudence influences not only the legislation and practices of the European countries, but also the jurisprudence of other global and regional human rights bodies (Merrils, 1993). As such it is a very powerful institution, widely perceived as a model of effectiveness (Ryssdall, 1996), which can significantly contribute to the advancement of women's rights in its member states and internationally. In its early years, this potential remained under-utilised as there were relatively few cases concerning women-specific abuses. However, in recent years, more cases concerning gender-based violence and other types of violations of women's rights have been adjudicated, which offers the Court an opportunity to set up standards in a gender-sensitive manner.

As of November 2014, the Court has examined (on merits) eight cases submitted by rape victims, of which seven concern ineffective criminal prosecution and one concerns a failure to establish mechanisms for prevention and detection of sexual violence in schools. Below, I analyse those cases concerning ineffective prosecution, as the one concerning sexual violence in schools is time- and place-specific.[4] The problems examined by the Court in these cases concerned a refusal to institute criminal proceedings, ineffective prosecution of rape by a state agent and private individuals (both in a context where there was direct proof of force and where there was none), and a delayed conviction and imposition of a short-term prison sentence.

Refusal to institute criminal proceedings

The Court's first rape case, *X. and Y. v. the Netherlands* (26 March 1985, Series A, no. 41), concerned the refusal to institute proceedings for a sexual offence (non-consensual sexual intercourse) that Ms Y. (a girl with intellectual disability, 16 years old at the time of the offence), suffered at the hands of the son of the director of the institution in which she lived. As Ms Y. was unable to report the crime, her father, Mr X. did. The prosecutor decided not to institute proceedings, a decision affirmed by the Court of Appeal, which considered it doubtful whether the charge of rape could be proved, as recourse to physical violence was a constituent element of the offence. The Court of Appeal held that the only applicable provision was one which prohibits 'causing a minor of blameless conduct to commit indecent acts or to suffer acts through gift, promises, abuse of dominant position, or deceit', which required the victim herself to take the action. The applicants argued that the failure to prosecute constituted a violation of Articles 3 (freedom from torture, inhumane and degrading treatment), 8 (the right to private and family life), 13 (right to an effective remedy) and 14 (freedom from discrimination)[5] in respect of Ms Y. and Article 8 in respect of Mr X.

The Court analysed the case under Article 8. It first clarified that this provision imposes positive obligations which 'may involve the adoption of measures designed to secure respect of private life even in the sphere of the relations of individuals between themselves' (*X. and Y. v. the Netherlands*, para. 23). This was at the time a progressive pronouncement which challenged the then particularly prominent public/private divide. The Court then assessed whether respect for private life in this case necessitated the adoption of criminal law provisions, or whether the availability of civil remedies was sufficient, as argued by the Dutch government. It stated that in rape cases 'fundamental values and essential aspects of private life are at stake', and held that 'effective deterrence is indispensable in this area and it can be achieved only by criminal law provisions' (*X. and Y. v. the Netherlands*, para. 27). Recognising that sexual violence implicates fundamental aspects of private life is an important achievement. However, the Court's refusal to analyse the claims under Article 3 – an absolute right enshrining one of the foundational values of democratic societies – is problematic, as it undermines the seriousness of rape.

In assessing compliance with Article 8, the Court did not analyse the Dutch legal framework on sexual violence, despite the problematic recourse to physical violence in a definition of rape and dubious wording of the applicable offence. It also did not challenge the domestic authorities' characterisation of the act as a relatively minor offence, thus failing to stress its serious nature. The only problem for the Court was that the applicable provision required the victim to institute proceedings, which left the applicant unprotected. This constituted a violation of Article 8 in respect of both the victim and her father.

Ineffective prosecution of rape by a state agent

The Court has also examined cases involving rape in custody committed by a state agent and the ineffective prosecution of these offences. In *Aydin v. Turkey* (25 September 1997, Reports of Judgments and Decisions 1997-V), a 17-year-old Kurdish girl was raped by military officers. In the course of the investigation, the military commander was questioned, the custody register subpoenaed and the applicant was sent to three gynaecological examinations. However, the officers who allegedly held her in custody and the villagers who might have seen her being taken into custody were not interviewed, while the gynaecological examinations, conducted by inexperienced doctors, were focused solely on establishing whether or not she had lost her virginity. While the proceedings were still pending at the time of the Court's judgement, there seemed to be no progress. The applicant argued that she was subjected to torture in violation of Article 3 and that she had no effective remedy in violation of Article 13.

In *Maslova and Nalbandov v. Russia* (no. 839/02, 24 January 2008), the first applicant[6] was repeatedly raped (and subjected to other forms of torture) by policemen when she was called for questioning as a witness in criminal proceedings. The investigation was immediately opened and evidence collected. A search of the location was conducted, which resulted in the discovery of two used condoms and two cleaning wipes bearing traces of the sperm of the officers and vaginal epithelium of the victim. This resulted in formal charges being laid against the Russian prosecution officers. However, there were serious violations of procedural rules, including disregard of a special procedure for opening an investigation in respect of prosecution officers, which rendered all previously collected evidence in the case inadmissible. This created a stalemate in the proceedings. The applicant argued that her ill-treatment and the failure to effectively investigate it violated Article 3 and Article 13.

With regard to so-called substantive violations,[7] the Court had to establish whether it could be considered proven that applicants were raped by state agents. The standard that the Court employs is 'beyond reasonable doubt', but this is not a criminal law standard. While it is incumbent on the applicant to prove her claim, inferences may be drawn from the state's failure to provide evidence in cases where the applicant has been held in the custody of the authorities. In both cases, the state's responsibility was established. In *Aydin*, the Court accepted the facts as established by the Commission,[8] and in *Maslova and Nalbandov*, it took account of evidence discovered during the domestic criminal proceedings.

Having established that rapes were committed by state agents, the Court looked at whether these acts could be classified as torture, the concept referring only to 'deliberate inhuman treatment causing very serious and cruel suffering', different from other forms of prohibited ill-treatment on account of the severity and special stigma attached to torture.[9] It held (para. 83):

> Rape of a detainee by an official of the State must be considered to be an especially grave and abhorrent form of ill-treatment given the ease with which the offender can exploit the vulnerability and weakened resistance of his victim. Furthermore, rape leaves deep psychological scars on the victim which do not respond to the passage of time as quickly as other forms of physical and mental violence…

In both cases the Court found that 'the accumulation of acts of physical and mental violence' inflicted on the applicants and the 'especially cruel act of rape' to which they were subjected amounted to torture in breach of Article 3 of the Convention (*Aydin*, para. 86; *Maslova and Nalbandov*, para. 106). The Court's pronouncements on rape acknowledge its severity as well as the intersectionality of discrimination. However, the focus on the vulnerability of the detainee in determining the severity of treatment is problematic, as it might imply a hierarchy of victims in relation to whether they were raped by a state agent or private persons.

The procedural obligations were analysed under Article 13 in *Aydin* and under Article 3 in *Maslova and Nalbandov* (the latter being typical now, see Mowbray, 2004). The Court first explained the state's duty to undertake official investigation into rape, a process to which the victim must also have access, and which has to be thorough and effective, capable of leading to the identification and punishment of those responsible. In both cases, a violation of this obligation was found: in *Aydin* the investigation could not be considered comprehensive as not all relevant evidence was collected, while in *Maslova and Nalbandov*, investigating officers seemed to have been manifestly incompetent. In *Aydin* (para. 107) the Court also criticised the way in which gynaecological examinations were conducted, clarifying that:

> [T]he victim [should] be examined, with all appropriate sensitivity, by medical professionals with particular competence in this area and whose independence is not circumscribed by instructions given by the prosecuting authority as to the scope of the examination.

The Court's imposition on the state of a duty to collect and assess all of the relevant evidence in a professional manner – in particular, an obligation to perform gynaecological examinations with sensitivity and competence – sets important standards in the prosecution of rape.

Ineffective prosecution of 'date rape'

Three cases heard by the Court concerned the ineffective investigation and prosecution of rape committed by a private individual where there was no direct proof of rape. In two of them the main issue was the prosecutor's focus on the lack of resistance by the victim, and in the third, the investigative judge's focus on the victim's character and behaviour.

In *M.C. v. Bulgaria* (no. 39272/98, ECHR 2003-VII), a girl aged 14 years and 9 months was allegedly raped by two acquaintances. The applicant admitted she did not actively resist but argued that she refused the advances. In the course of investigation, many witnesses were heard and expert reports ordered. However, little was done to test the credibility of the versions of the events proposed by the defendants. Emphasis was put on the fact that there was no evidence of the use of physical force or threats by the defendants, nor of active resistance by the applicant, even though it was noted that 'her young age and lack of experience meant that she was unable... to demonstrate firmly her unwillingness to engage in sexual conduct' (*M.C. v Bulgaria,* para.64). In light of that, the prosecutor terminated the proceedings, a course which was affirmed on appeals. The applicant argued a violation of Articles 3, 8 and 14.[10]

In *I.G. v. Moldova* (no. 53519/07, 15 May 2012) a girl, aged 14 years and 10 months, was allegedly raped by her acquaintances. She did not physically resist but claimed she had verbally rejected intercourse. During the investigation, a prosecutor who had not worked on the case cleared the defendant of all charges. This decision was annulled by the prosecutor who worked on the case, as he held that it was not based on the examination of all the circumstances of vulnerability relating to the applicant (as an intoxicated minor). The defendant was eventually convicted by the court of the first instance for sexual intercourse with a person younger than 16 years of age. However, the Court of Appeal annulled the judgement on the basis that the decision to discontinue prosecution had been unlawfully annulled, as this was not done by a prosecutor of a higher rank to the one who had discontinued the prosecution. It also held that there was no legal basis to annul the decision to discontinue proceedings, as rape could not be proven. The applicant argued that this constituted a violation of Articles 3 and 8. She also argued that the requirement of corroborative evidence of resistance had violated her right to non-discrimination on the basis of sex, which was in breach of Article 14, in conjunction with Articles 3 and 8.[11]

In the third case, *D.J. v. Croatia* (no. 42418/10, 24 July 2012), the applicant was allegedly raped by a work colleague after an evening out. The police failed to inspect the scene and collect all the evidence, while allegedly making derogatory comments about the applicant. The criminal investigation was also incomplete, as not all the relevant witnesses were called, and the skirt she was wearing was never taken for examination. The investigating judge made comments about the victim's drunken state and disorderly behaviour in his decision, expressing disagreement with the opening of investigation. He also subpoenaed her previous medical records and questioned her father about his relationship with her. When prosecuting authorities decided to discontinue proceedings, the applicant overtook the prosecution but eventually gave up, as she had not been granted any legal aid. She claimed violations of Articles 3 and 8. She also argued that these violations were rooted in gender prejudices and stereotypes and hence they constituted gender discrimination in violation of Article 14 in conjunction with Articles 3 and 8.

In *M.C.* and *D.J.*, the Court analysed both Articles 3 and 8, recognising that rape constitutes a violation of both physical integrity and personal autonomy. However, this approach was not followed in *I.G.*, which was analysed under Article 3 only. Gender discrimination claims were not examined, the Court holding that no separate issue arose under Article 14, even though several international standards on sexual violence consider it a form of gender discrimination (see, for example, CEDAW Committee's General Recommendation 19, 1992; Council of Europe Convention on Preventing and Combating Violence Against Women and Domestic Violence, 2012; UN Declaration on Elimination of Violence against Women, 1993). There were also strong indications that the prosecuting authorities held stereotypical views of women's appropriate sexual behaviour and subscribed to 'real rape' mythology.

In these case, the Court emphasised that both Articles 3 and 8 impose the obligation on states to effectively punish and investigate rape committed by a private individual. In all three cases it found this duty breached, as the respective authorities had failed to assess evidence in a comprehensive and context-sensitive manner, and did not take into account special psychological factors involved in cases concerning minors. In *M.C.* the Court stressed that the defendants' credibility should have been tested, as some of their statements aimed at presenting the applicant as a promiscuous girl signalled the need for caution. This is a positive pronouncement which challenges the stereotype that women want to be sexually possessed. However, in *I.G.* the Court failed to take into account another stereotypical assumption about women – that they lie about rape – when criticising the state for not testing the credibility of both the victim and the defendants, by, for example, questioning people known to them and ordering a psychological examination of the applicant.

Another myth at issue in the *I.G.* and *M.C.* cases, which the Court successfully challenged, was the 'real rape' myth that defines rape as a violent attack that the victim must physically resist (Temkin & Krahé, 2008). In *M.C.* the Court criticised the prosecutor's focus on the lack of direct proof of rape as overly restrictive, an approach which elevates physical force to an element of offence, which in the Court's view was instead a lack of consent. Basing the definition of rape on the lack of consent rather than force challenges the norm of possessive (hetero)sexuality, according to which men enjoy possessing women while women enjoy being possessed (Naffine, 1994). This approach is more supportive of a communicative model of sexuality, based on free agreement of the parties (Munro, 2008).

The Court also challenged certain rape myths and stereotypes about victims in *D.J.* In addition to examining failures in collecting evidence, the Court addressed the attitudes of the investigating judge, noting that he voiced quite a strong opinion of the applicant and based his disagreement with the prosecution largely on the applicant's conduct, which he viewed as problematic. The Court stressed that the allegation that a rape victim was under the influence of alcohol, or there were other circumstances concerning the victim's behaviour or personality, cannot dispense the authorities from the obligation to effectively investigate. The Court, however, did not problematise the subpoena of the victim's unrelated medical reports or the questioning of her father regarding his relationship with the victim. It thus failed to challenge the myth that rape victims contribute to their victimisation, which seems to be implicit in such conduct of the domestic authorities.

Ineffective prosecution of rape where the application of force was established

Two further cases of the Court concern ineffective prosecution of rape where the application of force was established. In both cases there was a failure to convict the defendants, for different reasons. In *P.M. v. Bulgaria* (no. 49669/07, 24 January 2012), the applicant was 13 years old when she was allegedly raped by two boys, on account of which she suffered injuries to her hymen and head. The proceedings were opened immediately after the event but were stayed for almost eight years, as one of the defendants could not be found (though he had not changed his address), and they were twice discontinued and resumed. The domestic proceedings finally ended 15 years later. One of the defendants was found guilty of aggregated rape but was relieved from liability and punishment as his prosecution was time-barred, while the proceedings against the other were terminated by the Court of Appeal as his prosecution also became time-barred. The applicant argued a violation of Articles 3, 8 and 13 of the Convention.

In *C.A.S. and C.A. v. Romania* (no. 26692/05, 20 March 2012), the alleged rape of a seven-year-old boy (the first applicant), who sustained injuries, was also left unpunished. The investigation did not start promptly as it took two months before the defendant was questioned and there were significant periods of inaction. Seven years after the event, the first instance court found the defendant not guilty of sexual corruption of a minor (the offence of rape was found inapplicable as males were not recognised as rape victims at that time). This finding was confirmed by the Court of Appeal. Domestic courts stressed the fact that the first applicant was not consistent in his account, was prone to fantasies and that his parents had not reacted promptly or appropriately when they had noticed the odd behaviour of their son. The applicants (the victim and his father) argued under Articles 3 and 8 that the investigation was neither prompt nor effective and that the legal classification given to the facts by the domestic courts contradicted the Convention requirements.[12]

The Court analysed these claims under both Articles 3 and 8 and found violations of these articles in both cases. It was critical of the lack of promptness in both cases, stressing the grave nature of the offences and the vulnerability of the victims as young children. In *C.A.S. and C.S.*, the Court also criticised the authorities for their failure to weigh up the conflicting evidence in a context-sensitive assessment. It noted that the domestic courts attached significant weight to the fact the family did not report the alleged crimes immediately. In the Court's view, this assessment was made without consideration of the particular psychological factors in cases involving minors as victims, which could have explained the victim's hesitation both in reporting the abuse and in his inconsistent descriptions of the facts. Referring to the principle of the child's best interest and the need for steps towards recovery and integration, the Court also expressed regret that the first applicant was not offered counselling, nor was he accompanied by a qualified psychologist during the proceedings or afterwards.

Recognition of the special vulnerability of young victims and the need for prosecuting authorities to promptly provide psychological and other types of support to such victims is a welcomed development – as is the challenge to victim-blaming attitudes. The Court, however, failed to address the problem of multiple questioning of (young) victims and their repeated expert examination in the domestic proceedings. As in *X. and Y.*, it also failed to provide guidelines with respect to what constitutes effective legislation on sexual assaults. For the Court, classifying the act as sexual corruption of a minor did not fall short of the Convention requirements.

Delayed conviction to short-term prison sentences for 'gang rape'

The most recent case concerned a delayed conviction to a short-term prison sentence. In *W. v. Slovenia* (no. 24125/06, 3 January 2014), an 18-year-old woman with learning disabilities was raped by a group of men. After the judgement of acquittal a couple of months after the event, the proceedings were resumed but no action was taken for 10 years, as two of the defendants were at large. There were also delays due to frequent changes of the president of the judicial chamber. All of the defendants were finally convicted almost 16 years after the event. They were all issued a prison sentence below the legally prescribed minimum (ranging from 8 to 12 months) on account of the passage of time. The applicant argued that these delays violated Articles 3 and 6. The Court (para. 69) agreed with the applicant that:

> ...the prolonged state of uncertainty and other negative implications of the lengthy proceedings, in particular having to relive the painful events a number of times in three separate retrials, caused her unnecessary suffering and frustration...

It held that this could not be justified by reference to problems within the organisation of the judiciary and was also critical that the proceedings against the defendants, who were at large, were severed only 10 years after the event. The Court also problematised short sentences issued against the defendants. It emphasised that these deficiencies were all the more serious in light of the applicant's particular vulnerability as a person with a disability, and so it found that the domestic authorities did not comply with their positive obligations under Article 3 of the Convention. The fact that the applicant was awarded damages for the state's delay of the maximum amount of €5,000 did not deprive the applicant of her victim status, as the amount was lower than those awarded in similar cases by the Court.[13]

A few crucial victim-sensitive pronouncements were made in this case: the Court recognised the uncertainty and pain victims suffer when proceedings are prolonged. It also noted the problem of short sentences, though this was linked to the ineffectiveness of the proceedings as a whole. It remains to be seen whether the Court will challenge short prison sentences itself; this seems to be unlikely in light of its jurisprudence on domestic violence (see *Irene Wilson v. the UK* (dec.) *no. 10601/09* 23 October 2012).

Potential and limits of the Court's jurisprudence

The Court has conceptualised rape as a serious violation of human rights, which falls under the scope of both Articles 3 and 8 of the Convention. Such a conceptualisation recognises that rape has implications for both physical and psychological integrity (primarily protected under

Article 3) and personal autonomy (primarily protected under Article 8), however, its approach has not been consistent, as in *X.* and *Y.*, the facts were analysed under Article 8, and in *I.G.*, under Article 3 only.

With respect to what type of treatment under Article 3 is constituted by rape, the Court differentiates between rape by a state agent and rape by a private individual, as it has only been willing to define rape as torture when committed by a state agent. This (largely symbolic) differentiation is problematic, as it implies a hierarchy of rape and rape victim based on the application of the gendered public/private divide. Whether rape occurs in the public or private sphere should not be relevant in assessing the severity of treatment (which is different to assessing the state's responsibility).[14] As noted by the International Criminal Tribunal for the former Yugoslavia Appeal Chamber in the *Kunarac et al* judgement (ICTY-96-23, 2 June 2002, paras. 149–151), 'Sexual violence necessarily gives rise to severe pain or suffering, whether physical or mental, and in this way justifies its characterisation as an act of torture'.

Furthermore, rape as a form of gender-based violence should be conceptualised as a gender equality issue. It is regretful that the Court has not analysed sex discrimination claims, as it has failed to acknowledge the gendered nature of sexual violence. It is hoped that in future the Court will be more willing to reconceptualise discrimination, in light of its jurisprudence on domestic violence (see *Opuz v. Turkey*, no. 33401/02, ECHR 2009; *Eremia v. the Republic of Moldova*, no. 3564/11, 28 May 2013).

The Court has imposed a number of positive obligations on states in relation to effective criminalisation and prosecution of rape. Most importantly, it has stressed that all forms of non-voluntary sex have to be prosecuted by member states. In this way it has given rape an autonomous definition centred on consent,[15] which is more supportive of a communicative model of sexuality (Munro, 2008; see also Gotell, Chapter 4).

With regard to the prosecution of rape, the Court has held that the official investigation has to be conducted in a way that allows the victim to have access to the investigation, and which is prompt and comprehensive, whether the act was committed by a state agent or a private individual. It has emphasised that all cases should be prosecuted, including where the victim does not physically resist (as in *M.C.*; *I.G.*). This is a very important statement, as in many jurisdictions, prosecuting authorities and judges view resistance as a necessary element of rape (Radačić, 2014b). Setting this standard has important normative and symbolic powers in promoting sexual relationships based on the equality and autonomy of both parties.

The Court has also emphasised that all victims deserve criminal law protection and that domestic authorities cannot dispense with its obligations to effectively prosecute on the basis of the victim's conduct or character (in *D.J.*). This is crucial because certain categories of women – such as consumers of alcohol or those with psychological problems – are seen as particularly untrustworthy (Radačić, 2014b). It is to be hoped that these standards will provide impetus for law reforms within European countries and challenge the practice of dismissals and acquittals in cases where victims are seen as lacking in credibility or reliability.

The Court has also clarified the requirements of effectiveness in the context of rape investigations. It has emphasised that evidence has to be collected and assessed in a comprehensive and context-sensitive manner and that special psychological factors should be taken into account when victims are particularly vulnerable, such as minors (in *M.C, I.G., C.A.S. and C.S.*). The Court has also stressed that proceedings must be conducted in a prompt manner and that this requirement can be breached even when proceedings result in conviction, especially when sentences are unreasonably short (in *P.M., W.*). Finally, the Court has emphasised that gynecological examinations need to be conducted by competent doctors in a sensitive manner (in *Aydin*) and that child victims should be provided with psychological support (in *C.A.S.* and *C.S.*). These are all very important developments that challenge problematic domestic practices in the prosecution of rape, and hence they have a potential to benefit victims.

However, the Court has failed to address certain issues that are of great importance for the realisation of the rights of victims of rape. First, it has been overly deferential to the state's classification of the sexual acts in question. While holding that all forms of non-consensual sex have to be prosecuted, it has not set up standards on the domestic classification of these acts. Where the domestic authorities excluded certain forms of non-voluntary sexual intercourse from its legal definition of rape and defined it as less serious offences ('causing minor of blameless conduct to... suffer sexual acts...' in *X and Y*, and a sexual corruption of a minor in *C.A.S. and C.S.*), the Court did not find a violation of the Convention on this account. It would have been better if the Court had given some guidelines with respect to the state's positive obligation to set up an effective legal framework regarding sexual offences.

The Court furthermore has failed to challenge certain problematic practices relating to the treatment of victims in criminal proceedings, such as subjecting victims to multiple medical examinations and multiple questioning of very young victims (as in *C.A.S. and C.S.*). Moreover, its pronouncement on the need to test the credibility of both parties, though not problematic in the context of the *I.G.* case, fails to take into account widespread myths about the untrustworthiness of rape victims.

Conclusion

In this chapter, I analysed the European Court of Human Rights' jurisprudence on rape (cases concerning ineffective prosecution), assessing its contributions and limitations as a mechanism of justice for rape victims. The analysis shows a mixed record. The Court has contributed to placing rape high on the human rights agenda, since rape has been conceptualised as a violation of the most fundamental human rights. The Court has also imposed a number of obligations on states, thus setting specific standards for the effective prosecution, which contributes significantly to the victim's rights in the European context (and more broadly through its influence on other international human rights mechanisms). But, as this analysis demonstrates, there is still room for improvement, particularly with respect to challenging different rape myths and stereotypes prevalent in the criminal prosecution of rape, such as the assumption of the law enforcement authorities that victims often lie and contribute to their victimisation. It is hoped that the Court will address this in its future cases.

Notes

1. Gender-based violence is defined as 'violence that is directed against a woman because she is a woman or that affects women disproportionately'. CEDAW Committee [Committee on Elimination of All Forms of Discrimination Against Women] 'Genera Recommendation no. 19 (1992)' in 'Note by the Secretariat, Compilation of General Comments and General Recommendations Adopted by Human Rights Treaty Bodies', HRI/GEN/Rev.7, 246.
2. Neither of these words (nor even the combination of both) expresses all aspects of the experience of being raped. The use of the word 'victim' emphasises the fact of victimisation and the responsibility of the perpetrator. The term 'survivor' emphasises the individual's resistance, her or his ability to take action in the face of immense obstacles, to survive (and thrive) despite the trauma. For the sake of simplicity, I use the term 'victim' throughout this chapter.
3. Before the entry into force of the Protocol 11 to the Convention (CETS no. 155), the responsibility was shared between the Commission on Human Rights (to which individual complaints were first submitted, provided that

the state in question accepted the right to individual petition), the part-time Court (which was only able to examine the case if the state in question recognised its jurisdiction when the Commission or the state brought the case before it) and the Committee of Ministers.

4. It concerned a lack of an effective regulatory framework for detecting and reporting sexual abuse in Irish national schools in the 1970s that were owned and managed by religious authorities (*O'Keeffe v. Ireland* [GC], no. 35810/09, ECHR 2014).
5. The applicant contended that the difference in treatment established by the legislature between various categories of persons deserving of special protection against sexual assaults amounted to discrimination and left persons in her situation unprotected. Article 14 is a subsidiary right, and can be argued only in conjunction with another substantive right.
6. The second applicant, the first applicant's boyfriend, also complained about mistreatment by police but as these acts were not of a sexual nature, his complaints will not be analysed here.
7. Substantive violation is analysed under the substantive aspect of Article 3 provides protection from state action (so-called negative obligations), while the procedural violation concerns the state's failure to conduct effective investigation (so-called procedural obligations, a type of a positive obligation).
8. Before entry into force of Protocol 11, it was the Commission who first analysed the case. It was the Commission who first examined the case, and the case could only be referred to the Court if the respondent state had accepted its jurisdiction. In cases concerning violations of Article 3 by state agents, the Commission (and the Court) often undertook a fact-finding mission.
9. Article 3 does not explicitly require the Court to draw a distinction between the forms of prohibited ill-treatment, but the Court has tended to do it. The distinction between various forms of ill-treatment derives principally from the intensity of suffering inflicted. The level of severity is assessed according to the facts at issue (duration of treatment, physical and mental effects on the victim, and in some cases personal characteristics of the victim, such as sex and age) and in light of 'social developments'.
10. She claimed that she was discriminated against on the basis of sexual orientation, as the age of consent was higher for homosexual sex.
11. Article 14 is a subsidiary right, prohibiting discrimination in enjoyment of Convention rights. It has no independent existence and has to be argued in conjunction with another substantive right.
12. Both applicants also argued that their right to home under Article 8 was violated as they had to move, but this complaint will not be analysed here, due to space constraints.
13. According to the Court's jurisprudence, the applicant loses the victim status when the state both acknowledges the violation and awards appropriate just satisfaction.
14. Under the Convention, state responsibility for torture is not limited to instances of involvement of the state official, as in the Convention Against Torture and Other Cruel, Inhuman and Degrading Treatment or Punishment, but is engaged when the state fails to exercise due diligence in securing that rights are respected by private individuals.

15. The Court interprets the terms in Convention autonomously, independent of domestic classifications. The theory of autonomous concepts was first espoused in *Engle and Others v. the Netherlands* (nos. 5100/71, 5101/71, 5102/71, 5354/72 and 5370/72) (1976) Series A no 22.).

References

Bartlett, K. T. (1990) 'Feminist Legal Methods', *Harvard Law Journal*, 103, 829–888.

CEDAW Committee's General Recommendation 19 Violence Against Women. Council of Europe Convention on Preventing and Combating Violence Against Women and Domestic Violence (adopted 12 April 2012).

Edwards, K. M., Turchik, J. A., Dardis, C. M., Reynolds, N. and Gidyez C. A. (2011) 'Rape Myths: History, Individual and Institutional-Level Presence, and Implications for Change', *Sex Roles*, 65, 761–773.

Merrils, J. G. (1993) *Development of International Law by the European Court of Human Rights*, 2nd ed. (Manchester: Manchester University Press).

Mowbray, A. W. (2004) *Development of Positive Obligations under the European Convention on Human Rights* (Oxford: Hart Publishing).

Munro, V. (2008) 'Constructing Consent: Legislating Freedom and Legitimating Constraint in the Expression of Sexual Autonomy', *Akron Law Review*, 41, 923–956.

Naffine, N. (1994) 'Possession: Erotic Love in the Law of Rape', *Modern Law Review*, 57, 10–37.

Radačić, I. (2014a) 'Rape Myths and Gender Stereotypes in Croatian Laws and Judicial Practice', *Feminist Legal Studies*, 22, 67–87.

Radačić, I. (2014b) Seksualno nasilje: mitovi, stereotipi i pravni sustav (*Sexual Violence: Myths, Stereotypes and the Legal System*) (Zagreb: TIM Press).

Rao, A. (1995) 'The Politics of Gender and Culture in International Human Rights Discourse', in J. Petters and A. Wolper (eds.) *Women's Rights, Human Rights: International Feminist Perspectives* (New York: Routledge), pp. 167–175.

Romany, C. (1994) 'State Responsibility Goes Private: A Feminist Critique of the Public/Private Distinction in International Human Rights Law', in R. J. Cook (ed.) *Human Rights of Women: National and International Perspectives* (Pennsylvania: University of Pennsylvania Press), pp. 85–115.

Ryssdall, R. (1996) 'The Coming of Age of the European Court of Human Rights', *European Human Rights Law Review*, 18, 18–29.

Temkin, J. and Krahé, B. (2008) *Sexual Assault and the Justice Gap: The Question of Attitude* (London: Hart Publishing).

UN Declaration on Elimination of Violence against Women (adopted on 20 December 1993), UN Doc A/RES/48/104 (UNDEVAW).

UNGA (2006) 'Indepth Study on All Forms of Violence Against Women: Report of the Secretary General', *UN* Doc. A/61/122/Add.1, paras 171–81.

9

Reforms, Customs and Resilience

Justice for Sexual and Gender-Based Violence in Liberia

Niels Nagelhus Schia and Benjamin de Carvalho

Introduction

In 2000, the UN Security Council adopted Resolution 1325 on women, peace and security, a resolution which highlighted the role of women in the prevention and resolution of conflicts, peace negotiations, peace-building, peacekeeping, humanitarian response and post-conflict reconstruction. It further stressed the importance of their equal participation and full involvement in all efforts for the maintenance and promotion of peace and security. This resolution propelled the formation of other resolutions on women, peace and security that focus particularly on women's security in conflict and post-conflict situations (S/RES/1820, S/RES/1888, S/RES/1889, S/RES/1960, S/RES/2106, S/RES/2122). Championing these initiatives as well as in their wake, there has been an increasing focus on the women–conflict nexus in research and policy work.[1] However, this body of work has come partly at the expense of a focus on the effects of these resolutions 'on the ground' in ongoing peace-building processes. The current chapter is an attempt at remedying that.

Based on empirical examples from the peace-building process in Liberia, this chapter shows how United Nations Security Council (UNSC) resolutions concerning the security of women and children in post-conflict countries often presuppose existing and well-functioning state institutions. Post-conflict countries, however, usually have poorly functioning state institutions. This implies that there is a mismatch between intentions in resolutions and the reality on the ground. In this chapter we proceed by describing the effects of this mismatch at the implementation level, where efforts often involve activities aimed at establishing the presupposed institutions rather than making use of already existing structures. More specifically, we investigate the tension that lies between addressing specific issues and viewing them within their broader context. Much of the problem may lie in the fact that sexual and gender-based violence (SGBV) is not dealt with in the broader context of (re)building rule of law institutions as a whole, or by taking into account how local traditions and systems of justice administration work in practice. The case of the rape law in Liberia would indicate that a certain amount of duality in the international community's efforts at addressing the shortcomings of the so-called rule of law institutions may be a viable road. Achieving the goals set by any international body aimed at improving such institutions in a post-conflict setting should take into account the realities on the ground – rather than pursuing at all costs these goals and principles from some generic blueprint. There is little to indicate that the best way to achieve justice for all in Liberia – especially for marginalised groups – is through strengthening the formal system at the expense of traditional arrangements. For many Liberians, justice seems to go through a dual administration which takes due account of local practices and traditional arrangements.

Resolutions and implementation

In UN peacekeeping there is a certain mismatch between the international level where policies are devised and the local level where these are implemented. This mismatch is due largely to the fact that the Security Council resolutions, providing the framework for the activities on the ground, are subject to international as well as national foreign policy agendas. These resolutions are drafted, agreed upon and adopted by diplomats and high-level policymakers who are more focused on big politics and diplomacy and less on the knowledge, perspectives and analytical means necessary to grasp the root causes of the challenges. The result of this mismatch, we argue here, is that international donors and the UN often assume that *nothing* is working and that everything in a post-conflict environment will have to be built anew. Measures implemented are often ineffective or counterproductive, and international actors are largely left to deal with the symptoms. Remedying these difficulties will require taking stock of how institutions worked before the intervention, and tackling the problems in a comprehensive, long-term manner, rather than in the piecemeal fashion that suits the agendas of donors. The problem in Liberia is not impunity only for SGBV crimes, but for crimes in general.[2]

Although Liberia has existing and well-functioning non-Western structures (Moran 2006, p. 6), these systems have in fact been generally neglected in the post-conflict reform process. Characteristically, there is little information on the customary law and traditional practices of Liberia. The best attempts at mapping Liberia's customary justice system are probably those made by Herman and Martin-Ortega (2011), Isser et al. (2009) and Moran (2006). Through documentation of the traditional system, these authors track how the system has survived years of civil war and remains active and functional in all communities throughout the country, at all levels. This material is vast and enables understanding of the many views present in Liberia on the topic. Whereas this literature is hinged on a mapping of the traditional structures and the customary justice system in Liberia, we build on this scholarship to illustrate and ultimately explain how some areas of society have been disconnected in UN peacekeeping missions.

The adoption of Resolution 1325 serves as a good illustration of how Security Council resolutions are extensive policies with far-reaching effects, but also that they are often characterised by an inwardly focused executive decision-making process.[3] Resolution 1325 was the result of an internally driven UN process promoting women's rights and heavily influenced by high-level diplomacy, non-governmental organisations (NGOs) and think tanks, but it also lacked voices on the ground. The nurturing of member states, networks of NGOs and international experts constituted the strength of Resolution 1325 (Anderlini, 2007, p. 197). Thus, with the passing of this resolution, and the follow-up resolutions, gender issues and combating sexual violence became anchored at the core of UN peacekeeping missions, but also at the international agenda on peace and security. Increasingly, problems specific to women and children which in the past had been left unaddressed were now being framed, addressed and attended to by UN peacekeeping missions through a top-down agenda-setting process. The specific evolution of these resolutions made women, peace and security an especially attractive topic within the peace-building enterprise for Western governments to fund. This in turn created a peace-building paradigm where an approach from below and *the needs on the ground* have been difficult to incorporate.

Since the end of the conflict in Liberia in 2003, a key priority of the UN Mission in Liberia (UNMIL), UN agencies, NGOs and international non-governmental organisations (INGOs) has been to deal with the very high levels of sexual violence against women and children. Central to these efforts have been a series of rule of law reform initiatives. In Liberia this area is particularly challenging as the country has a history of poor governance, corruption and a low degree of public trust in government. The judicial system in the country is outdated when compared with Western standards and suffers from a severe lack of infrastructure and human resources. After the war, this system had collapsed and international organisations, donor countries and the government were hesitant to engage with this sector. Five years into the peace process there was still no national strategy or long-term plans for the rule of law sector in the country (Hayner, 2007, pp. 19, 23). The result of this hesitancy was that the rule of law reform initiatives were either delayed or characterised by ad hoc initiatives. In Liberia, this situation created space for a substantial number of initiatives propelled by Resolution 1325 and the follow-up resolutions. One such initiative was the establishment of Women and Children Protection Sections (WACPS). The WACPS were physical units adjacent to over 30 police stations throughout the country, staffed by teams of police officers and dedicated to addressing SGBV. Later, the WACPS were accompanied by a number of other initiatives from the international community, including a joint UN and Government of Liberia national strategy on the implementation of S/RES/1325 (see Government of Liberia, 2009), the creation of a Ministry of Gender and Development, and several campaigns aimed at engendering awareness.

Despite these initiatives, the challenges continue. A few perpetrators are brought to justice and even fewer face trial and are found guilty. In September 2013, 10 years after UNMIL was established, the UNSC extended the mandate of the United Nations Mission in Liberia. During the briefings, Liberia's Minister of National Defence, Brownie Samukai, the Secretary-General's Special Representative in Liberia and head of UNMIL, Karin Landgren, and the chair of the Liberia configuration of the Peacebuilding Commission, Ambassador Staffan Tillander, were addressing the dire need for developing a capable and accountable justice and security sector. While acknowledging and welcoming the overall progress of the country towards greater peace and stability, the UNSC pointed at the continuing problems with violent crime and SGBV: 'Women and girls in Liberia continue to face a high incidence of sexual and gender-based violence'.[4] The Council further called on the government of Liberia for a continued focus, in coordination with UNMIL, on combating sexual violence and fighting impunity for perpetrators of such crimes in order to improve the situation for the victims.

The need for the government to 'develop and sustain a self-sufficient, capable and competent security sector to build the confidence of all Liberians' was particularly emphasised.[5] Despite the programmes, initiatives and efforts to combat SGBV, the problems and the degree of impunity continued.

Liberia's customary justice system

Due to a weak state, limits of the formal justice system, poor infrastructure, poverty and lack of transportation, access to the formal justice system in Liberia is often determined by social capital, social and familial networks and whether you reside in a rural or urban location. This is similar to the situations in most post-conflict countries (see also Davies and True, Chapter 10), but in Liberia this is especially relevant as the country has a dual justice system: a formal court hierarchy under the judiciary and a system of customary courts authorised under the Hinterland Regulations. This system was established in 1943 as the Rules and Regulations Governing the Hinterland of Liberia. This represented an attempt on the part of the Liberian state and the Ministry of Internal Affairs to extend its authority by using indirect rule. The landscape of the justice system in Liberia is a complex one, involving several different and parallel state-sponsored customary justice systems as well as community justice systems. The levels of the customary justice system range from senior members of a household to the county superintendent. Below is a brief overview of the hierarchy, in descending order: county superintendent, district commissioner, paramount chiefs, clan chiefs, town chiefs, quarter chiefs, senior member of a household/family.

This customary justice system involves 'non-binding arbitration with additional elements of mediation', whereby cases can be appealed to higher levels and to the formal system (Herman & Martin-Ortega, 2011, p. 146). If, for example, one of the parties disagrees with the decision of a town chief, the case can be taken to the next level, which might be the paramount chief or the formal system. However, the customary justice system is not permitted, by state law, to handle matters of serious crime such as murder and rape. In order to determine the truth and assign guilt in a case, the chiefs consult civil society – communities of elders, youth groups and families in the local community. Much scholarship describes how the customary justice system is anchored in the social community through this consultative process, and how the system is capable of addressing deeper social factors that inform behind conflicts

(Herman & Martin-Ortega, 2011; Isser et al., 2009; Moran, 2006; Piot, 1999). The process is said to be transparent and public. The decisions are part of a system that relies on the substantial role played by kinship and the elders in Liberian society. To date, Liberians seem to prefer this customary system. In general, it is seen as being more accessible and efficient than the formal system (Legal Working Group, 2009, p. 3). Moran (2006, p. 6) describes these structures as 'strong indigenous traditions of participation, voice, and empowerment, otherwise known as "democratic values", embedded in the governmental structures of local communities and in the operative conceptions of personhood used by these populations'. She further describes how these structures are a result of global historical processes involving indigenous people of Liberia and how they are 'fully modern' in the sense that they are part of people's everyday lives. As such, she continues, these systems constitute an 'alternative model of political process to that which has its origins in Western Europe' (Moran, 2006, p. 6).

Most of the disputes in Liberia are solved through recourse to the customary system. A temporary Legal Working Group, which was constituted by prominent legal scholars, members from relevant government institutions, the bar association, civil society and the law school, met four times in 2009 'to explore key issues including constitutional questions of separation of powers, due process and equality, and the legal framework governing the dual system' (Legal Working Group, 2009, p. 1). In their conclusions, the Working Group expressed concerns about constraining the customary system (p. 7). Furthermore, the group fears that undermining the customary system and the traditional leaders by limiting their authority might result in a justice vacuum that could destabilise communities and regions.

Herman and Martin-Ortega (2011) and Isser, Lubkemann and N'Tow (2009) note concerns about the customary system in regard to human rights, gender equality, trial by ordeal and separation of power. There are also challenges pertaining to a number of unresolved issues between the statutory and customary systems, chiefs overreaching their power and interference from the administration of the statutory justice system. The plurality of justice systems in the country also leads to a diversity of practices where the population in one area may have different rights to that in another. This is especially evident for women and children, as the different systems may operate with different sets of rules concerning number of wives, minimal marriage age and inheritance rights for women (Herman & Martin-Ortega, 2011, p. 147). That, however, does not mean the international community should not have strategies or programmes for building on these traditional structures, as long as the same concerns can be directed towards the formal justice system. The case study presented below shows the effects of this gap in justice-reform efforts and indicates that mapping and integrating customary structures in reform measures can provide a more comprehensive approach to building a sustainable peace in Liberia.

Planning challenges

The efforts of the international community to address SGBV in Liberia have been numerous and include building special WACPS adjacent to every county headquarters of the Liberian National Police (LNP) (see de Carvalho & Schia, 2011; Schia & de Carvalho, 2009, 2012). However, despite various action plans – both international and national – anti-SGBV efforts lack coherence and have not yielded the results initially hoped for. The UN has recognised this, stating that 'sexual violence against women and children remains a central reality of life in Liberia' (UNMIL, 2008). The reasons for the lack of results are many. Reporting a case of SGBV to the police can lead to stigmatisation of the victim by the community. Also, as the WACPS are based mainly in county capitals, reporting a crime can take the victim days of travelling. An NGO worker pointed this out: 'It's difficult to report to the police as there is no way of contacting them in the countryside' (Interview 1 Monrovia, 2009). Furthermore, the police often lack even basic logistical support. Some counties have only a single police car, and even fewer have the means to pay for fuel. The police often need to be pressured in order to investigate – and victims reporting a crime are routinely asked to contribute financially towards its solution.[6]

Those who do contact the police are often left in the difficult position of having reported a crime and identified the perpetrator only for the police to lack the means to investigate or otherwise follow it up. Furthermore, there is no proper back-up for police investigation and a few officers have received the necessary training. Most convictions happen either through concession or witness corroboration. Although international donors have sought to remedy this, much of what has been attempted is incompatible with Liberian police methods.

Finally, even if a case is investigated, proper prosecution routines are generally lacking. Outside of Monrovia, there are a few qualified judges and a few places which have all the elements of rule of law. As the situation is now, large numbers of people are jailed without ever having been prosecuted.[7] Faced with these challenges, the UN and international donors have set up various programmes with SGBV as a priority to be dealt with.

SGBV and the rule of law: A fragmented approach

The SGBV programmes are often disconnected or not based on actual local needs or contexts. As a UN official put it: 'The UN tends to fragment vulnerable issues. SGBV has become fragmented and rape has taken all the attention' (Interview 2 Monrovia, 2009). An NGO worker explained: 'GBV tends to be equated with rape, at the expense of other forms of gendered violence' (Interview 3 Monrovia, 2009).

This fragmentation of SGBV also occurs at the strategy level, where SGBV policies are implemented without taking into account the broader processes of (re)building rule of law institutions. As one interviewee put it, 'there is no question that rapes are bad, but the response is devised wrongly' (Interview 4 Monrovia, 2009). In many cases, a deeper understanding of the root causes of SGBV is entirely lacking in UN policies. One official in UNMIL's Gender Section told us (Interview 5 Monrovia, 2009), 'We are doing our research'. UNMIL's first report on the causes of rape was reported to be in preparation. Another UN official explained: 'The problem we have with these [strategies] is that we have hundreds and hundreds of strategies. It's just madness! It's why nothing ever gets done' (Interview 3 Monrovia, 2009).

It also seems that efforts to deal with SGBV have come to the fore at the expense of other processes such as judicial reform, training new legal specialists and fighting corruption. As one interviewee told us, '[SGBV work] is diverting the attention from the serious problem, corruption'. According to this legal specialist, more problematic issues are being left unaddressed: 'Everyone looks at [gender-based violence] at the expense of a holistic picture of the criminal justice system. The problem is the legal system as a whole' (Interview 6 Monrovia, 2009). Many of the interviewees said that the problem in Liberia in terms of impunity for SGBV crimes was not so much that the system was biased against women but that '[gender-based violence] programs do not address the root causes of why people can't get justice' (Interview 7 Monrovia, 2009). Work on tackling SGBV today focuses largely on the symptoms, without addressing the cause. As one interviewee exclaimed: 'Why can't victims of rape get justice? It's not because they're women; not because they're victims of rape; it's because *nobody* gets justice here!' (Interview 6 Monrovia, 2009). While the UN and international donors seek to deal with SGBV through various programmes, these are seldom coordinated, take little stock of the institutions already working and lack an understanding of the cause of the problems at hand. Thus, in order to secure a 'gender-just peace', it is necessary to focus holistically on the rule of law sector to enhance the accountability and acknowledgement of the system.[8]

Lack of local knowledge

As we have established, the UN has little understanding of the traditional customary system. Indeed, most UN people that were interviewed had only a marginal understanding of the Liberian penal code. As a case in point, UN personnel and NGO workers generally saw it as a great success that rape had been introduced in the penal code as a crime in 2005 as the result of pressure from the international community. Symptomatic of this lack of knowledge of the judicial system is IRIN News (Integrated Regional Information Networks, part of the UN Office for the Coordination of Humanitarian Affairs), which includes the following in the country profile of Liberia:

> Liberian law prohibits domestic violence; however, violence against women has become widespread. Several NGOs have programmes to help abused women and girls, and to increase awareness of their rights... In December 2005, parliament passed legislation to make rape illegal.
>
> (IRIN, 2007)

However, the new rape law did not formalise recognition of rape as a crime – rape was already on the statutes. What it did was to modify and add to existing legislation: for instance, making new provision for rape within marriage and criminalising sexual intercourse with minors between the age of 16 and 18 years. The views from most representatives of the international community during three fieldwork sessions in Liberia clearly indicate the extent to which the UN system is inadequately informed to deal with SGBV and the rule of law in a comprehensive manner.

This shortcoming is also evident in the logistical support provided to the national police. Equipment provided for the WACPS included personal computers and electricity generators. However, computer literacy is often limited and generators require scarce fuel, which is needed for driving. The dire lack of resources to actually go and investigate crimes is a much more pressing concern than providing computer equipment.

Indeed, it was unclear why these computers had been provided in the first place, as the working methods of the police did not require them. It seemed as if the logistical support provided for the WACPS was dispatched without having first considered the working methods of the local police, their needs and a budget for running costs.

On the other hand, having two systems working alongside each other also represents challenges, as described by Anthony Valcke of the American Bar Association: 'The problem with customary law is that no one has ever mapped the customs in Liberia. This represents a problem in terms of getting them [the two systems of law] to work together... [T]he customary law needs to be mapped' (Interview 7 Monrovia, 2009). Not much has changed since 2009, and this view is also supported by Herman and Martin-Ortega (2011, p. 157). Thus, while there are reform processes in the formal system, it is not clear whether there are any reform initiatives aimed at the customary sector, even though this could substantially improve access to justice throughout the country. Juan Obarrio, a social anthropologist focusing on law, violence and sovereignty, has pointed out how the rural parts of the population in African countries with weak states continue to use the customary justice systems (Obarrio, 2011). Most of our interviewees shared the same impression and believed that Liberians would continue to latch onto the customary system as long as this was considered the most efficient and accessible system of justice. What is happening in Liberia is, to a large extent, what Cliffe and Manning (2008, p. 165) have termed 'the fallacy of terra nullius' – the inability of the UN to take into account pre-existing institutions and the assumption that everything must 'start from zero'. Consequently, there should be some clear advantages in retaining and adapting customary justice systems rather than imposing new ones from above.

SGBV and traditional justice

If we for the moment agree that using the interplay between statutory and traditional customary systems may in many ways be more efficient and legitimate than imposing a Western liberal statutory system, several problems arise. First and foremost, the international community will need to understand how these traditional systems work.[9] While there has been a tendency to ignore traditional conflict management mechanisms, there is also a lack of understanding of how traditional arrangements work.[10] If these arrangements are to work in conjunction with a statutory court system, a precondition is knowledge of their functioning and areas of coverage in a manner generally acceptable by international standards. Here the research by Isser and colleagues (2009), Herman and Martin-Ortega (2011) and Moran (2006) shows not only how traditional systems operate, but also how they are embedded in everyday Liberian life. It has also shown the kinds of expectations Liberians have for conflict management systems, be they traditional or 'modern'. These studies make it possible to tentatively sketch how the interplay between different mechanisms and institutions for conflict management might work in addressing SGBV.

As noted above, while there seems to be a general dissatisfaction with the formal courts and their ability to handle cases, there is a widespread agreement that rape should fall under the jurisdiction of the formal court system. Liberians also criticise the new rape law 'for not allowing for restorative remedies that take into account broader social interests for "less egregious" types of rape' (Isser et al., 2009, p. 6). As a male respondent from Nimba County said, the traditional system has an element of reconciliation that the formal court system lacks due to its inefficiency and inaccessibility. There would appear to be a clear case for attempting to draw upon both systems in administering justice, for the traditional system does seem to take into account several elements which the formal court system does not. Liberians are dissatisfied with the formal system, and not only because it does not deliver effectively:

> Most Liberians would still be unsatisfied with the justice meted out by the formal system, even if it were able to deliver on the basics... This is because the core principles of justice that underlie Liberia's formal system, which is based on individual rights, adversarialism, and punitive sanctions, differ considerably from those valued by most Liberians. One of the consistent complaints levied by Liberians against the formal court system is that it is overly narrow in how it defines the problems it resolves and thus fails to get at the root issues that underlie the dispute... In order to be seen as adequate, justice must work to repair those relations, which are the ultimate and more fundamental causal determinant, rather than merely treat the behavioral expressions that are viewed as its symptoms.
>
> (Isser et al., 2009, pp. 6–7)

The formal court system does have problems of effectiveness. This contrasts with the customary system. Most Liberians report that:

> ... resolutions reached through customary processes are final and carried out... [I]n the absence of official enforcement mechanisms, the principle of voluntariness, together with a range of social pressures

> and a strong desire for reconciliation, serve to enforce customary resolutions.
>
> (Isser et al., 2009, pp. 6–7)

All this could easily be taken together and mounted as a strong defence of the traditional system at the expense of the formal system generally advocated by international organisations – but this is not the only conclusion to be drawn. As confirmed on several occasions through our own fieldwork as well, Liberians generally feel that egregious crime such as murder and rape should be handled by the statutory system. Such a view would also correspond to the practice of chiefs, who generally seem to refer these cases to the formal system. In a sense, then, the interplay between formal and traditional systems needs to take into account deep-rooted perceptions, beliefs and cultural practices. Although the formal system may enjoy a fair amount of legitimacy, it can at times be problematic. There are many examples that could be cited of cases in which traditional arrangements appear to work more effectively and enjoy greater legitimacy than formal arrangements. However, it is important to note that one reason for this is the emphasis that traditional institutions place on *restorative* justice:

> [I]n the resolution of most types of rape most rural Liberians continue to emphasize restorative and socially reconciliatory objectives as more important than punitive ones. The objective of reconciliation remains particularly important in a context in which the kinship relations that are so vital to all aspects of subsistence and social order itself are likely to socially link perpetrators and victims and their families.
>
> (Isser et al., 2009, p. 69)

There seems to be a clear argument here for a dual system of justice – at least in the shorter term – rather than for the international community to focus all its efforts on implementing a weak formal system throughout the country.[11] Our aim here has not been to make the case for one system over the other. Our argument is therefore not that peacekeepers should forget rule of law reforms altogether and praise the system of customary law, and there seems to be little doubt that in the longer term, the chiefs will give way to magistrates. However, a full overhaul of the justice sector may be too much to handle for a peacekeeping operation with fast-shifting (relatively young) personnel who oftentimes have little or no understanding of local customs and social relations. Seeking to address certain crimes within the framework offered by a dual system in the short term may not only give a more satisfactory treatment of cases through the customary system, as long as social norms collide to some extent with the Western statutory understanding of the rule of law; it may also give the court system a much-needed 'break' and allow it to focus on fewer cases, thus demonstrating to the Liberian and international community that these cases will get treated in a satisfactory way.

Just as there is no mechanism by which modern statutory systems *ipso facto* gain legitimacy by virtue of the principles they embody, neither are there any prescriptions for how such a system could become effective overnight. So far the pursuit of the rights of women in cases of SGBV does not seem to have greatly improved women's access to justice. From such a perspective:

> ... in its current form of operation and at the current pace of internal reformation, it would be difficult to conclude that the expansion of the formal system's local jurisdiction at the expense of customary alternatives is, in actual practice, promoting international standards of justice.
>
> (Isser et al., 2009, p. 86)

It would therefore seem advisable to operate with caution when reforming rule of law institutions, as operational failure of the new systems can easily result in not only a loss of support but also severe damage to the social fabric.

Conclusion

The international response to the situation for women in Liberia – although touted as one of the great success stories in implementing S/RES/1325 by the UN and the Liberian government – has not achieved what it set out to do. Efforts at reforming the institutions of the rule of law have had mixed success, to say the least.

The way the SGBV issues were pursued by the international community left little space for connection to the geographical site. The effect of this was that questions of justice and impunity often were dealt with through the customary justice system or traditional structures, rather than through the newly implemented formal system. The customary system remains disconnected from the larger international engagement in the country. The rule of law reform in Liberia has thus been characterised by a vertical loyalty towards the Security Council resolutions, leaving limited space for bureaucratic autonomy in the field. This in turn has not resulted in an improved situation for women and children in Liberia. The institutional disconnection to the site has led to a situation where the peace-building responses have focused on issues that fit the agendas of international donors, rather than local-level concerns such as customary systems and traditional structures. While the international 'quick impact' projects may be necessary they tend to dominate, obstructing a holistic reform of the rule of law institutions. As long as no one in Liberia gets justice, women and children will not get it either – no matter how many police stations and courthouses are built.

This does not mean that SGBV should be reduced to a legal problem or an issue of rule of law. A working justice system is necessary to address SGBV, but it may not be sufficient. UNMIL and the UN agencies in Liberia have begun addressing these challenges and established programmes aimed at combating such atrocities. However, the institutional logic seems to maintain a focus on small, manageable projects which can show quick, quantifiable progress – resulting in an impression that issues are being dealt with when they often are not. The international response to SGBV in Liberia has focused too much on symptoms and too little on causes. In fact, one could also say that it has focused too much on institution building and too little on peace-building. As shown in this chapter, the traditional structures seem to be more efficient and able than the statutory justice system.

Instead of connecting with the country's dual system of customary and statutory law, and seeing how the two branches may work together and complement each other, international actors often act as if Liberia were a modern-day *terra nullius* – a place where nothing of what existed prior to UN intervention can be used. Dealing with SGBV in Liberia requires a comprehensive response, one that can take into account all the institutions of the rule of law as well as addressing the underlying causes rather than reactively patching up the symptoms. Successfully addressing SGBV requires that the policies devised and implemented be based on close knowledge of the problem at hand and of the institutions and infrastructure available for solving them. A key problem today is the propensity to apply ready-made, generic solutions that resonate well with Western donors.

How to manage the interplay between different systems so that most victims – in this case, victims of SGBV – receive acceptable justice is still a matter of debate. However, the fact remains that the hinterlands of Liberia are neither *terra nullius* nor a savage jungle. In this chapter we have shown that customary systems include mechanisms allowing structurally subordinated voices to be heard, and they maintain traditions of legitimacy, reconciliation as well as institutional checks and balances. These are all features of the democratic values of the West. Relying on customary systems to address SGBV – within certain negotiated standard procedures – may also prove to be a powerful tool to change deep-rooted social views on rape and sexual violence.

Notes

1. See 1325 and 1820 follow-up resolutions, for instance: 1888, 1889 and 1960. See also de Carvalho and Lie (2011) and Lie and de Carvalho (2010).
2. The chapter builds on fieldwork undertaken in Liberia in December 2007, May 2008 and January/February 2009 and builds on visits to WACPS and interviews with NGO workers, UN officials and Liberian government officials.
3. For more on decision-making processes in the UNSC, see Schia (2013).
4. UN News Center: 'Security Council extends UN peace mission in Liberia for another year'; Retrieved from http://www.un.org/apps/news/story.asp?NewsID=45888&Cr=liberia&Cr1&utm_content=buffer6c50d&utm_source=buffer&utm_medium=twitter&utm_campaign=Buffer#.UkmIPryITcm
5. 'What's in blue: Liberia Mission Renewal: Phase Two of the Drawdown Begins'; Retrieved at: http://www.whatsinblue.org/2013/09/liberia-mandate-renewal-drawdown-phase-two.php#
6. Fieldnotes from fieldwork in four Liberian counties: Montserrado, Bomi, Grand Cape Mount and Lofa.
7. UNMIL's Correction Advisory Unit reported in 2008 that prison facilities are massively overcrowded, with over 90 per cent of the prison population in pre-trial detention.
8. A 'gender-just peace' is defined by Annika Bjørkdahl and Johanna Mannergren Slimovic (2013, p. 2) as 'a positive peace that provides for social justice and equity... [A] peace that contributes to a fundamental shift in the provision of specific rights related to women's gender roles, a transformation of gender relations in society, and redefinition of gender hierarchies'.
9. As de Carvalho and Lie (2015) argue, the problem here might be that how many international actors involved in the peace-building is more important than the results of this involvement. See also Neumann and de Carvalho (2015).
10. This seems the case in much of the literature on rule of law reforms in peace operations. See, for instance, Blume (2008) in which he reviews Call (2007), Carrothers (2006), Jones et al. (2005) and Stromseth et al. (2006).
11. See also Herman and Martin-Ortega (2011), Isser et al. (2009), Moran (2006) and Stromseth et al. (2006, p. 336).

References

Anderlini, S. N. (2007) *Women Building Peace – What They Do, Why It Matters* (Boulder, CO: Lynne Rienner Publishers).

Bjørkdahl, A. and Selimovic, J. M. (2013) 'Gendered Justice Gaps in Bosnia-Herzegovina', *Human Rights Review*, 15(2), 201–218.

Blume, T. (2008) 'Security, Justice and the Rule of Law in Peace Operations', *International Peacekeeping*, 15(5), 713–721.

Call, C. T. (ed.) (2007) *Constructing Justice and Security after War* (Washington, DC: United States Institute of Peace).

Carrothers, T. (ed.) (2006) *Promoting the Rule of Law Abroad: In Search of Knowledge* (Washington, DC: Carnegie Endowment for International Peace).

Center on International Cooperation (2010) *Annual Review of Global Peace Operations 2010* (Boulder, CO: Lynne Rienner).

Cliffe, S. and Manning, N. (2008) 'Practical Approaches to Building State Institutions', in C. T. Call and V. Wyeth (eds.) *Building States to Build Peace* (Boulder, CO: Lynne Rienner), pp. 163–184.

de Carvalho, B. and Lie, J. H. S. (2011) 'Chronicle of a Frustration Foretold? The Implementation of a Broad Protection Agenda in the United Nations', *Journal of International Peacekeeping*, 15(3/4), 341–362.

de Carvalho, B. and Lie, J. H. S. (2015) 'A Great Power Performance: Norway, Status, and the Policy of Involvement', in B. de Carvalho and I. B. Neumann (eds.) *Small State Status Seeking: Norway's Quest for International Standing* (London: Routledge), pp. 56–72.

de Carvalho, B. and Schia, N. N. (2011) 'Sexual and Gender-Based Violence in Liberia and the Case for a Comprehensive Approach to the Rule of Law', *Journal of International Relations and Development*, 14(1), 134–141.

Ellis, S. (2007) *The Mask of Anarchy – The Destruction of Liberia and the Religious Dimension of an African Civil War* (London: Hurst & Co.).

Government of Liberia (2009) 'The Liberian National Action Plan for the Implementation of United Nations Resolution 1325'; Retrieved from http://www.undp.org/cpr/documents/gender/lnap_gender.pdf

Hayner, P. (2007) *Negotiating Peace in Liberia: Preserving the Possibility for Justice* (New York: Center for Humanitarian Dialogue and ICTJ).

Herman, J. and Martin-Ortega, O. (2011) 'Narrowing Gaps in Justice – Rule of Law Programming in Liberia', in C. L. Sriram, O. Martin-Ortega and J. Herman (eds.) *Peacebuilding and Rule of Law in Africa – Just Peace?* (London: Routledge), pp. 142–160.

IRIN News (2007) 'Republic of Liberia: Humanitarian Country Profile', *IRIN News*; Retrieved from http://www.irinnews.org/country.aspx?CountryCode=LR&RegionCode=WA

Isser, D., Lubkemann, S. C. and N'Tow, S. (2009) *Looking For Justice: Liberian Experiences with and Perceptions of Local Justice Options* (Washington, DC: United States Institute of Peace).

Jensen, E. G. (2008) 'Justice and the Rule of Law', in C. T. Call and V. Wyeth (eds.) *Building States to Build Peace* (Boulder, CO: Lynne Rienner), pp. 119–142.

Jones, S. G., Wilson, J. M., Rathmell, A. and Riley, K. J. (2005) *Establishing Law and Order after Conflict* (Santa Monica, CA: RAND).

Legal Working Group (2009) 'Findings of the Legal Working Group', Ministry of Justice and UNMIL, *Monrovia*; Retrieved from http://www.usip.org/files/Liberia%202009/LWG%20%20Findings%20Final_Updated.doc

Lie, J. H. S. and de Carvalho, B. (2010) 'Between Culture and Concept: The Protection of Civilians in Sudan (UNMIS)', *Journal of International Peacekeeping*, 14(1/2), 60–85.

Moran, M. (2006) *Liberia: The Violence of Democracy* (Philadelphia, PA: The University of Philadelphia Press).

Neumann, I. B. and de Carvalho, B. (2015) 'Introduction: Small States and Status', in B. de Carvalho and I. B. Neumann (eds.) *Small State Status Seeking: Norway's Quest for International Standing* (London: Routledge), pp. 1–21.

Obarrio, J. (2011) 'Traditional Justice as Rule of Law in Africa: An Anthropological Perspective', in C. L. Sriram, O. Martin-Ortega and J. Herman (eds.) *Peacebuilding and Rule of Law in Africa – Just Peace?* (London: Routledge), pp. 23–43.

Piot, C. (1999) *Remotely Global: Village Modernity in West Africa* (Chicago, IL: University of Chicago Press).

Schia, N. N. (2013) 'Being Part of the Parade – "Going Native" in the United Nations Security Council', *Political and Legal Anthropology Review (PoLAR)*, 36(1), 138–156.

Schia, N. N. and de Carvalho, B. (2009) 'Nobody Gets Justice Here!' *Addressing Sexual and Gender-based Violence and the Rule of Law in Liberia* (Oslo: NUPI).

Schia, N. N. and de Carvalho, B. (2012) 'The Protection of Civilians, Sexual and Gender-Based Violence and the Rule of Law in Liberia', in B. de Carvalho and O. J. Sending (eds.) *The Protection of Civilians in UN Peacekeeping: The Evolution of a Concept and Its Implementation in Practice* (Baden-Baden: Nomos), pp. 181–196.

Sending, O. J. (2009) *Why Peacebuilders Fail to Secure Ownership and be Sensitive to Context* (Oslo: Norwegian Institute of International Affairs).

Sriram, C. L., Martin-Ortega, O. and Herman, J. (2011) *Peacebuilding and Rule of Law in Africa* (London: Routledge).

Stromseth, J., Wippman, D. and Brooks, R. (2006) *Can Might Make Rights? Building the Rule of Law after Military Interventions* (Cambridge: Cambridge University Press).

UNMIL (2008) *Liberia: UNMIL Humanitarian Situation,* Report No. 156, 24 November 2008; Retrieved from http://www.reliefweb.int/rw/rwb.nsf/db900SID/EGUA-7LPQBP?OpenDocument

UNMIL (2009) 'Quality of Personnel Essential for Restoring Confidence in Justice System, Says UN Deputy Envoy'; Retrieved from http://unmil.org/1article.asp?id=3344&zdoc=1.

10

The Pandemic of Conflict-Related Sexual Violence and the Political Economy of Gender Inequality

Sara E. Davies and Jacqui True

Introduction

Since the 1998 Rome Statute recognised widespread and systematic acts of sexual and gender-based violence (SGBV) as an act of genocide, a war crime and crime against humanity, the last decade has seen historic recognition that egregious acts of sexual violence merit international political and legal attention (UN General Assembly, 1998). Notably, there are now no fewer than seven United Nations Security Council resolutions on the cross-cutting theme of Women, Peace and Security.[1] This significant international attention on sexual violence in armed conflict was further heightened with the launch of the United Kingdom's Prevention of Sexual Violence Initiative (PSVI) in May 2012 by Foreign Secretary William Hague. Thus far, the PSVI has prompted a G8 Declaration (April 2013), a Security Council Resolution,[2] the United Nations General Assembly Declaration of Commitment to End Sexual Violence in Conflict (September 2013) supported by 150 states and a new International Protocol on the Documentation and Investigation of Sexual Violence in Conflict (June 2014) (UK FCO, 2014). These actions illustrate the high-level political actions being taken to address sexual violence in conflict around the world. Yet current research on the early warnings of 'widespread and systematic' sexual violence in conflict discounts the relevance of structural gender inequality in the prevention of these atrocities.

In this chapter we examine the extent to which structural gender inequality is considered in studies of conflict-related sexual violence that are informed by these international developments. We argue that researchers have not adequately or consistently established the presence or absence of a relationship between gender inequality and sexual violence in armed conflict. Rather, they have selectively used conflict data, definitions of SGBV, thresholds for mass sexual violence and single sources of evidence to support their arguments. Thus the findings from this body of research are neither sufficiently rigorous nor generalisable to be able to eliminate structural gender inequality as an explanation for the conditions giving rise to widespread and systematic SGBV. We illustrate this argument with reference to the pattern of SGBV in both conflict and post-conflict periods in Sri Lanka. Addressing the key problematic of the volume, we argue that promoting gender justice for victims of conflict-related SGBV involves recognising sexual violence crimes as political crimes that seek to deny representation and redistribution towards those targeted.

The chapter unfolds in three parts. First, we explore the causal analysis of SGBV and argue that it fails to understand the gendered nature of the drivers of SGBV (Cohen & Nordas, 2014; Wood, 2012). Second, we illustrate why a critical feminist insight into SGBV is essential to illuminate the early contributory risk that gender inequality poses in SGBV. Here, we turn to the case of Sri Lanka since the end of the civil war in 2009. Third, we summarise why an understanding of SGBV that incorporates the gendered political relationship between SGBV and structural gender inequality is essential to restore access to justice. To recognise the dangers of silence on SGBV in conflicts and to begin addressing political representation and recognition for survivors requires us to move beyond criminal justice and the socialisation and accountability of perpetrators.

The emerging international norm against sexual violence in armed conflict

'Widespread and systematic' SGBV was first defined under international law in the 1998 Rome Statute of the International Criminal Court (ICC). SGBV crimes, which include rape and other forms of sexual and non-sexual attacks on women and girls, boys and men, are defined as such by the ICC because of 'persecution on the grounds of gender' (Office of the ICC Prosecutor, 2014, p. 12). 'Gender' here does not refer to 'biological sex' or to people called 'women', but rather to the attempt to achieve masculine dominance over 'others' through rape and sexual and other forms of violence where the intention is to 'feminise' and shame victims, their families and communities. The Office of the ICC Prosecutor considers sexual violence crimes in addition to rape, such as sexual assault, slavery, abduction and forced pregnancy. Sexual violence crimes are perpetrated by more than one side in a conflict, by state and non-state actors, by males and females. They are also crimes occurring outside of conflict, with few victims and one or many locations. What defines all of these acts is that they involve persecution on the basis of gender (masculine dominance over feminised subjects) and are carried out by individuals, but where institutions (military/militia, prisons, equipment, laws, security and justice) implicitly or explicitly support them (Office of the ICC Prosecutor, 2014).

The UN Security Council (UNSC) recognises SGBV crimes under the Rome Statute but also recognises SGBV as a threat to international peace and security since the adoption of Resolution 1325 (UNSC 2000). As noted, there have been seven UNSC resolutions on the cross-cutting thematic Women, Peace and Security agenda, passed since Resolution 1325 (UNSC 2000). These refer to the responsibility of Member States to pursue violators of sexual violence in armed conflict (SVAC) and recommend measures to prevent these acts. Resolutions 1888 (UNSC 2009a), 1889 (UNSC 2009b), 1960 (UNSC 2010), 2106 (UNSC 2013a) and 2122 (UNSC 2013b) have increasingly focused on sexual violence only in armed conflict situations. Resolution 1888 (2009) requires the Secretary-General to provide annual reports on SVAC. This is arguably the most successful and compelling call to action to protect victims of SVAC (Kirby, 2012).

In the 2012 inaugural report on situations of SVAC, the UN Secretary-General referred to cases under the categories 'conflict', 'post-conflict' and 'elections, political strife and/or civil unrest' (at the time, the political protests in Egypt fell into this last category). Some Member States of the UNSC opposed that report, including two permanent members (China and Russia). It led to the successive 2013 and 2014 reports to remove the 'elections, political strife and/or civil unrest' category (Security Council Report, 2014, p. 5). However, the 'post-conflict' category of cases has remained on the Security Council agenda and the Secretary-General still raises 'other situations of concern' (UN Secretary-General, 2013, 2014). The reference to 'sexual violence in conflict' is a political attempt by the Security Council to delimit the discussion of SGBV and does not follow from the legal norm as established in the Rome Statute.

The defining feature of SGBV crimes in pre-conflict, conflict and post-conflict contexts is that they have become 'normalised' within a given environment and there is a risk of them becoming 'systematic' (Baaz & Stern, 2013; Kirby, 2012). Key markers of 'widespread and systematic' are when additional identifying features lead to particular groups being targeted for attack, being subjected to the same type of attack, being attacked by the same group of perpetrators, and when there is impunity for the attacker (Goetz, 2008). Given this, much of the focus on early warning and prevention of SGBV crimes should be dedicated to situations *outside* of conflict, and countries where there are *serious levels* of societal gender inequality that would highlight the groups further vulnerable to SGBV. However, this is not the case in most of the research on the cause(s) of SGBV, as is discussed below.

Explaining the causes of sexual violence in conflict

Since the passage of Resolution 1325 (2000), in the current literature there have been two major explanations provided for mass SGBV based on the study of patterns across four or more cases of armed conflict.[3] One explanation is that mass SGBV is caused by the presence or existence of armed conflict. Sexual violence occurs when there are perpetrator dynamics, such as type of recruitment and socialisation in the armed group that fuel these crimes. In this research, sexual violence is viewed as a primarily opportunistic crime carried out by individuals in armed groups. The other major explanation is that mass sexual violence is a deliberate collective strategy deployed against civilians for the purpose of war gain or plunder, enabling the acquisition of resources, land and power. Neither explanation, as we will illustrate, is informed by an analysis of the relationship between structural gender inequality and political violence. We turn to this third, alternative explanation – critical feminist analysis of sexual violence – to provide new insight into the factors that could identify high-risk situations of SGBV toward the development of more effective early warning frameworks.[4]

Wood's (2006) study of eight cases ranging from the Second World War to the Salvadoran civil conflict and the US-led war in Vietnam is one of the first to examine the varied use of SVAC. Wood asks: if sexual violence is a 'strategic tool' for waging war, then why do armed groups inconsistently use it? She draws on existing studies to compare 'non-event' cases where allegations of the perpetration of sexual violence by at least one-armed group involved in the conflict were ostensibly 'absent'. She defines 'absence' as the rare or minimal reporting of sexual violence. Exploring a number of existing hypotheses, she found little support for explanations of the use of sexual violence based on the type of conflict, the instrumentality of SGBV to the group, the militarisation of masculinity or pre-existing, uneven gender relations. For each of these potential explanations, Wood uses the method of falsification, pointing to an anomalous case that she claims disproves it. The presence of gender inequalities that predate conflicts is dismissed, because to include it would imply that sexual violence should be more prevalent in wars in which traditional gender norms are disrupted (Wood, 2006, p. 325).[5] She also states that gendered social relations cannot account for the targeting of particular individuals and groups for sexual violence because all groups have these unequal, power dynamics, but not all groups perpetrate sexual violence.

Based on her falsification of potential explanations, Wood (2006) argues that the most compelling explanation for sexual violence was the individual opportunity to commit violence, facilitated by the lack of a hierarchical command structure and explicit norms against sexual violence within armed groups. Wood's study has spurred a debate within political science and international relations on the primary drivers of SVAC; between those scholars who argue that SGBV is largely 'opportunity-driven' (Butler et al., 2007; Cohen, 2013) and those who argue it is a 'deliberate strategy' informed by the context of the conflict itself (Farr, 2009). Studies that distinguish strategic SGBV from opportunistic SGBV tend to focus on the scale of sexual violence (low to high prevalence) being reported (isolated reports versus numerous reports) (Butler et al., 2007; Cohen, 2013). However, this attention to the scale of sexual violence perpetrated in a conflict ignores the selective but widespread use of gendered violence against a group or members within it. This is explored by Butler and colleagues (2007), who focus on the opportunistic sexual violence facilitated by the breakdown of control and discipline within the perpetrator armed group.

Farr (2009) challenges the studies by Wood (2006) and Butler and colleagues (2007), suspecting that there may be crucial differences in the use of SGBV across types of conflict and perpetrator. She compares war rape in 27 armed conflicts reported by Project Ploughshares in 2007. Like others, Farr (2009, p. 6) does not refer to the 1998 Rome Statute's definition of 'widespread and systematic' SGBV, but notes the studies of 'extreme war rape', defined as 'regularized, war-normative acts of sexual violence accompanied by intentional serious harm, including physical injury, physical and psychological torture, and sometimes murder'. Farr's study is one of the few references to sexual violence as being part of a broader pattern of political violence against a particular group. Similar to Bastick and colleagues (2007), Farr (2009, p. 10) is less concerned with explaining the *scale* of sexual violence in war than with understanding 'differences in the prevalence and prominence of particular rape sites, perpetrator groups, and victim targets'. From 27 cases, she identifies

4 war rape patterns: field-centred/opportunistic; field-centred/woman-targeted; state-led/ethnic-targeted; and state-led/enemy-targeted.

Contesting previous findings, Wood's analysis reveals varied reports of conflict-related sexual violence and different motivations and targets of violence depending on the context of the conflict and what combatants were fighting over. In the conflicts she analysed, such as those in Liberia and the Democratic Republic of Congo, where strong rebel groups were fighting to gain control over valuable resources in a country, SGBV tended to be highly prevalent and perpetrated by both rebels and state agents in the field area where the fighting was occurring (field-centred/opportunistic). Thus, rape may have a strong opportunistic component as well as a 'strategic' purpose. Field-centred/woman-targeted rape occurred more often in conflicts such as Afghanistan and Iraq where both state and rebel groups were perpetrators, with women specifically targeted for their 'deviant' social behaviour, including dress, appearance in public, political activism and so on. State-led/ethnic-targeted rape was perpetrated in contexts like Chechnya and Myanmar, where a powerful, controlling state attempted to quash a smaller secessionist or minority-representing group. In this category, rape victims were often targeted based on ethnicity. Finally, state-led/enemy-targeted rape tends to target victims based on ideological affiliations with rebel groups and activism critical of the state. In this situation, large and powerful rebel groups appear to have committed little SGBV, while state security forces tend to have employed SGBV as a means of repression (for example, in Sri Lanka, see below). However, as Farr (2009) acknowledges, these findings are limited to situations already involving violent conflict. What is not clear is whether the motivations for different groups to deploy SGBV shift across the phases of conflict, before, after and during armed fighting.

Like Farr, Green (2006) examines 'collective' rape as a gendered form of political violence, but she explores the phenomenon irrespective of the presence of conflict and draws from multiple sources for reports of sexual violence. Collective rape is defined as 'a pattern of sexual violence perpetrated on civilians by agents of a state, political group and/or politicized ethnic group' (Green, 2006, p. ii). Patterns of 'collective' rape on a global scale are measured drawing on English language news reports of mass rape from 1980 to 2003. Green finds confirmation for the hypothesis that conflict intensity and militarisation drive collective rape. On the question of the relationship between gender inequality and SGBV, however, she argues that the presence of conflict would have affected the gender indicator scores.[6] Green does not appear to take into account that gender inequality is a political objective and that SGBV crimes are political acts in those situations where gender oppression enables the achievement of political objectives.

More recently, Cohen (2013) has examined sexual violence specifically in civil conflicts (defined by the Fearon and Laitin (2003) Civil War data set). Sexual violence is measured on a scale of intensity (0–4) and the reporting source (US State Department annual reports) is replicated from the study of Butler and colleagues' (2007). Cohen finds no statistically significant evidence of a relationship between sexual violence and ethnic hatred, ethnic cleansing or genocide, nor any relation to gender inequality operationalised using proxy variables from the Cingarelli and Richards Human Rights data set on women's economic, social and political rights and fertility rates. Above all, Cohen identifies perpetrator socialisation to be the most likely cause of SGBV. She suggests that early warning analysis should consider reports of abductions by armed groups as a sign of the escalating threat of wartime rape, which is especially acute under conditions of state collapse and in the presence of resources for plunder. However, we contend that the recruitment strategies or moral codes of armed groups cannot be considered 'gender-neutral' explanations. Soldiers and rebels are affected by socially constructed and culturally specific gender norms, which influence their treatment of groups, their tactical use of violence and the norms within their group depending on their gender make-up.

The findings of Wood, Butler et al., Green and Cohen about the permissive environment enabling perpetrator rape (more than the presence of gender inequality, ethnic grievances or the genocidal intent of the regime) have been corroborated by Cohen and Nordas (2014) using a larger conflict database (Uppsala Conflict Data Program) and expanded reporting sources, including UN and non-governmental organisation reports as well as US State Department annual reports. These studies demonstrate the extent to which current attempts to identify the 'levers' and 'mechanisms' essential to preventing SVAC do not address gendered structures, institutions and identities as 'triggers' for such violence. In particular, they do not address *why* combatants (military or rebels groups) use sexual and gender-based forms of violence in particular, nor do they explain *which* populations are going to be targeted for this form of violence. Even if we accept the opportunistic and instrumental arguments, they do not illuminate why acts of SGBV are strategically advantageous and time-efficient versus, for example, killing or (only) forcibly displacing populations.

Understanding the characteristics of a particular population targeted for this violence requires understanding why this population is being attacked – inevitably this requires an understanding of the existence of gendered inequalities and discrimination that may explain why it is instrumental or/and opportunistic to use SGBV in the first place (Baaz & Stern, 2013; Enloe, 2000; Goldstein, 2001; Kirby, 2012; True, 2012). Fertility rates, used as the proxy for gender equality in statistical studies like Cohen's (2013), for example, tell us little about the degree of gendered inequality and discrimination within a society. They also have limited utility in revealing short- to medium-term changes in gender relations.[7] One objection given to the study of levels of gender violence within a society prior to the onset of SGBV in conflict is the questioning of why sexual violence needs to be examined in this way when 'other forms of conflict-related violence are not subjected to continuity arguments?' (Quijano & Kelly, 2012, p. 489).[8] However, the Office of the ICC Prosecutor refers to these crimes as 'persecution on the grounds of *gender*' (Office of the ICC Prosecutor, 2014, p. 12, emphasis added). Variations in norms regarding rape and gender within and across groups, and in the phases and intensity of political violence and conflict, including situations prior to armed conflict, are relatively neglected as causal factors. This results in the relationship between political violence and the use of 'widespread and systematic' SGBV being poorly understood. The dominance of 'opportunistic' versus 'strategic' explanations of SGBV ignores the ontologically prior relationship between structural gender inequality and political violence. Even if prohibition norms are vital to addressing mass SGBV and perpetrator attitudes, values, beliefs and interests, these must themselves be explained more fully as they do not arise 'naturally' or spontaneously, nor can they explain why SGBV (and not other forms of violence) is overwhelmingly perpetrated against women and children. Indeed, the targeting of civilian populations disproportionately made up of women and children should logically lead us to want to interrogate whether structural gender inequalities affect the patterns and location of SGBV crimes. Such violence is always constructed and legitimised within a gendered social context (Enloe, 2000; True, 2012). These gendered contexts need to be understood as both part of the problem and the solution to mass sexual violence. As the Office of the ICC Prosecutor argues, understanding the differences in status, power, roles and needs between males and females enables the Office to 'gain a better understanding of the crimes, as well as the experiences of individuals and communities in a particular society' (Office of the Prosecutor, 2014, p. 3).

As well as critically analysing the gendered contexts affecting the behaviour of suspected perpetrators of SGBV crimes, we should also interrogate the collection of sexual violence data. Given that we know women are less likely to be politically represented in post-conflict situations (Buvinic et al., 2013), and that deaths (including indirect deaths due to health and disability) disproportionately affect women in post-conflict situations (see Ghobarah et al., 2004; True, 2012),[9] the opportunity and incentive to report sexual violence is likely to be compromised. Moreover, as the Sri Lanka case reveals in the second part of this chapter, a gender analysis may reveal deeper insight into whether the 'reported' volume of cases relates to the actual volume given the pre-conflict existence of ethnic and political discrimination. In studies where it has been claimed that SGBV did 'not' occur, we have little understanding of what gender-sensitive analysis informed this finding (see Human Security Report Project, 2012; Wood, 2009). What the Sri Lanka case demonstrates below is that we must be careful in assuming that silence on SGBV means it did not occur. In Sri Lanka, the prevalence of structural gender inequality is a crucial explanation and predictor of SGBV. Once we identify the risks attached to those who report these crimes, we are able to recognise and bring about gender-responsive redistribution, restoration, recognition and representation in a post-conflict society.

Sri Lanka and the silence on SGBV

In exploring the brutality against civilians in the last stages of this 30-year civil war, the UN Secretary-General's 2011 Panel of Experts on Accountability in Sri Lanka found that both the Sri Lankan armed forces and Tamil Tigers (LTTE) committed grave acts of violence, including sexual violence, amounting to crimes against humanity and war crimes (UN Secretary-General Internal Review Panel, 2012, para. 151). In particular, the report documents how Tamil women were targeted for rape and sexual violence in the final stages of the conflict by Sri Lankan armed forces. These acts were 'greatly under-reported' due in part to 'cultural sensitivities and associated stigma [which] often prevented victims from reporting such crimes, even to their relatives' (UN Secretary-General Internal Review Panel, 2012, para. 152). In March 2014, the UN Human Rights Council passed a resolution declaring that the Sri Lankan government was failing in its responsibility to prosecute individuals for these crimes (UN Human Rights Council, 2014). In that resolution, the Office of the High Commissioner for Human Rights was called upon to investigate allegations of war crimes and crimes against humanity committed by all parties during the civil war, and to specifically address ongoing 'violations of human rights in Sri Lanka, including SGBV' (UN Human Rights Council, 2014).

It is important to analyse the Sri Lanka case in light of our current understanding of mass SGBV for two reasons. First, those scholars who view SGBV as instrumental or opportunistic tend to agree that the perpetrator is the source of prevention, but this explanation insufficiently accounts for why SGBV persists after the end of the war, with the victory of the Sri Lankan government. Second, in the few times researchers have sought to explain the Sri Lanka case it has been proposed that the existence of sexual violence within the conflict is one-sided (Farr, 2009; Human Security Report Project, 2012; Wood, 2009). Specifically, it is contended that the LTTE did not engage in sexual violence during or after the conflict due to strict prohibitions concerning sexual relations among the membership (Human Security Report Project, 2012; Wood, 2006, 2009). However, a critical feminist analysis of the gendered structures within Sri Lanka contests these explanations of the occurrence and reporting of SGBV crimes in the country. First, as we examine further below, impunity for gender violence is pervasive in Sri Lanka. Because of pervasive gender oppression, the stigma and shame attached to this violence rests with the survivor, not the perpetrator. As such, gender-based violence is being deployed to solidify the victory of the Sri Lankan government post-2009 and to further political victory over an ethnic minority population. Such violence can only be effective if we understand the constitutive relationship between gender inequality, gender violence and the nationalisation project in Sri Lanka.

This leads to the second point: given the political situation in Sri Lanka, the absence of reported SGBV violations (by either party of the conflict, LTTE and Sri Lankan armed forces) does not mean such violations have not taken place. Ethnic and religious division within Sri Lanka, coupled with creeping authoritarian rule, make it nearly impossible to appreciate the extent to which widespread and systematic SGBV crimes have been perpetrated by *both* LTTE rebels and the Sri Lanka military against civilian populations (as suggested in the UN Secretary-General Internal Review Panel, 2012). This is problematic for drawing a conclusive understanding about the prevalence of SGBV in Sri Lanka. However, this case does serve to illustrate the objective of SGBV – to secure political gains through the use of violence that is stigmatising and shameful within that society within existing gender norms and which thus represses political opposition or resistance.

The political utility of gender violence in peace

In the Sri Lanka case, the majority of reported SGBV victims are returning displaced persons in the impoverished northern provinces of Sri Lanka. (Nearly 500,000 were forcibly displaced during the final months of the Sri Lankan military assault on those provinces in 2009.) These victims are predominantly female returnees, including former Tamil combatants and war widows. They are in situations of extreme vulnerability due to the political and economic restrictions on Tamil access to land rights, compensation, resources and income (Minority Rights Group International, 2013). However, 'the quest for truth, justice and accountability at the community level is primarily led by women, in a way that is relatively unusual in the rest of Sri Lanka' (Minority Rights Group International, 2013, p. 14). Many Tamil women have asserted their right to compensation and land and have demanded investigation of family members in a way that is unprecedented in 'heavily patriarchal' Sri Lankan society (Minority Rights Groups International, 2013, p. 3). Consequently, it may not be a mere coincidence that Tamil women in the northern and eastern provinces have experienced extreme acts of sexual intimidation and violence by Sri Lankan military and police in a heavily policed security zone upon their return (Sooka, 2014; UN Secretary-General, 2012, p. 18).

In a patriarchal, militarised society such as Sri Lanka, the use of sexual violence by the military and police is effective because gender norms within that society promote women's subordination and modesty (Fulu et al., 2013; Gupta, 2014).[10] Women and men, whether Tamils, Muslims or human rights activists, who do not agree with the political agenda of the Sri Lankan government, are being subjected to SGBV to reinforce their need to comply with Sri Lankan authorities (Sooka, 2014). The UN Human Rights Council (2014) resolution noted that the continuation of political violence against minority groups within Sri Lanka – including the strategic use of SGBV – points to sustained efforts by the Sri Lankan government to ensure its decisive political victory since 2009. However, we can only understand why SGBV consolidates political victory if we understand its effects in the context of pervasive structural gendered inequality and normalisation of violence against women in Sri Lanka.

Kodikara (2014) argues that since the 2009 victory against the LTTE, there has been a 'resurgence of Sinhala Buddhist nationalism' in post-war Sri Lanka. Kodikara (2014) describes the 'valorisation' of the Sri Lankan military and the resurgence of nationalism, particularly directed towards the Sri Lankan military and police to populate the country, with bonus rewards for large families.[11] Civilian women are experiencing a dramatic curtailment of their reproductive rights, with a comprehensive crackdown on institutions that provide emergency abortions, contraceptive advice and devices. Police and public health administrators (within hospitals) are enforcing a (never repealed) decades-old ban on sterilisation procedures to prevent a 'diminishing Sinhala race' (Kodikara, 2014). At the same time, there are reports of women of Tamil ethnicity or Muslim faith being forced to use birth control with injectable contraceptives. Other reports have suggested that the continued military and police occupation of northern and eastern Tamil-populated states is fuelling a sex trafficking industry among the population of internally displaced returnees (most women) who traditionally relied on livelihoods from the land which is now military owned (ICAN, 2013). Young girls and women who are trafficked face being ostracised within their communities. It is suspected that many returning women are choosing not to report their experience of sexual violence to avoid stigma within their own community and to avoid risks of consequent sex trafficking, and that young girls are being forced to marry older men within their community (ICAN, 2013; Minority Rights Group International, 2013).

The myth of the non-event

Those perpetrating SGBV crimes during and after the Sri Lankan civil war have committed these crimes with anonymity and impunity by virtue of the gendered inequality and racism that the state permits and encourages (Kodikara, 2014; Sooka, 2014). In a United Nations Development Programme (UNDP)-commissioned report on Violence Against Women in the Asia Pacific, Sri Lanka had one of the highest rates (31 per cent) of male respondents reporting that they had committed non-intimate partner rape (Fulu et al., 2013, p. 41).[12] Across three provinces, including one Tamil-populated province in the north, Sri Lanka also had the highest percentage of men (95 per cent) who reported they had committed rape but were not punished for their act (Bangladesh and Indonesia were, respectively, second and third; Fulu et al., 2013, p. 45). The UNDP report reveals a pervasive impunity for egregious acts of gender violence: one-third of men self-report committing an act of non-intimate partner rape in a society where 95 per cent of men who admit to rape are not punished (Fulu et al., 2013; ICAN, 2013, p. 3). A recent World Bank study on violence against women in South Asia noted that Sri Lanka had 'one of the highest prevalence rates of violence against women' (Solotaroff & Pande, 2014, p. 57).

A gendered analysis of sexism and racism in Sri Lanka demands that we scrutinise the accepted logic that LTTE soldiers did not engage in rape because there was a moral code against it to maintain group cohesion, and scrutinise allegations that the Sri Lankan military and police did so (only) because of a permissive environment of impunity. In fact, because of the permissive environment of impunity, the minority status of Tamil women and men, and the pervasive gender inequality across Sri Lankan society, we need to interrogate the silence around who *did* and *did not* commit SGBV crimes in Sri Lanka.

Local and international supporters of LTTE have as much of a vested interest in maintaining silence as the Sri Lankan government given that both face allegations of war crimes and systematic violations of human rights. Both sides have equally engaged in a war of propaganda during the decades-long civil war (Gupta, 2014). However, as the International Crisis Group reported (2007, p. 31), 'the government's human rights abuses have tended to take some attention away from LTTE violations. The lack of media access to LTTE areas also plays a part'. As noted in the UN Secretary-General Internal Review Panel report on Sri Lanka (2012) and the Human Rights Council (2014), both sides have committed human rights abuses. Specifically, the LTTE has reportedly committed 'political killings and refused to allow any pluralism or freedom of expression in areas' under their control (International Crisis Group, 2007, p. 1). The LTTE has been accused of forced abductions of children to secure village support, and the torture as well as murder of political opponents (Farr, 2009, p. 21; UN Secretary-General Internal Review Panel, 2012). Given the pervasive culture of impunity for sexual violence at the national level, it is hardly surprising that few Tamil individuals would be willing to come forward with sexual violence allegations against the LTTE. This is particularly so in an environment where the LTTE carries out extrajudicial killings against political opponents and the Sri Lankan security forces have acted in a climate of impunity and lawlessness.

The Report of the UN Secretary-General's Panel of Experts on Accountability in Sri Lanka determined that both sides had committed grave acts of sexual violence. It noted that both the Human Rights Watch and UN Special Representative for Children in Armed Conflict had concerns about the gendered forms of violence the LTTE were committing to increase conscript numbers and coerce civilian support (UN Secretary-General Internal Review Panel, 2012, para. 151). Farr (2009, p. 21) argues that given the LTTE were engaging in other violations including forced abduction of children and the torture and extrajudicial killing of political opponents, it seems unlikely that they were not also engaging in acts of SGBV against these groups. Given the state of lawlessness and discrimination within Sri Lanka, it is surprising the degree to which scholars have interpreted the absence of allegations of SGBV against non-state armed groups as an absence of crimes. Even if there exist rebel groups and militaries that prohibit sexual violence, to suggest that the absence of reports indicates the absence of crime is misleading, especially given that the purpose of gender-based crimes is typically to secure silence and submission. In situations where sexual violence is 'opportunistic', military training and socialisation may be effective. However, in situations like post-conflict Sri Lanka where SGBV is a gendered form of violent persecution delivered to achieve maximum political ends, socialisation techniques and legal prosecution regimes must work to overcome the gender norms that have permitted long-standing political and social impunity for these crimes.

Implications for justice

Current understandings of SGBV as a strategic 'weapon of war' or an opportunistic act in a permissible 'rape culture' fail to see the ways in which sexual violence may be a 'political' act. This is because they do not examine the gendered structural inequalities that make these acts thinkable and plausible before and during conflict. They do not see gender inequality as an inherently political phenomenon that determines the distribution of power and resources, and thus, which groups are subject to these SGBV crimes. We need to significantly improve our knowledge of when sexual violence is deployed as political violence, against whom, and why. Our analysis of the Sri Lanka conflict, particularly during the 2009–2014 post-conflict period, reveals a pattern of SGBV used to intimidate and silence political opposition. However, we can only understand the effectiveness of this violence if we understand the unequal gendered conditions in which sexualised violence takes place. SGBV is most effective in societies not merely because there is a culture of impunity for sexual and gender-based crimes but because political, economic and social structures create pervasive gender inequality. This environment of gendered inequality allows SGBV to be a widespread and systematic act deployed to further erode survivors' claims to retribution and restoration of their civil and political rights.

In the case of Sri Lanka, we know from their claims to asylum that both male and female human rights defenders and Tamil survivors of the 2009 war have experienced persistent harassment, sexual torture under arrest in their homes and continued sexual intimidation and harassment after release, as well as during the war itself (Sooka, 2014). Those who remain within Sri Lanka appear unable to report their experiences due to both the political danger and the social stigma within their family and their community.

In Sri Lanka, the use of SGBV to silence activists and the political opposition corresponds to a broader pattern of the denial of justice to those who have experienced physical and sexual violations. In a UNDP-commissioned report, *Violence Against Women in the Asia Pacific*, the survey (located across three provinces, including one Tamil-populated province) found that Sri Lanka had the third highest rate of male respondents reporting that they had committed non-intimate partner rape (31 per cent) (Papua New Guinea [44 per cent] and Indonesia [33 per cent]; Fulu et al., 2013, p. 41). However, Sri Lanka had the highest percentage of men who reported they had committed rape but *were not punished for their act* (95 per cent) (Fulu et al., 2013, p. 45). The UNDP report reveals that Sri Lanka has high levels of acceptance, amongst men and women, of families using violence to control female members (Fulu et al., 2013). Because these crimes are not considered to be crimes that should be recorded and investigated by the police, official figures on SGBV in Sri Lanka may be indicative of a silent epidemic (ICAN, 2013, p. 3).

In this broader context in Sri Lanka, SGBV becomes an effective, even legitimate form of political violence to (re-)establish gender order and ethnic dominance. It is facilitated by the fact that that there are few opportunities to receive reports on the extent to which this violence may be widespread and systematic among non-state armed groups versus state armed groups. Justice in this environment may be continually denied to survivors, who are expected to remain silent to preserve their status and/or safety. The adoption of the Human Rights Council Resolution in early 2014 led to the creation of a Commission of Inquiry to address the lack of evidence concerning war crimes and crimes against humanity committed by all parties near the end of the civil war, and in the years following (UN Human Rights Council, 2014). The outcome of this commission is currently unknown with change of government in Sri Lanka in late 2014 leading to a delay in the release of the Commission's report.

Until the Sri Lankan government conducts its own enquiry into the actions of all parties during the civil war (and afterwards), there will be few opportunities within the country to investigate and uncover the true of extent of SGBV crimes. State-level recognition of the extent of these crimes begins to restore the criminal and legal redress for these crimes, and it will help to achieve international recognition of the need for collective reparations to be targeted at survivors of SGBV and to address the economic, social and political disempowerment that has been produced from such violence. In recognising that this violence has taken place, there is an opportunity not only to identify the perpetrators, but to identify the pattern of systematic and widespread targeting that occurred. With this understanding, Sri Lanka can then begin addressing the politics of exclusion and institutional shortcomings that led to these populations being attacked in the first place.

In a country such as Sri Lanka, with entrenched patriarchy across its social, political and economic institutions, combined with the extreme vulnerability of ethnic, religious or political minorities, the non-reporting of SGBV cannot constitute good evidence that sexual violence has not been systematically employed. We contend that the failure to predict the sexual violence that occurred in Sri Lanka and to explain the continued prevalence of SGBV since 2009 is due to a general failure of political science scholarship. In particular, scholarship on the causes of sexual violence in conflict has failed to appreciate how the scale of gendered inequality in the Sri Lankan community, taken together with the political oppression of those critical of the Sri Lankan government, constrains reporting of any SGBV violence.

Conclusion

Current research on mass sexual violence tends to view it as a by-product of armed conflict, either as opportunistic acts that occur in the theatre of war (Cohen, 2013; Wood, 2006) or as instrumental acts of war used to achieve other tangential aims, such as displacement, seizure of land and political repression (Farr, 2009). These studies conceive gendered structural conditions within a society as pervasive across all conflicts, and as part of the normal(ised) background to conflict. However, they do not conceptualise SGBV specifically as an act of *political violence*. We contend that this research fails to attend to the powerful effects their knowledge claims have in international politics, in this case silencing and reinforcing gendered discrimination and the culture of impunity for SGBV (Ackerly & True, 2008; Kirby, 2012). The risk of such studies is a failure to consider the relationship between gender inequality and gender-based crimes, potentially compounding the likelihood that victims, especially women and girls, will be denied access to justice. As Daly

(Chapter 3) describes, the 'dark figure' of non-reported, non-adjudicated and non-convicted cases of sexual violence risks amplification when the political violence of SGBV is underplayed or ignored.

At present, causal research on SGBV has not adequately appreciated the politicised context of sexual violence reporting and data collection on the ground. Very real challenges with sexual violence data collection, including gaining access to SGBV reports, has led researchers to analyse the causes of sexual violence globally with incomplete data, despite the potential biases and selectivity of this approach. For instance, scholars have narrowed their focus to a particular type of armed conflict, perpetrator or form of sexual violence where the data exist but not necessarily where the problem lies (*The Lancet*, 2014). Most studies relying on quantitative analysis of existing data sets or on secondary qualitative data do little to contextualise the serious limitations of the data. Equally problematic is that much of this research has assumed that because gender inequality is everywhere it cannot logically explain SGBV anywhere. From a feminist methodological perspective, such a conclusion is not justified objectively by the research question. The multifaceted concept of gendered inequality is poorly operationalised in the majority of causal studies, and thus structural gender discrimination cannot be ruled out as an explanation for widespread and systematic sexual violence. At the very least, to allow us to assess their knowledge claims, scholars should highlight the limitations of their research designs on sexual violence in conflict. Even if a crucial cause of sexual violence is a social environment that enables perpetrators, it is not the sole cause and the gendered social construction and legitimation of perpetrators' attitudes, values, beliefs and interests must also be explained. The latter are intimately related to the 'value' of women and men and their political, economic and social relationships in a given society.

A gendered perspective on mass SGBV is crucial for the prevention of conflict. Current policy recommendations on conflict-related sexual violence focus on ending impunity for individual (male) perpetrators and addressing the lack of hierarchy and rape prohibition norms within armed groups. Such recommendations neglect to examine the significance of gendered inequalities and discriminatory practices that make the use of sexualised violence extremely effective and especially harmful in destabilising communities, and likely to continue to be used while gendered inequalities and discrimination endure. Though in some cases armed groups consciously choose sexual violence, it is not so much the active intent that makes sexual violence in times of conflict a concern, but how in their aggregation these activities serve to reinforce the material relations of inequality between men and women during and after conflict and the culture of impunity. Without the tools of gender analysis we cannot understand the material structures and cultural orders of perpetrators and the victim-survivors of conflict-related SGBV. This lack of knowledge undermines our effort to end this violence. In particular, the prevention of future SGBV violence must direct attention to the survivors of past SGBV crimes by creating political spaces for their representation in post-conflict institutions. It must also provide opportunities for the redistribution of material resources to eliminate structural gender inequalities. The focus on prevention, moreover, demands that we rethink the retribution focus on perpetrators and resist efforts to restore the pre-conflict gender order.

Notes

1. See United Nations Security Council [UNSC], S/Res/1820 (19 June 2008); S/Res/1888 (30 September 2009); S/Res/1889 (5 October 2009); S/Res/1960 (16 December 2010); S/Res/2106 (24 June 2013); S/Res/2122 (18 October 2013).
2. UN Security Council Resolution S/Res/2106 (June 2013).
3. See Bastick et al. (2007); Butler et al. (2007); Cohen (2013); Cohen and Nordas (2014); Farr (2009); Green (2006); Mroz (2011); Nordas and Cohen (2012); Wood (2006, 2009).
4. Examples of a critical feminist analysis of the root causes of sexual violence in conflict include Baaz and Stern (2013); Cockburn (2010); D'Costa (2011); Enloe (2000); Henry and Kirby (2012); Mackenzie (2012).
5. Wood (2006, pp. 325–326) also questions the relationship between gender and sexual violence in conflict by asking why gender inequality produces sexual violence in one setting, but in another leads to the participation of women in rebel militias.
6. Similarly, Green (2006) finds that the presence of ethnic cleavages was most likely informed by the presence of conflict, and as such, was not strongly correlated with the presence of SGBV. These findings are corroborated by Cohen (2013), Nordas and Cohen (2012) and Wood (2006, 2009).
7. The relationship between gender equality and fertility rates is a J-shaped curve; that is, after initially declining with greater gender equality, fertility increases, as observed in countries which come closest to gender parity in education and economic and political participation, such as Sweden and New Zealand (Myrskyla et al., 2009).
8. Quijano and Kelly (2012, p. 489, n. 154) note in a personal communication with Cohen: 'scholars who study wartime killing are rarely asked to calculate rates of pre-war murder to determine if the culture was especially murderous before the outbreak of conflict'.
9. SGBV studies that examine direct deaths due to armed conflict do not include indirect deaths in their analysis (Farr, 2009; Mroz, 2011).

10. Sri Lanka has the lowest representation of women in parliament in South Asia, at 5.8 per cent (Solotaroff & Pande, 2014, p. 77).
11. The government provides rupee cash benefits to military and police personnel (overwhelmingly Sinhalese) who have a third child (Kodikara, 2014).
12. Only Papua New Guinea (44 per cent) and Indonesia (33 per cent) reported higher rates of non-intimate partner rape than Sri Lanka.

References

Ackerly, B. and True, J. (2008) 'Reflexivity in Practice: Power and Ethics in Feminist Research on International Relations', *International Studies Review*, 10(4), 693–707.

Baaz, M. E. and Stern, M. (2013) *Sexual Violence as a Weapon on War?* (London: Zed Books).

Bastick, M., Grimm, K. and Kunz, R. (2007) *Sexual Violence in Armed Conflict: Global Overview and Implications for Security Sector* (Geneva: Geneva Centre for the Democratic Control of Armed Forces).

Butler, C. K., Gluch, T. and Mitchell, N. J. (2007) 'Security Forces and Sexual Violence: A Cross-National Analysis of a Principal Agent Argument', *Journal of Peace Research*, 4, 669–687.

Buvinic, M., Das Gupta, M., Casabonne, U. and Verwimp, P. (2013) 'Violent Conflict and Gender Inequality: An Overview', *World Bank Research Observatory*, 28(1), 110–138.

Cockburn, C. (2010) 'Gender Relations as Causal in Militarization and War: A Feminist Standpoint', *International Feminist Journal of Politics*, 12(2), 139–157.

Cohen, D. K. (2013) 'Explaining Rape during Civil War: Cross-National Evidence (1980–2009)', *American Political Science Review*, 107(3), 461–477.

Cohen, D. K. and Nordas, R. (2014) 'Sexual Violence in Armed Conflict: Introducing the SVAC Dataset, 1989–2009', *Journal of Peace Research* 51, 418–428.

Connell, R. W. (1990) 'The State, Gender and Sexual Politics: Theory and Appraisal', *Theory and Society*, 19(5), 507–544.

D'Costa, B. (2011) *Nationbuilding, Gender and War crimes in South Asia* (London; New York: Routledge).

Enloe, C. (2000) *Manoeuvres: The International Politics of Militarizing Women's Lives* (Berkeley, CA: University of California Press).

Farr, K. (2009) 'Extreme War Rape in Today's Civil-War-Torn States: A Contextual and Comparative Analysis', *Gender Issues*, 26(1), 1–41.

Fearon, J. D. and Laitin, D. D. (2003) 'Ethnicity, Insurgency, and Civil War', *American Political Science Review*, 97(1) 75–90.

Fulu, E., Warner, X., Miedema, S., Jewkes, R., Roselli, T. and Lang, J. (2013) *Why Do Some Men Use Violence Against Women and How Can We Prevent It? Quantitative Findings from the United Nations Multi-country Study on Men and Violence in Asia and the Pacific* (Bangkok: UNDP, UNFPA, UN Women and UNV); Retrieved from http://www.partners4prevention.org/node/515

Ghobarah, H. A., Huth, P. and Russett, B. (2004) 'Comparative Public Health: The Political Economy of Human Misery and Well-Being', *International Studies Quarterly*, 48(1), 73–94.

Goetz, A. (2008) 'Women Targeted Or Affected By Armed Conflict: What Role For Military Peacekeepers?' Conference Summary Report, 27–29 May 2008, Wilton Park, Sussex, UNIFEM, June; Retrieved from http://www.securitycouncilreport.org/atf/cf/%7B65BFCF9B-6D27-4E9C-8CD3-CF6E4FF96FF9%7D/WPS%20SUMMARY%20REPORT%20WP.doc

Goldstein, J. (2001) *War and Gender: How Gender Shapes the War System and Vice Versa* (New York: Cambridge University Press).

Green, J. L. (2006) 'Collective Rape: A Cross-National Study of the Incidence and Perpetrators of Mass Political Sexual Violence, 1980–2003', submitted PhD thesis, Ohio University.

Gupta, R. (2014) 'Sri Lanka Women in Conflict', *Open Democracy* 50.50, 7 March 2014; Retrieved from https://www.opendemocracy.net/5050/rahila-gupta/sri-lanka-women-in-conflict

Henry, M. and Kirby, P. (2012) 'Rethinking Masculinity and Practices of Violence in Conflict Settings', *International Feminist Journal of Politics*, 14(4), 445–449.

Human Security Report Project (2012) *Human Security Report 2012: Sexual Violence, Education, and War: Beyond the Mainstream Narrative* (Vancouver: Human Security Press).

ICAN (International Civil Society Action Network) (2013) 'Elusive Peace, Pervasive Violence: Sri Lankan Women's Struggle for Security and Justice', *What the Women Say,* Report Brief No. 8, Spring; Retrieved from http://www.icanpeacework.org/wp-content/uploads/2013/06/Slanka-final.pdf

International Crisis Group (2007) 'Sri Lanka's Human Rights Crisis', *Asia Report,* No. 135, 14 June; Retrieved from http://www.crisisgroup.org/~/media/Files/asia/south-asia/sri-lanka/135_sri_lanka_s_human_rights_crisis.pdf

Kirby, P. (2012) 'How is Rape a Weapon of War?: Feminist International Relations, Modes of Critical Explanation and the Study of Wartime Sexual Violence', *European Journal of International Relations*, 19(4), 797–821.

Kodikara, C. (2014) 'State Racism and Sexism in Post-war Sri Lanka', *Open Democracy*, 10 November; Retrieved from https://www.opendemocracy.net/5050/chulani-kodikara/state-racism-and-sexism-in-postwar-sri-lanka.

Mackenzie, M. (2012) *Female Soldiers in Sierra Leone: Sex, Security and Post-Conflict Development* (New York: New York University Press).

Minority Rights Group International (2013) 'Living with Insecurity: Marginalization and Sexual Violence Against Women in North and East Sri Lanka', Minority Rights Group International Report; Retrieved from http://www.minorityrights.org/download.php@id=1297.

Mroz, M. (2011) *Wartime Sexual Violence: The New Kalashnikov? A Test of Three Hypotheses on the Use of Sexual Violence as a Weapon of War* (Saarbrucken: Verlag).

Myrskyla, M., Kohler, H-P. and Billari, F. (2009) 'Advances in Development Reverse Fertility Declines', *Nature,* 460, 741–743.

Nordas, R. and Cohen, D. K. (2012) Sexual Violence by Militias in African Conflicts: Not a Question of 'Delegation' by States, CSCW Policy Brief 1; Retrieved from http://file.prio.no/publication_files/cscw/Nordas-Cohen-Sexual-Violence-Militias-African-Conflicts-CSCW-Policy-Brief-01-2012.pdf

Office of the ICC Prosecutor (2014) Policy Paper on Sexual and Gender-Based Crimes, June; Retrieved from http://www.icc-cpi.int/iccdocs/otp/OTP-Policy-Paper-on-Sexual-and-Gender-Based-Crimes–June-2014.pdf

Quijano, A. A. and Kelly, J. (2012) 'A Tale of Two Conflicts – An Unexpected Reading of Sexual Violence in Conflict through the Cases of Colombia and Democratic Republic of Congo', in Morten Bergsmo, Alf B. Skre and Elisabeth Jean Wood (eds.) *Understanding and Proving International Sex Crimes* (Oslo: Torkel Opsahl Academic Epublisher), pp. 437–494.

Security Council Report (2014) *Cross-Cutting Report on Women Peace and Security: Sexual Violence in Conflict and Sanctions*; Retrieved from http://www.securitycouncilreport.org/women-peace-and-security/

Solotaroff, J. L. and Pande, R. P. (2014) *Violence against Women and Girls: Lessons from South Asia*, World Bank Group; Retrieved from https://openknowledge.worldbank.org/handle/10986/20153.

Sooka, Y. (2014) *An Unfinished War: Torture and Sexual Violence in Sri Lanka, 2009–2014*, Bar Human Rights Committee; Retrieved from https://barhumanrights.org.uk/sites/default/files/documents/news/an_unfinihsed_war._torture_and_sexual_violence_in_sri_lanka_2009-2014_0.pdf

The Lancet (2014) 'Ending Sexual Violence in Conflict and beyond', *The Lancet*, 383 (9934), 2019.

True, J. (2012). *The Political Economy of Violence against Women* (New York: Oxford University Press).

UN General Assembly (1998) Rome Statute of the International Criminal Court, 17 July 1998; Retrieved from http://www.unhcr.org/refworld/docid/3ae6b3a84.html.

UN Human Rights Council (2014) *Promoting Reconciliation and Accountability in Sri Lanka*, 26 March 2014, A/HRC/25/L.1/Rev.1 2014.

UN Secretary-General (2012) *Conflict Related Sexual Violence*, Report of the Secretary-General Prevention of Sexual Violence in Armed Conflict, S/2012/33.

UN Secretary-General (2013) *Conflict Related Sexual Violence*, Report of the Secretary-General, Prevention of Sexual Violence in Armed Conflict, S/2013/149.

UN Secretary-General (2014) *Conflict Related Sexual Violence*, Report of the Secretary-General, Prevention of Sexual Violence in Armed Conflict, S/2014/181.

UN Secretary-General Internal Review Panel (2012) *Report of the Secretary-General's Internal Review Panel on United Nations Action in Sri Lanka*, November; Retrieved from http://www.un.org/News/dh/infocus/Sri_Lanka/The_Internal_Review_Panel_report_on_Sri_Lanka.pdf

United Kingdom (UK) Foreign Commonwealth Office (FCO) (2014) *Summit Report: Global Summit to End Sexual Violence in Conflict*. 10 December; Retrieved from https://www.gov.uk/government/publications/summit-report-the-global-summit-to-end-sexual-violence-in-conflict-june-2014

UNSC [United Nations Security Council](2000) Resolution 1325, S/RES/1325.

UNSC [United Nations Security Council] (2008) Resolution 1820, S/RES/1820.

UNSC [United Nations Security Council] (2009a) Resolution 1888, S/RES/1888.

UNSC [United Nations Security Council] (2009b) Resolution 1889, S/RES/1889.

UNSC [United Nations Security Council] (2010) Resolution 1960, S/RES/1960.

UNSC [United Nations Security Council] (2013a) Resolution 2106, S/RES/2106.

UNSC [United Nations Security Council] (2013b) Resolution 2122, S/RES/2122.

Wood, E. J. (2006) 'Variation in Sexual Violence During War', *Politics and Society*, 34(3), 307–342.

Wood, E. J. (2009) 'Armed Groups and Sexual Violence: When Is Wartime Rape Rare?', *Politics and Society*, 37(1), 131–162.

Wood, E. J. (2012) 'Rape during War is Not Inevitable: Variation in Wartime Sexual Violence', in M. Bergsmo, A. B. Skre and E. J. Wood (eds.) *Understanding and Proving International Sex Crimes* (Oslo: Torkel Opsahl Academic Epublisher), pp. 389–419.

11
Combatting Violence Against Indigenous Women

Reconciliation as Decolonisation for Canada's Stolen Sisters

Rosemary Nagy

Introduction

Indigenous women around the world face endemic levels of violence within their communities and at the hands of state and non-state actors (UNPFII, 2012). This is typically at higher rates than that experienced by non-indigenous women. In Canada, indigenous women are also almost three times more likely to be the victim of a violent crime (sexual assault, physical assault, robbery) than non-indigenous women (Brennan, 2011). In the United States, indigenous women are 2.5 times more likely to be raped or sexually assaulted than non-indigenous women (Amnesty International, 2006, p. 2). In Australia, this rate of victimisation is three times higher for indigenous women than it is for non-indigenous women (Australian Law Reform Commission, 2010, para. 24.27)

As is argued throughout this book, part of moving towards 'rape justice' requires going outside the confines of criminal law. In settler societies, the criminal justice system has too often failed indigenous women as a result of ineffective, indifferent or biased policing and judicial processing. This chapter moves beyond the focus of criminal justice by locating sexual, and indeed other gender-based, violence in its structural contexts. An intersectional approach to violence against women takes into account the multifaceted identities and overlapping contexts of discrimination, privilege and subordination that compound to produce distinct experiences of violence (AWID, 2004; Crenshaw,

1991; FIMI, 2006). Sexual violence is entangled with gender, race, economics, colonialism, globalisation and land, and this is highly evident in the experience of indigenous women. While criminal justice is indeed important, we must take fully into account the complex landscape of violence against indigenous women in order to better prevent and redress its occurrence. Thus, this chapter explores a more holistic response that is based on decolonisation, reconciliation and full respect for the human rights of indigenous women.

In this chapter I first examine the gendered, racialised and socio-economic nature of violence against indigenous women that occurs within ongoing processes and structures of colonisation. The second part of the chapter focuses on the 'Stolen Sisters' or 'Sisters in Spirit', which refers to the almost 1200 indigenous women who have gone missing or murdered in Canada since 1980 (RCMP, 2014).[1] While indigenous women constitute 4.3 per cent of the Canadian population, they are greatly over-represented at 11.3 per cent of total missing females and 16 per cent of all female homicides (RCMP, 2014, pp. 8–9).[2] Actors within the United Nations (UN) and in Canada have repeatedly called upon Canada to meet its human rights obligations by establishing a national inquiry into the matter and developing a national action plan. The Canadian government's refusal to do so is emblematic of deep divides in the indigenous–Canada relationship. Thus, in the third part of the chapter I argue that meeting human rights obligations could help to advance reconciliation by challenging the gender violence at the heart of colonisation and stimulating substantive sociopolitical change.

Reconciliation on this account is a process of decolonisation, one where acknowledging and dismantling relational structures of inequality enable the healing of relationships. This process of decolonisation could be understood as correcting the injustices of cultural misrecognition, inequitable socio-economic distribution, political misrepresentation and unequal civic participation that are explored throughout this volume. However as I argue here, it is essential to centre the concept and process of reconciliation on indigenous ways of knowing and being, and to unsettle settler narratives of 'truth' and 'justice' that neglect, exclude, distort or harm indigenous peoples (see Regan, 2010).

Comparative overview: Violence against indigenous women

The gendered violence of colonisation

Cherokee scholar Andrea Smith (2003, p. 78) writes that historically the egalitarian status of women in indigenous societies on Turtle Island

(North America) was a threat to white patriarchy. The 'demonization of Native women' was part of 'white men's desires to maintain control over white women', as well as the key to subjugating indigenous peoples as a whole. She further demonstrates that racialised indigenous bodies were seen as 'immanently polluted with sexual sin', and indigenous women were therefore intrinsically 'rapeable' (Smith, 2003, p. 73). The willingness to treat indigenous women and men as violable objects was embedded within a larger European worldview that saw nature as an object of domination and conquest, rather than something to live with in a state of harmony and interdependence (Smith, 2003, p. 80). Moreover, as McClintock (1995, p. 23) shows, Africa, Asia and the Americas were themselves feminised in the European explorer imaginary, the female interior awaiting male penetration. With the myth of *terra nullius*, the virgin lands were 'passively awaiting the thrusting, male insemination of history, language and reason' (McClintock, 1995, p. 30).

Settler colonialism, my focus here, 'strives for the dissolution of native societies' and 'erects a new colonial society on the expropriated landbase' (Wolfe, 2006, p. 388). Indigenous populations were seen as obstacles to the land and consequently fell victim to conquest and genocide. This transpired through massacres, extermination, forced removals, the introduction of disease and forced assimilation. Forced assimilation occurred through control of native identity, Christianisation, residential schooling and the abduction of thousands of indigenous children for placement in white families. Forced assimilation was a gendered process, resulting in the 'imposition of European gender relationships on Native communities', without which, Smith (2005, p. 139) argues, colonisation would never have occurred.[3]

Many indigenous peoples in the United States, Canada and Australia had matrilineal descent systems and women had significant roles to play in family and community. However, the imposition of patrilineal descent and property patterns during colonisation greatly reduced the strength of indigenous women. In Canada, with the 1876 Indian Act, the granting of 'Indian status' through a patrilineal system effectually reduced the number of status Indians because every time a woman 'married out', both she and her children were considered white. This enabled settlers to control who had access to reservation land and drastically reduced the number of 'status Indians' across the country (Lawrence, 2004). Aboriginal women in Australia suffered similar penalties for marrying out. They also had no recourse if their indigenous spouses decided to 'sell them out' of status by voluntarily enfranchising (becoming legally assimilated citizens) – a change in status that prohibited any further association with aboriginal relations and also resulted in greater rates of alcoholism and family violence (McGrath & Stevenson, 1996, pp. 43–44).[4]

Alongside these forms of 'arithmetical genocide' (Ward Churchill cited in Lawrence, 2004, p. 77), the forcible removal of children for foster care, adoption and boarding schools was a central pillar in getting rid of the 'Indian problem'. In these institutions of forced assimilation, children commonly experienced racism and denigration, loss of language and culture, loss of family and community life, harsh living conditions and sexual and physical abuse (HREOC, 1997; Milloy, 1999; Smith, 2005). A gender analysis of the residential schools shows that the schools were 'designed to destroy women's traditional roles within clan, kinship and governance systems, preparing them instead to become the "property" of individual men as good "Christian" wives' (NWAC, 2010a, p. 11). The separation of siblings by gender at the schools served to reinforce male–female disconnection (NWAC, 2010a, p. 12) and the gendered hierarchy of religious orders running the schools modelled settler values of male authority. The loss of language and parenting skills further deprived women of their traditional roles as mothers, grandmothers, caregivers, teachers and family decision makers (Jacobs & Williams, 2008, p. 127).

Understanding contemporary violence against indigenous women

Colonisation is a 'structure, not an event' (Wolfe, 2006, p. 388), and it continues today by way of broken treaty promises, the loss of indigenous knowledge and languages, huge gaps in quality of life indicators, non-recognition of sovereignty and identity, and environmental degradation and encroachment upon indigenous homelands. Indigenous women's experiences of violence and strategies of resistance continue to be affected by gender inequality, discrimination, poverty, social exclusion and dispossession from ancestral homelands (UNICEF et al., 2013). Globalisation also represents for many indigenous peoples a continuation of colonisation. Whereas colonisation may be understood as the exploitation of indigenous lands and resources, globalisation arguably builds on this by adding 'more direct exploitation of dispensable bodies for profit... especially female bodies in its dependence on cheapened labour of women' (Kuokkanen, 2008, p. 218).

International studies on contemporary manifestations of violence against indigenous women and girls define it holistically, recognising that violence may have spiritual, psychological, physical, sexual, political, economic and/or social dimensions. Violence manifests in different yet often overlapping forms. The UN Permanent Forum on Indigenous Issues (UNPFII, 2013) offers the following multifaceted categorisations:

- *Interpersonal violence,* including assault, murder and sexual violence;
- *Private-sector violence,* such as corporate environmental pollution which has profound implications for traditional ways of life and negative health effects for women, including on their reproductive health;
- *Public-sector violence,* including the over-representation of indigenous women in poverty and prison, state failure to act in the face of interpersonal violence and discrimination in the delivery of public services;
- *Customary/traditional/cultural violence,* meaning misogynistic practices carried out in the name tradition such as sex-selective abortion and the treatment of women as the property of men;
- *Colonisation-related violence,* such as community dysfunction, internalised racism, low self- and group esteem, and the acceptance by indigenous women of (or a reluctance to speak out against) violence due to 'a desire not to further marginalise their men or bring shame upon their communities';
- *Trafficking in indigenous women and girls* for the purpose of sexual exploitation.

Sami scholar Rauna Kuokkanen (2012) argues that it is important to distinguish between gender-specific forms of targeted violence and more general forms of violence that disproportionately burden indigenous women and girls. In order to produce effective strategies, rather than conflating the two, it is necessary to analyse systematically how violence operates and interacts at different levels (Kuokkanen, 2012a, p. 7). She argues that indigenous women are vulnerable to violence, exploitation and abuse at the levels of 'interpersonal violence, violence rooted in systemic gendered racism in society, and state violence' (Kuokkanen, 2012a, p. 7).

The interrelationship between these levels can be seen, for instance, in domestic violence and sexual abuse arising out of the breakdown of community and family structures as a consequence of intergenerational colonial trauma. The configuration of colonial and settler spaces can also play into abusive encounters – violence is naturalised in the 'degenerate' spaces that marginalised indigenous women might occupy, such as zones of prostitution, while white male violence is enacted as entitlement to that space and the bodies in it (Razack, 2000). This is not to suggest that violence against indigenous women is simply the negative result of colonialism or the only factor in all forms of violence. Furthermore, while colonialism shapes relations of power within families, communities and societies, the perpetrators of and bystanders to violence, whether settler or indigenous, must be considered as agents who bear responsibility for their actions.

Indigenous femicide

Turning to the killing of indigenous women, a crime that is often paired with sexual violence, a quick comparative look also shows the interrelated levels of interpersonal, state and structural violence at work. Guatemala's 36 years of state terror and counter-insurgency were deeply rooted in colonial history and its subsequent environment of racism, exclusion and inequality. The state bears responsibility for 93 per cent of human rights violations, including acts of genocide against the Mayan people, and 83 per cent of all identified victims were Mayan (CEH, 1999, paras 1 and 15). Mayan women and girls were systematically targeted for gender-based violence, including femicide and rape (UNICEF et al., 2013, p. 39). Post-war Guatemala sustains high levels of gender-based violence, including one of the world's highest femicide rates. Despite the introduction of specialised femicide courts in 2008, there has been little impact on reducing violence against women or addressing cultures of impunity and sexism (Amnesty International, 2012).

Waves of femicide in Mexico, most notoriously in the industrial border town of Ciudad Juárez, also demonstrate the ways in which neoliberal globalisation, corruption in the justice system and machismo gender norms impact marginalised women. In Ciudad Juárez, an estimated 370 women were murdered between 1993 and 2003 and even more are said to have disappeared (Amnesty International, 2003; Ensalaco, 2006). Since then, the killings have continued at the same rate or higher, but the murder of women has become normalised and lumped into statistics for regular murder in an extremely violent city (Riley, 2012). One category of murders is associated with high rates of domestic violence and drug trafficking; the other main category is serial killings (often committed with brutal sexual violence and sexual mutilation) of teenage women employed in the *maquiladoras* (Ensalaco, 2006, p. 240). It is likely that many of these victims were indigenous, having migrated from rural areas to work in the factories, and they are known colloquially as '"*les inditas del sur*", the little Indian girls from the south of Mexico – poor, dark-skinned and indigenous looking' (de Alba & Guzmán, 2010, p. 1).

The population of Juárez swelled in the 1990s with the implementation of the North American Free Trade Agreement, which fuelled the expansion of the largely US-owned *maquiladora* industry (Pantaleo, 2010, p. 350). While young female employees get higher wages than they might have received elsewhere in Mexico, the high costs of living in a border town and the *maquiladora* designation of 'female' jobs as 'unskilled' labour (compared with 'male' jobs as 'skilled' labour) render these women poor, exploited and working in conditions of sexual harassment and discrimination. Moreover, Mexicans 'resent both the multinationals who profit and the women who work for them', and the women are viewed as symbolising the prostitution of Mexico (Livingston, 2004, p. 65). They also transgress gender norms, having a degree of independence. Police and politicians have made statements to the effect that only 'bad girls' could have been targets because, often in their view, prostitutes and *maquiladora* workers are one and the same (Ensalaco, 2006). Such dismissive remarks contribute to the impunity of perpetrators, as do gross police incompetence and deliberate inaction. In sum, the missing and murdered women are constructed as worthless and disposable, both sexually and economically. In a city where impunity reigns, social exclusion renders these young women vulnerable targets of male backlash against changing gender norms and the 'displacement of economic frustration' (Livingston, 2004, p. 68).

The Stolen Sisters: Canada's missing and murdered indigenous women

Intersecting vulnerabilities and biases

In Canada, the story unfolds similarly to the examples above: the social exclusion of racialised and sexualised victims, dismissive police and social indifference and bias. Of the 1181 missing and murdered indigenous women across Canada, perhaps the most infamous case is that of Vancouver's Downtown Eastside, a highly disadvantaged area beset with poverty, homelessness, addictions and prostitution. Of the approximately 65 missing and murdered women from the Downtown Eastside, one-third are indigenous, despite the fact that they represent only 3 per cent of the general population in that area (Stanton, 2013, p. 69). Media representations have characterised the missing women as 'drug-addicted sex workers', thereby reinforcing a 'blame the victim' mentality and erasing colonialism and race from the story (Jiwani & Young, 2006).

Vancouver police investigations into the missing women were a 'blatant failure' (MWCI, 2012, vol. 1). Despite families' concerns that a serial killer was at work, police refused to acknowledge this possibility for years. This meant that 18 more murders occurred between the 1997 arrest and release of Robert William Pickton for attempted murder and the eventual discovery of the remains of 33 women on his farm in 2002.[5]

Despite the infamy of the Downtown Eastside/Robert Pickton case, most of the missing and murdered women across Canada did not work in the sex trade. In her independently compiled database, University of Ottawa researcher Maryanne Pearce (2013) puts the number of aboriginal sex workers in Canada at 20 per cent; the RCMP (2014) puts it at 12 per cent.[6] Nonetheless, it is worth noting the high over-representation of indigenous women in the sex trade, and especially in the lowest tier, street prostitution, where they are most vulnerable to crime, violence and trauma (Farley et al., 2005).

As Pearce (2013, pp. 257–259) puts it, vulnerabilities lead to vulnerabilities: sex work, addiction, substance abuse, criminal records, histories of hitchhiking between or across cities, histories of homelessness or running away and childhood separation from family in foster care, group homes or residential school. In addition to these risk factors, the Native Women's Association of Canada (NWAC) also notes 'heightened vulnerabilities' in connection to foetal alcohol spectrum disorder (FASD), gang involvement and lack of awareness and preparation for the move from small communities to large urban centres (NWAC, 2010b, p. 37). All this occurs in a context of indigenous women's overall 'higher levels of poverty, lower educational attainment, higher unemployment, poorer physical and mental health and lack of housing' (NWAC, 2010b, p. 11).

'Each vulnerability is another reason for Other-ing individuals... Thus, the layering of vulnerabilities leads to less support from both the wider society and the agents of the state, but also results in the greater likelihood of being targeted as victims' (Pearce, 2013, p. 256). As Amnesty International (2009, p. 22) argues, apathy and social attitudes that condone or encourage violence apply to indigenous women not because they have so-called high-risk lifestyles but 'because they are Indigenous women'. It appears that some men specifically target indigenous women with acts of extreme violence due to racism or the expectation that social indifference will guarantee impunity (Amnesty International, 2009, p. 2). 'Bias among police may mean that family concerns over a missing person or a suspicious death are ignored, leading to investigations that are inadequately resourced or closed prematurely' (Amnesty International, 2014, p. 3). The RCMP (2014,

p. 3) reports that there is little difference in solve rates (close to 90 per cent) between aboriginal and non-aboriginal victims. However, this does not counteract longstanding concerns with and distrust of police in the face of the bungling of the Downtown Eastside murders and abusive and apathetic policing along northern British Columbia's 'Highway of Tears', where many indigenous women have disappeared (Human Rights Watch, 2013). To this we can add a history of Royal Canadian Mounted Police (RCMP) involvement in the removal of children for residential school, indigenous deaths in custody and 'starlight tours', where police drop inebriated indigenous men at the outskirts of town, where they sometimes freeze to death.

Concerns with policing are but one part of a wider societal problem that is rooted in colonialism. Residential schooling is a direct explanation for the over-representation of indigenous female homicides, particularly in the case of the most vulnerable women. In interviews conducted with the families of missing and murdered women, NWAC found that in most cases, the women's parents or grandparents attended Indian Residential School: 'Many spoke of the resulting family dysfunction or disconnect as impacting their lives and placing the women in a vulnerable situation' (Jacobs & Williams, 2008, p. 133). Many of these women had also been displaced from their communities due to gender-discriminatory status provisions of the Indian Act or due to the 'Sixties Scoop', which saw 11,000 First Nations children, along with many other indigenous children, taken into the child welfare system and adopted out to mainly white homes, sometimes without the consent or knowledge of their families (NWAC, 2010b). This resulted in cultural dislocation, confused identities and 'many were believed to have suffered sexual and other abuse and continue to deal with the trauma' (NWAC, 2010b, p. 8). Research indicates these experiences can be linked to higher levels of domestic violence, sexual exploitation, involvement in the sex trade and conflict with the law (NWAC, 2010b, pp. 9–10). Indigenous women suffer staggering levels of domestic violence, but socio-economic marginalisation and the lack of on-reserve shelters and other supports reduce their ability to escape violence (Amnesty International, 2009, p. 8).

Stolen Sisters crisis: An obstacle to reconciliation

The issue of missing and murdered women is closely related to the challenges of reconciliation within Canada, particularly in light of the Prime Minister's 2008 apology for residential schools and the work of the Truth and Reconciliation Commission (TRC) from 2009–2015 on the history and legacy of the schools. While the government tends to approach reconciliation in terms of closure on the past, individual healing and having compensation and a truth commission in place, many indigenous activists and residential school survivors argue that reconciliation is inseparable from issues such as land dispossession, treaty, governance structures, underfunding of First Nations education and child welfare, and, of course, the missing and murdered women (see Nagy, 2013). As advocates for the Stolen Sisters have noted, families 'may be reluctant to even consider reconciling with a society whose institutions have failed them so profoundly' (Jacobs & Williams, 2008, p. 136).

At the international level, the Committee on the Elimination of Racial Discrimination (CERD), the Committee on the Elimination of Discrimination Against Women (CEDAW), the Committee on the Rights of the Child (CRC), the Committee Against Torture (CAT), the UN Special Rapporteur on the Rights of Indigenous Peoples and 24 state members of the Human Rights Council have all expressed significant concern about disproportionate levels of violence against indigenous women and girls in Canada and the lack of progress in combatting it (Amnesty International, 2014, pp. 5–6). The Canadian Feminist Alliance for International Action (FAFIA) and NWAC have also submitted complaints to the CEDAW committee and the Inter-American Commission on Human Rights. After country visits, both human rights bodies issued reports in 2015 and 2014 respectively, voicing strong concerns and detailing the call for action.

Transnational political advocacy is particularly focused on establishing a national public inquiry into the Stolen Sisters and developing a national action plan. In February 2014, NWAC presented the federal government with a petition with 23,000 signatures calling for a national inquiry. Groups such as the Assembly of First Nations, Amnesty International, Human Rights Watch, FAFIA, opposition MPs, the UN Special Rapporteur on the Rights of Indigenous Peoples and nine member states of the Human Rights Council have supported this call.

The Canadian Government's steadfast refusal to establish a national inquiry is widely seen as undercutting its purported commitment to reconciliation. For example, at a TRC event in April 2013, a Quebec provincial minister announced as a gesture of reconciliation that nine provinces would be jointly pressing the federal government to hold a national inquiry.[7] A public inquiry would provide an independent, comprehensive national investigation that considers overlapping levels of government responsibility; increases public awareness; and 'begins to address the crisis in confidence felt within aboriginal communities in relation to government and justice system responses' (NWAC, 2013, p. 1). While no inquiry can solve all problems, building trust and confidence is key to the advancement of reconciliation, and a national inquiry is perceived to be an important step. Furthermore, an inquiry could arguably help fulfil international human rights obligations, including the expectation that Canada undertake an analysis of causes in order to determine whether there was a racialised pattern to the disappearances and to examine the reason for failures to investigate (CEDAW, 2008).

Canadian Prime Minister Stephen Harper has been sceptical of the effectiveness of an inquiry, saying it is time for action, not further study (CBC News, 2014). In the autumn of 2014, the government allocated CAD$25 million over five years for community safety plans, victim services and healing and risk reduction strategies. While the urban-based Congress of Aboriginal Peoples supports this approach, most other indigenous groups are disappointed and frustrated, and some feel like the blame is being placed on aboriginal communities (Walker, 2014). This funding policy flows out of a 2013 Parliamentary Special Committee report, which, unsurprisingly, did not call for an independent national inquiry because government MPs dominated the committee. Furthermore, as NWAC noted in its response to the report, 'there is no mention of the impacts of colonization and the need for real and comprehensive reconciliation. Healing cannot be a one sided affair, as it leads to victim blaming, discrimination, and racism' (NWAC, 2014). The fact that current policy does not address systemic patterns and factors no doubt reflects the Prime Minister's belief that these women's deaths are a 'criminal matter' and should not be viewed as a 'sociological phenomenon' (Stephen Harper cited in McLean, 2014).

Yet, as demonstrated in the section above, indigenous femicide *is* a sociological phenomenon – one that is deeply rooted in the gendered violence of colonialism. The systemic factors fuelling high levels of violence against indigenous women in Canada necessitate comprehensive measures, including tackling racialised and gendered socio-economic gaps; revitalising indigenous ways of being; improving police investigations; challenging pervasive stereotypes of missing indigenous women as somehow responsible for their fates; providing better, equitable and culturally relevant social supports; and implementing and realising the rights set out in the CEDAW and the UN Declaration on the Rights of Indigenous Peoples (Amnesty International, 2009, 2014; NWAC, 2010b). In the section below, I examine how compliance with international human rights – and ongoing transnational pressure to comply – might help to advance reconciliation from outside the confines of the settler state.

Combatting violence against indigenous women: Reconciliation as decolonisation

One potential argument against relying on international human rights as the framework for reconciliation is that the state-centric nature of international law assumes the legitimacy of settler state sovereignty. However, complaints procedures and reviews can serve to call that legitimacy into question, and transnational activism can be seen as 'as the very exercise of autonomy and self-determination' (Kuokkanen, 2012b, p. 245). This argument in turn speaks to two related levels of reconciliation. Meeting the obligations of human rights and indigenous peoples' rights may strengthen the nation-to-nation relationship between Indigenous Peoples and Canada, including the relationship between marginalised indigenous women and the Canadian state. Additionally, 'bottom-up' pressure from Canadian citizens against the state to ameliorate or re-examine aspects of its aboriginal policy may also be evidence of reconciliation across social divides.

While we may typically think of reconciliation as a domestic process, the Canadian TRC (2012, p. 9) has pointed toward the Universal Declaration of the Rights of Indigenous Peoples as a 'framework for working towards ongoing reconciliation'. However, the TRC has not specified what this might mean in a general context or specifically linked it to the missing and murdered women. While the Declaration should be read as a holistic document, specific to our purposes is Article 22 (2):

> States shall take measures, in conjunction with indigenous peoples, to ensure that indigenous women and children enjoy the full protection and guarantees against all forms of violence and discrimination.

Moreover, the UN Expert Group on Combatting Violence Against Indigenous Women and Girls writes:

> Combating violence against women and girls in the indigenous context must be achieved holistically and not addressed in isolation from the range of rights recognized for indigenous peoples in general. In that regard, violence cannot be seen as separate from the history of discrimination and marginalization experienced by indigenous peoples as a whole.
>
> (UNPFII, 2012, para. 17)

James Anaya, former UN Special Rapporteur on the Rights of Indigenous Peoples, has called upon governments worldwide to provide the basis for reconciliation with indigenous peoples:

> Full respect for treaties, agreements and other constructive arrangements is a crucial element in advancing toward reconciliation with indigenous peoples and in addressing persistent deep-rooted problems related to historical wrongs, failed policies of the past, and continuing barriers to the full realization of indigenous peoples' rights... [this] can go far in helping to build trust among indigenous peoples and to rebuild relationships between States and indigenous peoples in a true spirit of good faith, partnership, and mutual respect... [This should be part of a broader dialogue] to help build understanding between indigenous peoples and others, and to help shift any persistent negative attitudes or misunderstandings about indigenous peoples and their rights.
>
> (UNPFII, 2013)

Building on this, and as I have argued elsewhere (Nagy, 2013), reconciliation is best understood not as an end point, but as a process of decolonisation. Decolonisation means 'revealing and dismantling colonialist power in all its forms' (Ashcroft et al., 2000, p. 63). This includes structures of power (such as land, laws, governance structures, education systems, socio-economic distribution) and the attitudes, values and identities that are produced by and inform the structures. It involves challenging decision-making structures for inclusion, self-determination and recognition of indigenous knowledge (e.g. oral history, legal custom), and investing mutual processes and institutions with respect and reciprocity.

Furthermore, decolonisation is inseparable from gender justice because 'it has been precisely through gender violence that we have lost our lands in the first place' (Smith, 2005, p. 137). Decolonisation as a gendered process is attuned to the fact that indigenous women and girls specifically face *gender-based* violence as it intersects with other forms of oppression. Therefore their struggles for equality should not be subsumed under collective struggles for sovereignty. Rather, as Kuokkanen (2012b, p. 248) argues, individual and collective self-determination are interrelated: '[i]f women are not surviving as individuals in their communities due to physical or structural violence, collective survival as a people is also inevitably called into question'. In other words, indigenous peoples' rights and indigenous women's rights exist on a continuum. The realisation of both is part of the groundwork for ongoing processes of decolonisation, and consequently is the kind of reconciliation that is promoted through substantive social change that challenges the gender violence at the heart of colonisation.

Conclusion

Reconciliation between states and indigenous peoples must address gender injustices and staggering levels of violence against indigenous women. In this chapter, I have suggested that the international human rights framework for combatting violence against indigenous women necessitates a process of decolonisation that addresses intersectional gaps and divides in social structures and attitudes. Reconciliation on this view is a process, not an end point, and one that addresses the gendered, violent legacy of colonialism as being more than a criminal matter. In Canada, violence against indigenous women has been, and should continue to be, framed as both a human rights issue and an issue of reconciliation. Even if the specific demand for a national inquiry remains unmet, transnational pressure on the government to better respond to the Stolen Sisters may yet force Canada to take more comprehensive action and thereby substantiate its rhetoric of reconciliation. As the headline of the indigenous newspaper, *Windspeaker*, proclaimed in 2012: 'UN to do the job that Canada will not' (Ashawasegai, 2012). This suggests that human rights might provide a powerful advocacy tool that can help carve a path toward justice and reconciliation for indigenous women through ongoing transnational pressure, activism and dialogue.

Notes

1. The Royal Canadian Mounted Police (RCMP) report identifies 164 missing and 1017 homicide victims – 1181 aboriginal women in total.
2. Over-representation is even more marked in the Western provinces, with the aboriginal homicide victim proportion in Manitoba being 49 per cent, in Saskatchewan 55 per cent, in Alberta 28 per cent and in British Columbia 19 per cent (RCMP 2014, p. 9).
3. This is not to say that gender violence did not occur in precolonial societies. But in the context of Turtle Island (North America), gender relations were much more egalitarian than the deeply patriarchal nature of European societies. Women served as spiritual, political and military leaders; and many societies were matrilineal (Smith, 2005, pp. 18–19). Indigenous cultures also recognised more than two genders, such as with two-spirited people, in contrast to European heteropatriarchy.
4. Enfranchised men in Australia gained the right to drink alcohol, vote, handle their own money and receive a pension.

5. Pickton has since been convicted for 6 murders and 20 other charges were stayed. He once boasted that he killed 49 women.
6. Pearce's data are based on publicly available information and therefore have a lower count of indigenous victims (824) than the RCMP's report, which came out after Pearce's dissertation.
7. Field notes, 25 April 2013, Montreal event, Call to Gather. While the province of British Columbia did establish a commission of inquiry, the process was defective from the outset due to perceptions of bias and illegitimacy and to the province's unprecedented refusal to fund legal counsel for indigenous, women's and community organisations to participate in hearings (see Stanton, 2013).

References

Amnesty International (2003) *Intolerable Killings: 10 Years of Abductions and Murders of Women in Ciuddad Juárez and Chihuauhua* (New York: Amnesty International).

Amnesty International (2006) *Maze of Injustice: The Failure to Protect Indigenous Women from Sexual Violence in the USA* (New York: Amnesty International).

Amnesty International (2009) *No More Stolen Sisters: The Need for a Comprehensive Response to Discrimination and Violence against Indigenous Women in Canada* (London: Amnesty International).

Amnesty International (2012) *Annual Report: Guatemala* (London: Amnesty International).

Amnesty International (2014) *Violence Against Indigenous Women and Girls in Canada: A Summary of Amnesty International's Concerns and Call to Action*, submission to the Special Parliamentary Committee on Violence Against Indigenous Women (IWFA), 7 February 2014.

Ashawasegai, J. (2012) 'UN to Do the Job that Canada Will Not', *Windspeaker*, 29(10), 8–10.

Ashcroft, B., Griffiths, G. and Tiffin, H. (2000) *Post-Colonial Studies: The Key Concepts* (London: Routledge).

Australian Law Reform Commission (2010) *Family Violence – A National Legal Response*, ALRC report 114 (Canberra, Australia: Commonwealth of Australia).

AWID [Association for Women's Rights in Development] (2004) *Intersectionality: A Tool for Gender and Economic Justice* (Toronto: Association for Women's Rights in Development).

Brennan, S. (2011) 'Violent Victimization of Aboriginal women in the Canadian Provinces, 2009', *Juristat* (Ottawa: Statistics Canada).

CBC News (2014) 'Premiers Back National Inquiry on Missing Women', *CBC*, 24 July 2014.

CEDAW [Committee on the Elimination of Discrimination Against Women] (2008) *Concluding Observations of the Committee on the Elimination of Discrimination Against Women, Canada*, CEDAW/C/CAN/CO/7.

CEH [Commission for Historical Clarification] (1999) *Guatemala: Memory of Silence*, report of the Commission for Historical Clarification (Guatemala City: United Nations Office of Project Services).

Crenshaw, K. (1991) 'Mapping the Margins: Intersectionality, Identity Politics, and Violence Against Women of Color', *Stanford Law Review*, 43, 1241–1299.

de Alba, A. G. and Guzmán, G. (2010) '*Feminicidio*: The "Black Legend" of the Border', in A. G. de Alba and G. Guzmán (eds.) *Making a Killing: Femicide, Free Trade, and La Frontera* (Austin: University of Texas Press).

Ensalaco, M. (2006) 'Murder in Ciudad Juárez: A Parable of Women's Struggle for Human Rights', *Violence Against Women*, 12(5), 417–440.

Farley, M., Lynne, J. and Cotton, A. (2005) 'Prostitution in Vancouver: Violence and the Colonization of First Nations Women', *Transcultural Psychiatry*, 42(2), 242–271.

FIMI [International Indigenous Women's Forum] (2006) *Mairin Iwanka Raya: Indigenous Women Stand Against Violence* (New York: International Indigenous Women's Forum).

HREOC [Human Rights and Equal Opportunity Commission] (1997) *Bringing Them Home: Report of the National Inquiry into the Separation of Aboriginal and Torres Strait Islander Children from Their Families* (Sydney: Human Rights and Equality Opportunity Commission).

Human Rights Watch (2013) *Those Who Take Us Away: Abusive Policing and Failures in Protection of Indigenous Women and Girls in Northern British Columbia, Canada* (United States: Human Rights Watch).

Jacobs, B. and Williams, A. J. (2008) 'Legacy of Residential Schools: Missing and Murdered Aboriginal Women', in M. B. Castellano, L. Archibald and M. DeGagné (eds.) *From Truth to Reconciliation: Transforming the Legacy of Residential Schools* (Ottawa: Aboriginal Healing Foundation).

Jiwani, Y. and Young, M. L. (2006) 'Missing and Murdered Women: Reproducing Marginality in News Discourse', *Canadian Journal of Communication*, 31(4), 895–917.

Kuokkanen, R. (2008) 'Globalization as Racialized, Sexualized Violence', *International Feminist Journal of Politics*, 10(2), 216–233.

Kuokkanen, R. (2012a) 'Addressing Violence Against Indigenous Women and Girls as a Human Rights Issue', paper presented at International Expert Group Meeting, Combating Violence Against Indigenous Women and Girls: Article 22 of the United Nations Declaration on the Rights of Indigenous Peoples, New York, 18–20 January 2012.

Kuokkanen, R. (2012b) 'Self-Determination and Indigenous Women's Rights at the Intersection of International Human Rights', *Human Rights Quarterly*, 34(1), 225–250.

Lawrence, B. (2004) *'Real' Indians and Others: Mixed-Blood Urban Native Peoples and Indigenous Nationhood* (Vancouver: UBC Press).

Livingston, J. (2004) 'Murder in Juárez: Gender, Sexual Violence, and the Global Assembly Line', *Frontiers: A Journal of Women Studies*, 25(1), 59–76.

McClintock, A. (1995) *Imperial Leather: Race, Gender and Sexuality in the Colonial Contest* (New York: Routledge).

McGrath, A. and Stevenson, W. (1996) 'Gender, Race, and Policy: Aboriginal Women and the State in Canada and Australia', *Labour/Le Travail*, 38, 37–53.

McLean, S. (2014) 'Harper Says No to Renewed Calls for Public Inquiry into Missing and Murdered Indigenous Women', *APTN*, 21 August 2014.

Milloy, J. (1999) *A National Crime: The Canadian Government and the Residential School System 1879 to 1986* (Winnipeg: University of Manitoba Press).

MWCI [Missing Women Commission of Inquiry] (2012) *Forsaken*, report of the Missing Women Commission of Inquiry, British Columbia.

Nagy, R. (2013) 'The Scope and Bounds of Transitional Justice and the Canadian Truth and Reconciliation Commission', *International Journal of Transitional Justice*, 7(1), 52–73.

NWAC [Native Women's Association of Canada] (2010a) *Culturally Relevant Gender-based Models of Reconciliation* (Ohsweken: Native Women's Association of Canada).

NWAC [Native Women's Association of Canada] (2010b) *What Their Stories Tell Us: Research Findings from the Sisters in Spirit Initiative* (Ohsweken: Native Women's Association of Canada).

NWAC [Native Women's Association of Canada] (2013) 'Why Support a National Public Inquiry?' (Ohsweken: Native Women's Association of Canada).

NWAC [Native Women's Association of Canada] (2014) 'Response to Special Committee on Violence Against Indigenous Women' (Ohsweken: Native Women's Association of Canada).

Pantaleo, K. (2010) 'Gendered Violence: An Analysis of the Maquiladora Murders', *International Criminal Justice Review*, 20(4), 349–365.

Pearce, M. (2013) *An Awkward Silence: Missing and Murdered Vulnerable Women and the Canadian Justice System.* (Doctorate in Laws) Doctoral dissertation, University of Ottawa.

Razack, S. (2000) 'Gendered Racial Violence and Spatialized Justice: The Murder of Pamela George', *Canadian Journal of Law and Society*, 15(2), 91–130.

RCMP [Royal Canadian Mounted Police] (2014) *Missing and Murdered Aboriginal Women: A National Operational Overview* (Ottawa: Royal Canadian Mounted Police).

Regan, P. (2010) *Unsettling the Settler Within: Indian Residential Schools, Truth Telling, and Reconciliation in Canada* (Vancouver: UBC Press).

Riley, J. (2012) 'Brutal Female Homicides Continue in Ciudad Juarez With No End in Sight', *Examiner.com*, 6 April 2012.

Smith, A. (2003) 'Not an Indian Tradition: The Sexual Colonization of Native Peoples', *Hypatia*, 18(2), 70–85.

Smith, A. (2005) *Conquest: Sexual Violence and American Indian Genocide* (Cambridge, UK: South End Press).

Stanton, K. (2013) 'Intransigent Justice: Truth, Reconciliation and the Missing Women Inquiry in Canada', *Transitional Justice Review*, 1(2), 59–96.

TRC [Truth and Reconciliation Commission of Canada] (2012) *Interim Report* (Ottawa: Truth and Reconciliation Commission of Canada).

UNICEF et al. [United Nations Children's Fund (UNICEF), the United Nations Entity for Gender Equality and the Empowerment of Women (UN Women), the United Nations Population Fund (UNFPA), the International Labour Organisation (ILO) and the Office of the Special Representative of the Secretary-General on Violence against Children (OSRSG/VAC)] (2013) *Breaking the Silence on Violence Against Indigenous Girls, Adolescents and Young Women: A Call to Action Based on an Overview of Existing Evidence from Africa, Asia Pacific and Latin America* (New York: United Nations Children's Fund).

United Nations Permanent Forum on Indigenous Issues (2013) Broken Treaties Must Become a Thing of the Past, UN Expert Calls for Reconciliation with Indigenous Peoples, UN Press release, 9 August 2013.

UNPFII [United Nations Permanent Forum on Indigenous Issues] (2012) *Combating Violence Against Indigenous Women and Girls: Article 22 of the United Nations Declaration on the Rights of Indigenous Peoples*, report of the International Expert Group meeting (New York: United Nations E/C.19/2012/6).

UNPFII [United Nations Permanent Forum on Indigenous Issues] (2013) *Study on the Extent of Violence Against Indigenous Women and Girls in Terms of Article 22(2) of the United Nations Declaration on the Rights of Indigenous People* (New York: United Nations E/C.19/2013/9).

Walker, C. (2014) 'Assembly of First Nations Says Its Proposals on Missing Women "Tossed Aside" by Ottawa', *CBC News*, 17 September 2014.

Wolfe, P. (2006) 'Settler Colonialism and the Elimination of the Native', *Journal of Genocide Research*, 8(4), 387–409.

12

The Law of the People

Civil Society Tribunals and Wartime Sexual Violence

Nicola Henry

Introduction

After the Second World War, the Allies convened a major trial in Tokyo of 28 military and political leaders of the Japanese Empire. The Tokyo Tribunal, officially known as the International Military Tribunal for the Far East (IMTFE), tried individuals for war crimes, crimes against peace and crimes against humanity. Although the tribunal prosecuted and convicted defendants for the mass rapes of Chinese women during the 1937 invasion of Nanjing, the systematic sexual enslavement of 'comfort women' during the Asia-Pacific War was all but ignored by the Tokyo Tribunal (Askin, 1997; Henry, 2013).[1] Up to 200,000 girls and women who were forced, coerced, tricked or lured into sexual servitude and slavery never saw 'justice done' in the aftermath of the war. Moreover, no persons were prosecuted for the crimes against approximately 100 Filipino women from the town of Mapanique who were raped after Japanese troops had castrated and burned alive the men and boys from the town.

For 50 years, many victim-survivors harboured their stories in silence and shame, and the plight of the comfort women was temporarily cast into the shadows of history. Although the existence of comfort women was widely documented in diaries, novels and personal memoirs of ex-soldiers, and the issue was the subject of investigation by members of the Korean diasporic community in the 1970s and 1980s (Soh, 2008), it was not until the early 1990s that the comfort women issue started to receive widespread, international attention and response. This attention included, among other things, a series of lawsuits in Japanese, Korean and Filipino courts; official investigations, including United Nations reports; public apologies by state and public officials; books, documentaries, films and public memorials; and enormous academic, political and media debate and controversy.

In response to the injustices of the past wrongdoings of sexual enslavement, as well as the failure of legal mechanisms to provide justice to comfort women, in December 2000 a civil society 'people's tribunal' was established. The Women's International War Crimes Tribunal on Japan's Military Sexual Slavery (hereinafter 'the Women's Tribunal') was convened to examine the criminal liability of high-ranking Japanese military and political leaders of the Japanese Empire, using the Tokyo Trial as a starting point to pronounce judgement about historical wrongdoings. In total, 35 former comfort women came together to testify at the Women's Tribunal.

Focusing on the Women's Tribunal, this chapter considers the efficacy of civil society war crimes tribunals as a 'justice model' for addressing past forms of conflict-related sexual violence. The first section explores how crimes against the comfort women have been responded to using a range of legal mechanisms both within and beyond the state. The second section draws on civil society theory and Nancy Fraser's (1998, 2007) model of justice in order to examine the potentials and limitations of civil society tribunals for addressing conflict-related sexual violence.

Legal redress for comfort women

The term 'comfort woman' is an English translation of *ianfu*, which is an abbreviated Japanese euphemism for 'military comfort woman'. It refers to between 50,000 and 200,000 women and girls who were kidnapped, rounded up, coerced, lured, tricked, sold and otherwise recruited into military 'prostitution' for the Japanese military during the Asia-Pacific War (1931–1945) (see Hicks, 1997; Tanaka, 2002; Yoshimi, 2000). While the majority of comfort women were Korean, a large number were also from China (see Qui, Zhiliang & Lifei, 2013), as well as from other Southeast Asian, Pacific Island and European countries. It is important to note, however, that the term 'comfort woman' is highly insulting to many victims (Ruff-O'Herne, 1994) and is the subject of heated debate (see Soh, 2008). Relatedly, terms such as 'comfort station', 'brothel', 'enforced prostitution' and 'sexual slavery' have also caused much controversy because of the debate that exists around the method of recruitment of comfort women; namely, whether the women were voluntary sex workers or victims of mass rape or enforced prostitution. These debates about terminology are not merely semantic or academic disputations, but rather form the basis of social, legal and political judgements about the plight of the comfort women and the justice responses to this issue.[2] While there have been several Japanese governmental investigations into the comfort women issue and various government officials have issued public apologies to victims, revisionists claim that there is no evidence to substantiate the claim that women were abducted, forced or coerced into military brothels. Revisionists also deny the involvement of the Japanese military and state in the establishment and operation of the comfort stations. In particular, Japan as a nation continues to deny legal liability for the victimisation of comfort women, and past and current political leaders have publicly declared that there is no evidence supporting their claims. As such, many survivors and their advocates accuse the Japanese government of failing to provide an unequivocal statement about the role of the Japanese state in establishing the comfort stations, and/or how the crimes constituted violations under international law (Henry, 2013). Resolutions from a variety of different countries have called on Japan to once and for all apologise in clear and unambiguous terms and accept *direct state responsibility* for its involvement in the military brothels during the Asia-Pacific War (Hayashi, 2008).

Survivors have sought compensation through Japanese courts and also within their own jurisdictions. In the summer of 1991, for instance, South Korean former comfort woman Kim Hak-sun came forward at a press conference held in Seoul. She detailed how in 1941, at the age of 17, she was taken to Beijing by her foster father to look for a job. She was then detained for four months in a house being used as a brothel until she escaped with the assistance of a Korean itinerant merchant, who would later become her husband (Soh, 2008). Hak-sun and two other unnamed victim-survivors unsuccessfully filed a lawsuit against the Japanese government in December 1991, seeking an apology and compensation. The government's response was that the comfort stations had been owned and run by private operators and that the issue of reparations had been resolved with the 1965 bilateral treaty between Japan and South Korea, where the latter had agreed to demand no further wartime compensation from Japan.

A number of other unsuccessful lawsuits from litigants in different countries have followed. Each time, Japan has declared that claims to reparations have been settled by the post-war treaties made with other states, and that a statute of limitations applies (see Coomaraswamy, 1997). Compensation has also been sought by victim-survivors through their own courts. In August 2011, the Constitutional Court of Korea ruled that the South Korean government was in violation of the

Constitution for not doing enough to resolve the compensation claims for comfort women with Japan (Noriko, 2014). In 2004, after likewise proving unsuccessful in their attempts to claim reparations in Japanese courts, a Filipino organisation called Malaya Lolas ('liberated grandmothers') filed a lawsuit in the Philippine Supreme Court over the mass rapes of women during the 1944 Japanese siege of the town of Mapanique. The complainants similarly sought an apology and compensation from Japan, claiming that the Philippine government had violated its legal obligation in various international court proceedings against Japan. In a unanimous decision in August 2014, the Philippine Supreme Court dismissed the Malaya Lolas' claims for compensation on the basis of the 1951 San Francisco Treaty of Peace with Japan, where, in exchange for war reparations, the government had waived any claims for compensation from Japan (Kyodo, n.d.).

The issue of Japanese military and state involvement in the establishment and operation of the comfort stations remains outstanding. During the 1990s, the United Nations Special Rapporteur issued reports based on Japan's guilt and liability for the establishment of the wartime military brothels (Coomaraswamy, 1997; McDougall, 1998). The reports condemned the Tokyo Tribunal's failure to prosecute the major Japanese political and military leaders for these crimes, and affirmed that the crimes against the comfort women specifically fall under the international definition of slavery, which was illegal at the time of the Tokyo Trial, and which was also included in the Charter of the Tokyo Tribunal. This, and the aforementioned claims about compensation and apology, serves as the backdrop to the establishment of the Women's Tribunal in December 2000. Below I consider civil society initiatives more broadly as justice mechanisms for past forms of violence, before analysing the nature, impact and scope of the tribunal in addressing wartime sexual violence.

Civil society tribunals and the horizon of the 'lifeworld'

Civil society tribunals are an innovative transitional justice approach to addressing the past wrongdoings of the state or state-like actors. The first known civil society tribunal was the 1967 Russell Tribunal that was established by British philosopher and Nobel Prize winner Bertrand Russell, and hosted by French philosopher and writer Jean-Paul Sartre. The Russell–Sartre Tribunal (as it is also known) convened two sessions in Sweden and Denmark with representatives from 18 different countries. The aim of the tribunal was to conduct an investigation into US acts of aggression against Vietnam, Cambodia and Laos, and war crimes against civilians and prisoners of war under international law. The tribunal examined different sources of evidence and unanimously found that the US government had committed acts of aggression and that government and armed forces were guilty of the 'deliberate, systematic and large-scaled bombardment of civilian targets...'. It also found that the US was guilty of genocide against the people of Vietnam (see Duffett, 1968; Falk, 1988).

Based on the same model, more tribunals have been set up in the decades that followed, including a number of women's tribunals. Examples of the latter include the 1976 International Tribunal on Crimes Against Women, which sought to bring attention to violence and discrimination against women (see Russell & Van de Ven, 1976); the 2010 International Tribunal on Crimes Against Women of Burma, which aimed to document violations against women and act as a catalyst for democratic change in Burma; and the Women's Court for the Former Yugoslavia, that formally opened on 7 May 2015, providing a space for women to talk about their experiences of past and present forms of violence. Most feminist attention to date, however, has focused on the 2000 Women's International War Crimes Tribunal on Japanese Military Sexual Slavery (see Chinkin, 2001; Dolgopol, 2003; Dudden, 2001; Knopp, 2011; Matsui, 2001; Sakamoto 2001).

The Women's Tribunal was supported by women's NGOs throughout Asia and instigated by the Violence against Women in War Network, Japan (VAWW-Net). The tribunal was established to hear the testimonies of the suffering endured by comfort women and to determine the criminal liability of leading military figures, political officials and the Japanese state. The tribunal was set up to adjudicate gendered crimes that the Tokyo Tribunal failed to address, and the tribunal sat 'as if it were a continuation of the [1946] IMTFE [Tokyo Tribunal] and the subsidiary trials held in the Asia-Pacific' (Women's Tribunal Judgement, 2001, p. 19). As Richard Falk (1988, p. 28) claims, 'law is an instrument of civil society' and people's tribunals can exist outside the realm of the state, and indeed are utilised as a challenge to state power. This was affirmed by the Women's Tribunal, established as a people's tribunal 'to fill lacunae in international law and to forge new ground in the development of international law by creating a "law of peoples" arising from principles of humanity and justice' (Women's Tribunal Judgement, 2001, p. 15). But to what extent can or do civil society initiatives of justice enhance or even supplant 'justice' mechanisms of the state? And do such mechanisms extend beyond the delimiting, depoliticising and individualising currents of conventional legal responses to injustice?

Civil society: a model of and for justice?

Originally, the term 'civil society' (*civilis societas*) referred to a politically organised association of peoples living in a civilised (as opposed to 'barbaric') community. According to classical Greek philosophers, the common good could be fostered through public debate and dialogue as a rational way to uncover the truth and ensure the 'good life'. In this context, political power enabled civility, helping shape and guide the common moral project of the community (Ehrenberg, 1999). Civil society then was not autonomous from political power or the state, but rather its essential elements consisted of both ruling and being ruled. More modern conceptions of civil society, on the other hand, tend to treat the essential elements of civil society as 'autonomous forms of discourse, associations and solidarity [from the state]' (Cohen & Arato, 1992, viii). As Robert Fine (2014, p. 9) maintains, civil society theory 'places civil society on the side of *agency, creativity, activity, productivity, freedom, association, life itself*' (original emphasis) in opposition to the institutions of modernity, including consumerism, conformity and coercion. The occupation of political spaces 'from below' – a people's justice – represents an anti-politics or alternative *polis* – a site of problem-solving, resistance or subversion; an 'incarnation of ethical life' and a *ressentiment* against the power and violence of the state (Fine, 2014, p. 9).[3]

Of relevance to the Women's Tribunal, Jürgen Habermas' (1987) 'lifeworld' provides a useful way of thinking about the exchanges of communication between people in a global civil society. According to Habermas, the lifeworld is a personal, intersubjective, lived and experienced world. Communicative action, Habermas theorises, takes place on the 'horizon of the lifeworld' where, through language, ordinary people ('speaking and acting subjects') acquire knowledge, make meaning of the world and make plans of action through engagement with one another. Habermas' civil society or 'public sphere' exists at the interface of the private and public spheres of the lifeworld, where the state is open to challenge and critique. Civil society thus consists of 'more or less spontaneously emergent associations, organizations and movements that, attuned to how societal problems resonate in the private life spheres, distil and transmit such reactions in amplified form to the public sphere' (Habermas, 1996, p. 367).

More recently, ideas about civil society have transformed due to mass communication in online spaces and transnationalisation, although social movements both within and outside of the state system continue to exist as a site of contestation where alliances are forged, and values and identities are consolidated in a 'global civil society' (Lipschutz, 1992). These imagined political communities challenge the nation-state system from below and are arguably more distinct than civil societies from *within* the state, given their perceived autonomy from sovereign boundaries (Lipschutz, 1992) (what Nancy Fraser (1997) calls 'postnational constellations' or the 'transnational public sphere'). Examples of global civil societies include transnational networks that are mobilised around a common cause, such as human rights, feminist, indigenous, environmental and other global movements (Lipschutz, 1992; see also Walzer, 1995). Fraser (1990) argues that Habermas' idea of the public sphere is indispensable to social theory but inadequate as a critique of democracy in late capitalist societies because of its territorial, Westphalian frame. She argues (1990, p. 67) that the proliferation of subaltern counterpublics – defined as 'parallel discursive arenas where members of subordinated social groups invent and circulate counterdiscourses, which in turn permit them to formulate oppositional interpretations of their identities, interests, and needs' – is crucial for reducing disparities in stratified societies and redrawing the boundaries between public and private.

It is important to avoid romanticising civil society as Fraser (1990) warns, or abstracting it from its social, cultural and historical constitutive meaning and context (Fine, 2014). Micro-examinations of the *impact* of specific transnational movements, or their mechanisms of justice, rather will help to shed light on both their legitimacy and efficacy (Fraser, 1997). In relation to civil society tribunals, for instance, it is important to consider whether they are an effective medium for redressing harm, and whether the communicative power that they generate is capable of contributing to change in state or international laws, policies and practices. As Fraser claims (1997), the public sphere is increasingly transnational and the 'who', 'what', 'where' and 'how' of communication are now characterised by amorphous, dispersed, deterritorialised and translinguistic relations – making the task of assessing both legitimacy and efficacy difficult due to the extraterritoriality of these spaces.

Another way to assess transnational movements or accountability mechanisms is through Fraser's (2007) three-dimensional model of justice. This model, I contend, is useful for examining the intersection between violence, economic inequalities, culture and discourse, and the political struggles in transnational civil societies. Her model encompasses the three concepts of recognition, redistribution and representation, serving as a useful sociological theory on stratification, encompassing the intersectionality of axes of social injustice on the basis of gender, class, sexuality and race. These three concepts are analytically useful for thinking about the different (but related) dimensions of justice in the aftermath of sexual violence, regardless of historical, social or political context.

Recognition

First, according to Fraser (1998, p. 7), the politics of *recognition* targets cultural injustices, which are 'rooted in social patterns of representation, interpretation, and communication'. Such injustices include cultural domination from one culture by another; non-recognition or invisibility within one's own culture; and disrespect through disparaging stereotypes and representations in everyday life. On the other hand, regardless of context, recognition is intersubjective because it requires at least one other person to acknowledge the status or identity of the other. Although Fraser's focus is on status as identity politics on the basis of gender, race, class and sexuality, and not specifically on victimisation as a form of identity (which in and of itself is a problematic for the politics of recognition), her ideas about the importance of recognition as a component of social justice are nonetheless applicable to thinking about responses to gross human rights violations. In the context of past forms of sexual violence, for example, recognition is a form of validation that promotes respect, dignity and worth of the 'collective subjects of injustice' (Fraser, 1998, p. 8), addressing not only the misplaced stigma and shame of past violence, but also the injustice of 'misrecognition' (a term Fraser (1998, 2008) uses) of cultural, social, political and legal amnesia and denial.

Justice for comfort women thus entails recognition from the Japanese state in various forms, including an unambiguous apology that acknowledges the full extent of state and military involvement in the establishment and running of the comfort stations. Justice also includes recognition of the failure of the Tokyo Tribunal and other war crimes courts after the Second World War to prosecute individuals for sexual enslavement and enforced prostitution. The Women's Tribunal explicitly and unequivocally acknowledged the harm of this past misrecognition; an injustice in and of itself. The tribunal also recognised individual and collective responsibility for the harms perpetrated against the comfort women. The Women's Tribunal, therefore, played a number of interconnected and important roles for recognising the injustice of both sexual enslavement and the failure of law and politics to respond to this harm. First, it provided a clear statement about individual and collective criminal responsibility. Second, it used legal language and the format of a trial to name and condemn criminal behaviour under the rubric of international law, through terms such as 'slavery', 'crimes against humanity' and 'war crimes'. Third, the tribunal raised awareness of the prevalence of sexual violence in armed conflict in both historical and contemporary contexts. Fourth, it consolidated the collective memory of past wrongdoing through creating a permanent, public record through the lengthy tribunal judgement as well as other documents and materials, such as websites, videos, personal memoirs and documentaries. Fifth, it provided a safe space for victim-survivors to be heard in a supportive, non-adversarial context. And sixth, the tribunal acknowledged the psychosocial and socio-economic harms of gender-based violence, as well as the harm of past and present silence and denial.

In the absence of qualitative data on the experiences of victim-survivors who testified at the Women's Tribunal, it is not possible to conclude how successful the tribunal was in providing recognition on an interpersonal level. Existing studies on motivations for testifying in war crimes trials, however, tend to suggest that victims of mass atrocities have a compelling need to bear witness and tell their story; that they are motivated to testify in order to speak on behalf of the dead or loved ones; obtain further information; receive public acknowledgement; contribute to rebuilding social relations; educate the broader local and global community about what happened; and ensure perpetrator accountability and punishment (see e.g. Stepakoff et al., 2014; Stover, 2005). Empirical studies on truth commissions, war crimes courts, national courts and other transitional justice mechanisms reveal that victims may find it painful to testify about past forms of suffering in a public forum and may experience frustration, disappointment or psychological distress with unmet expectations, baffling bureaucratic procedures, inadequate preparation, offensive encounters with tribunal or commission staff, or adverse consequences in the aftermath of testimony (see e.g. Cody et al., 2014; Stover, 2005). Despite mixed results about the actual experiences of testifying, overall, these empirical studies unequivocally support the notion that having one's experience recognised in a public forum is highly valued among victim-survivors of mass atrocities (see also Clark, Chapter 2; and Powell, Chapter 13).

Recognition, however, is not solely an individualised justice need, but also has an important collective dimension. Fraser (1998, p. 26) claims that viewing misrecognition as a form of injustice rather than as a psychological malady prompts solutions that are geared towards cultural change, including changing social practices and institutions to ensure parity of participation in social life. Indeed, the Women's Tribunal provided an official, judicial pronouncement about criminal wrongdoing that many victim-survivors longed for. Although the tribunal could not make arrests, or prosecute or convict individuals, it was able to pronounce the guilt of individual perpetrators and, perhaps more importantly, the Japanese state. The Women's Tribunal concluded that the Emperor of Japan knew or should have known about the establishment and operation of the comfort stations, and that he failed to do his duty and was criminally liable for all of the charges contained in the tribunal's indictments (with the exception of the charge pertaining to the rape of the Mapanique women). The judges concluded that the other named accused were also guilty of superior and individual responsibility for the crimes committed against the comfort women and the women from Mapanique. In a statement about collective responsibility, the tribunal found that Japan bears state responsibility for the crimes of sexual violence and made a number of recommendations which included that the Japanese government compensate victim-survivors, provide a sincere apology that takes legal responsibility and give guarantees of non-repetition (see pp. 262–263 of the Tribunal Judgement for a full list of recommendations). In the context of this discussion, it is interesting to note that in the summary judgement for the Women's Tribunal, the audience gave a standing ovation to the judges' pronouncement of the emperor's guilt for the rape and sexual enslavement of comfort women.[4]

Redistribution

Fraser's (1998, 2007) second component of social justice is *redistribution*, which she defines as the fair distribution of benefits and burdens. Redistribution is a practical socio-economic tool, which Fraser (1998) claims is separate from, but not distinct to, that of recognition. She refers to a 'bivalent conception of justice' that encompasses both redistribution and recognition, but without collapsing them together as one. Justice therefore involves 'social arrangements that permit all (adult) members of society to interact with one another as peers' (Fraser, 1998, p. 30).

A reparative model that seeks to provide victims with an array of redistributive remedies may include: satisfaction (symbolic measures arising out of a duty to remember, such as an apology or commemorations); restitution (restoring victims to their original situation where possible); and monetary compensation for material and emotional damages (see Women's Tribunal Judgement, 2001, pp. 251–261). Compensation for past wrongdoings, for instance, helps to acknowledge not simply the psychosocial harms, but also the socio-economic and intergenerational impacts of egregious acts. Compensation also aims to redistribute both benefits and burdens. In 1995, monetary compensation was made available to victim-survivors through the establishment of the Asian Women's Fund (AWF). Although the AWF was set up and run by the Japanese government, compensation was provided solely through private donations and, as such, the AWF was the subject of deep controversy (Soh, 2003). Many viewed the donations as 'atonement money' and in violation of international law given that compensation was not provided for by the state. The rejection of donations by many comfort women demonstrates the complexity of redistribution as a component of justice. Victim-survivors and their advocates believed that compensation should come from the Japanese state, accompanied by statements of recognition, including a full and frank apology.

But individual reparative measures are not the only means of redistribution in the context of gross human rights violations. Redistribution would also entail economic restructuring; the reorganisation of the division of labour; and other fundamental transformations to the political economy (Fraser, 1998, p. 7). Although the Women's Tribunal did address the impacts of victimisation on comfort women's lives, acknowledge poverty as a causal factor and appreciate these harms beyond the crimes themselves, broader structural changes were not specifically listed in the tribunal's recommendations. In the context of my discussion here, the harms or injustices against the comfort women should be seen on multiple levels: the harm of sexual enslavement; the harm of social, political and legal misrecognition; and the resulting harms of economic deprivation and social exclusion that have prevented many comfort women from participating as equals in social and political life. Efforts therefore should be geared towards uncovering the complex causes underlying these crimes and preventing them from happening again.

Representation

Finally, Fraser's (2007) third component of justice is *representation* through symbolic 'just' language. This entails full social and political participation in subaltern counterpublic spaces, but equally important is the manner in which explications of past wrongdoing are represented in social, legal and political contexts. Parity of participation and symbolic representation have relevance both interpersonally and at the collective level. Here I wish to focus on post-colonial critiques of the comfort women movement, and the ways in which the testimonial narratives of victim-survivors are positioned under a redress or human rights paradigm. Specifically, I consider three questions: (1) Did the tribunal's representation of comfort women as victims of sexual enslavement entail a denial of agency? (2) Did these representations obscure or mask the complexity of comfort women's lives? And (3) Was the tribunal able to adequately capture the intersectionality of violence underlying the systematic enslavement of comfort women?[5]

The transnational violence against women movement more generally has been criticised by post-colonial scholars for reinforcing a one-dimensional, paradigmatic narrative of victimhood. This is reflected in a 'dominant discourse' that is inflected by a legacy of colonial rule, with the effect of denying women agency as empowered subjects. Post-colonial feminist scholars argue that the subaltern is represented in dominant discourse as inferior and in need of being rescued by Western liberators (Spivak, 1988). Reflecting on the dominant narrative of contemporary forms of sex trafficking, Jo Doezema (2000, p. 31), for instance, describes the use of spectacle, sensation and emotive language; of 'gut wrenching testimonies of broken dreams, withered illusions, rape and humiliation'. Similarly, Ratna Kapur (2002) claims that the image that is produced in these discourses 'is that of a truncated Third World woman who is sexually constrained, tradition-bound, incarcerated in the home, illiterate, and poor'. These representations pose a critical challenge in the violence against women field; that is, how to capture the complex and varied experiences of women's lives, including the array of intersectional disadvantages on the basis of race, ethnicity, class, age, ability and sexuality, and at the same time, avoid constructing cultural and gender essentialisms that serve to deny women agency. As Kimberle Crenshaw (1991, p. 1242) claims, frequently identity politics conflates or ignores difference. She argues that 'this elision of difference... is problematic, fundamentally because the violence that many women experience is often shaped by other dimensions of their identities, such as race and class'. She further states that 'through an awareness of intersectionality, we can better acknowledge and ground the differences among us and negotiate the means by which these differences will find expression in constructing group politics' (Crenshaw, 1991, p. 1299).

Relatedly, many scholars claim that identity politics can culminate in exclusionary stratifications. For instance, those who do not fit the ideal model of victimisation may not have the same access to legitimacy or claims to redress and, as such, a parity of participation cannot be said to exist. The 'authentic victim subject', as Kapur (2002) calls it, is a young, innocent victim who is incapable of expressing resistance or negotiation, and is denied any opportunity for self-representation within the hegemonic discourse. As Wendy Brown (1995, p. 27) also argues, the identity of the injured becomes fixed and the effect is to legitimise law and the state 'as appropriate protectors against injury' and the injured as being in need of protection 'by such protectors'.

In applying post-colonial feminist critiques about agency, intersectionality and victimhood to the comfort women movement, C. Sarah Soh (2008, p. 229) argues that Korean victim-survivors tell of 'much *more complex and varied lived experiences anchored to the painful sediment of their lifelong suffering* than the paradigmatic, one-dimensional story of the Japanese military comfort system as a war crime can satisfactorily explain' (emphasis added). She argues that the dominant story of the comfort women is of forcible recruitment through kidnapping or trickery, and that this has the effect of ignoring the 'wide range of varying experiences of victimized women and of the organization diversity of the comfort stations'. Soh (2008, p. 47) criticises feminist humanitarianism for framing the comfort women issue as exclusively a Japanese war crimes issue, which she claims diverts attention from other structural causes, such as imperialism, capitalism and patriarchy, and how hierarchically ordered gendered, class, racial and ethnic social relations played a pivotal role in the recruitment, establishment and operation of the comfort stations. Soh (2008, pp. xv–xvi) writes: '[t]heir biographical narratives reveal not only the unbelievably wretched life conditions of the poor in colonial Korea, but also the remarkable levels of agency, aspirations for autonomy, life-affirming perseverance, and resilience – characteristics that have been ignored or downplayed in most studies'.

Katharina Ramo Mendoza (2011, p. 7) likewise criticises the construction of the 'eternal victim' within the comfort women redress movement, noting that comfort women often are forced to tell their 'brutal and lurid' stories through the 'highly constructed and encoded' language of law that drains such narratives of both affect and context. This produces, Mendoza claims, a testimonial narrative that is 'selectively spectacular, explicit, and violent' (p. 67), and that obscures the 'many faces of the comfort women – their vulnerabilities and their strengths, their despair and fortitude, the small, essential details of their lives...' (p. 3).

Indeed, the Women's Tribunal was far from perfect. It was constrained in many ways by the overarching framework of international criminal law and as such, it prioritised the *legal* harms of sexual violence, at the expense of articulating broader ethical, structural and political wrongs (Sakamoto, 2001). The tribunal judgement, however, did make mention of the structural injustices before, during and after the Asia-Pacific War (see Women's Tribunal Judgement, 2001, p. 73), for instance, noting women's socio-economic vulnerability due to age, poverty, class, family status, education, nationality and ethnicity, and that girls were forced to go to work at an early age in order to support their families. Yet, by and large, the structural conditions of colonialism, patriarchy and capitalism, in which multiple states, institutions and other collectivities were also complicit, were sidelined in favour of a depoliticising, individualising criminal liability model. Although the tribunal attributes some blame to the 'internationally constituted' Tokyo Tribunal, the primary responsibility for the harms against the comfort women 'lies and remains with the state of Japan for its continuing failure... to prosecute perpetrators of all rank, to officially and fully apologise, and to provide reparations and other meaningful remedies for the crimes' (Women's Tribunal Judgement, 2001, p. 1). In addition, the focus, like most conventional international and domestic war crimes courts, was squarely on individual accused persons, and on proving the charges laid out in the indictments around rape and sexual slavery as a crime against humanity. Essentially, the proceedings were 'not a fake trial, but essentially a real trial without legal force' (Women's Tribunal Judgement, 2001, p. 16). In this way, the law is perceived as the remedy for injury (Brown, 1995); albeit not the only remedy.

While it may be true that the Women's Tribunal focused predominantly on eliciting details of the methods of recruitment, and the conditions and operation of the comfort stations in order to prove the charges contained in the indictments, it would be unrealistic to expect an alternative approach given the tribunal's specific goal was to perform as a legal trial, as if the tribunal were a continuation of the Tokyo Tribunal. There were, though, innovative and creative elements contained in the tribunal proceedings that differed substantially from those found in conventional war crimes courts. Victim-survivors at the Women's Tribunal, for instance, were given a safe space to tell their stories and to reclaim their dignity. The tribunal was able to make recommendations on reparations beyond the realm of law, and it was able to deliver judgement not only on individual criminal responsibility, but also on the collective responsibility of the Japanese state. Importantly, the tribunal documented how the methods of recruitment of women and girls into the comfort stations were extremely varied, and was careful to acknowledge that this does not factor into determinations about whether or not women were victims of sexual enslavement. This, and other parts of the tribunal's judgement, importantly sought to capture the diversity of comfort women's lives.

Conclusion

Civil society initiatives for seeking 'rape justice' represent a critical challenge to the hegemony of state-centric, institutionalised remedies at both the domestic and international level (see also Powell, Chapter 13). Civil society tribunals have the potential to transcend the individualising and depoliticising tendency of more conventional measures of justice, such as domestic or international criminal law. Civil society initiatives can serve to challenge state power and state crime and, in doing so, provide a more nuanced and complex version of criminal responsibility for past atrocities. Civil society tribunals also provide a unique truth-seeking forum for victims of historical wartime sexual violence. These mechanisms have the potential to resurrect state and collective responsibility for mass violence, contribute to the preservation of memory and, as such, provide an important (and sometimes) discordant narrative of the past.

Yet, there is scope for moving beyond the individual criminal responsibility model and the almost exclusive focus on the law as the sole remedy for sexual violence. Framing of the comfort women issue as a war crimes issue comes at the expense of more deeply articulating the broader socio-economic and political context of wartime exploitation, and the depth and diversity of survivor experiences of these harms. More attention, for example, could be directed to the recognition of broader structural harms, as well as primary prevention measures for ensuring that these crimes do not happen again.

A lack of acknowledgement of the harms perpetrated by acts of wartime sexual violence constitutes a grave injustice for victims of these crimes. The plight of the comfort women should serve as a lesson about the injustice of past misrecognition, as well as the importance of recognition, redistribution and representation, particularly in non-conventional, transitional justice mechanisms that seek to expand the boundaries of justice in potentially radical political ways. Above all, the stories of the comfort women are a reminder that justice for past harm is never straightforward, and never solely the domain of one realm.

Notes

1. There was only one trial at the 1948 Dutch Ad Hoc Military Court in Batavia, Java, which prosecuted and convicted military officers and brothel owners for the 'enforced prostitution' of 35 Dutch Indonesian women (see Hicks, 1997; Soh, 2008).

2. I will desist from using quotation marks for any of these terms for ease of reading, yet I wholeheartedly acknowledge the problematic connotations associated with the various terms used in this chapter, especially that of 'comfort women' and 'comfort stations'.
3. Note that the distinction between civil society and the state, and civil society and the family sphere, remains an issue of much debate. Wendy Brown (1995, pp. 146–147), for instance, notes that for Marxists, civil society is also the economic realm '...the domain where rights are exercised and individuality is expressed, hence a domain of *particularity*; and the stratification within it constitutes the domain of "real political life"...' (emphasis original).
4. See http://fightforjustice.info/?page_id=2818&lang=en.
5. Another critique of the transnational feminist movement around sexual violence has been that it fixates on sexual violence at the expense of ignoring other harms, such as those against men and boys, or non-sexually-based harms. Some have also argued that the 'over-criminalisation' of sexual violence has deleterious effects (for a discussion of these and other criticisms, see Henry, 2014).

References

Askin, K. D. (1997) *War Crimes Against Women: Prosecution in International War Crimes Tribunals* (Leiden; Boston: Martinus Nijhoff).

Brown, W. (1995) *States of Injury: Power and Freedom in Late Modernity* (Princeton, NJ: Princeton University Press).

Chinkin, C. (2001) 'Women's International Tribunal on Japanese Military Sexual Slavery', *The American Journal of International Law*, 95(2), 335–341.

Cody, S., Koenig, A., Mejia, R. and Stover, E. (2014) *Bearing Witness at the International Criminal Court: An Interview Study of 109 Witnesses* (Berkeley, CA: Human Rights Center, University of California Berkeley School of Law).

Cohen, J. L. and Arato, A. (1992) *Civil Society and Political Theory* (Cambridge, MA: MIT Press).

Coomaraswamy, R. (1997) *Report of the Special Rapporteur on Violence Against Women, Its Causes and Consequences, Ms. Radhika Coomaraswamy, in accordance with Commission on Human Rights Resolution 1994/45: Report on the Mission to the Democratic People's Republic of Korea, the Republic of Korea and Japan on the Issue of Military Sexual Slavery in Wartime*. U.N. Doc.E/CN.4/1996/1996/53.

Crenshaw, K. (1991) 'Mapping the Margins: Intersectionality, Identity Politics, and Violence Against Women of Color', *Stanford Law Review*, 43(6), 1241–1299.

Doezema, J. (2000) 'Loose Women or Lost Women? The Re-emergence of the Myth of White Slavery in Contemporary Discourses on Trafficking in Women', *Gender Issues*, 18(1), 23–50.

Dolgopol, T. (2003) 'The Judgment of the Tokyo Women's Tribunal', *Alternative Law Journal*, 28, 242–249.

Dudden, A. (2001) '"We Came to Tell the Truth": Reflections on the Tokyo Women's Tribunal', *Critical Asian Studies*, 33(4), 591–602.

Duffett, J. (ed.) (1968) *Against the Crime of Silence: Proceedings of the Russell International War Crimes Tribunal, Stockholm, Copenhagen* (Bertrand Russell Peace Foundation).

Ehrenberg, J. (1999) *Civil Society: The Critical History of an Idea* (New York: New York University Press).
Falk, R. (1988) 'The Rights of Peoples (In Particular Indigenous Peoples)', in J. Crawford (ed.) *The Rights of Peoples* (New York: Oxford University Press), pp. 17–37.
Fine, R. (2014) 'Civil Society Theory, Enlightenment and Critique', in R. Fine and S. Rai (eds.) *Civil Society: Democratic Principles* (Hoboken: Taylor and Francis), pp. 7–28.
Fraser, N. (1990) 'Rethinking the Public Sphere: A Contribution to the Critique of Actually Existing Democracy', *Social Text*, 25/26, 56–80.
Fraser, N. (1997) 'Transnationalizing the Public Sphere: On the Legitimacy and Efficacy of Public Opinion in a Post-Westphalian World', *Theory, Culture and Society*, 24(4), 7–30.
Fraser, N. (1998) 'Social Justice in the Age of Identity Politics: Redistribution, Recognition and Participation', in G. Peterson (ed.) *The Tanner Lectures on Human Values XIX* (Salt Lake City: University of Utah Press), pp. 1–67.
Fraser, N. (2007) 'Reframing Justice in a Globalizing World', in D. Held and A. Kaya (eds.) *Global Inequality* (Cambridge: Polity Press), pp. 252–272.
Fraser, N. (2008) *Scales of Justice: Reimagining Political Space in a Globalizing World* (New York: Columbia University Press).
Habermas, J. (1987) *The Theory of Communicative Action: Reason and Rationalization of Society*, trans. T. McCarthy (Cambridge, UK: Polity Press).
Habermas, J. (1996) *Between Facts and Norms: Contributions to a Discourse Theory of Law and Democracy*, trans. W. Rehg (Cambridge, MA: MIT Press).
Hayashi, H. (2008) 'Disputes Over the Japanese Military "Comfort Women" System and its Perception in History', *Annals of the American Academy of Political and Social Science*, 617(1), 123–132.
Henry, N. (2011) *War and Rape: Law, Memory and Justice* (London; New York: Routledge).
Henry, N. (2013) 'Memory of an Injustice: The "Comfort Women" and the Legacy of the Tokyo Trial', *Asian Studies Review*, 37(3), 362–380.
Henry, N. (2014) 'The Fixation on Wartime Rape: Feminist Critique and International Criminal Law', *Social & Legal Studies*, 23(1), 93–111.
Hicks, G. (1997) *The Comfort Women* (New York; London: W.W. Norton & Company).
Kapur R. (2002) 'The Tragedy of Victimization Rhetoric: Resurrecting the "Native" Subject in International/Post-colonial Feminist Legal Politics', *Harvard Human Rights Journal*, 15, 1–37.
Knopp, K. (2011) 'The Tokyo Women's Tribunal and the Turn to Fiction', in F. Johns, R. Joyce and S. Pahuja (eds.) *Events: The Force of International Law* (New York: Routledge), pp. 145–164.
Kyodo (n.d.), 'Philippine Top Court Ends "Comfort Women" Group's Legal Battle', *Japan Times*; Retrieved from http://www.japantimes.co.jp/news/2014/08/13/national/crime-legal/philippine-top-courts-denial-ends-filipino-comfort-women-groups-legal-battle/.
Lipschutz, R. D. (1992) 'Reconstructing World Politics: The Emergence of Global Civil Society', *Millennium-Journal of International Studies*, 21(3), 389–420.
Matsui, Y. (2001) 'Women's International War Crimes Tribunal on Japan's Military Sexual Slavery', *East Asia*, 19(4), 119–142.

McDougall, G. J. (1998) *Contemporary Forms of Slavery: Systematic Rape, Sexual Slavery and Slavery-like Practices: Final Report Submitted by Ms Gay J. McDougall, Special Rapporteur*. U.N. Doc.E/CN.4/Sub.2/1998/13.

Mendoza, K. R. (2011) ' "In War, and After It, a Prisoner Always": Reading Past the Paradigm of Redress in the Life Stories of the Filipino Comfort Women', PhD thesis, University of Iowa; Retrieved from http://ir.uiowa.edu/etd/1025.

Noriko, K. (2014) 'Korean Courts Order Japanese Firms to Compensate Wartime Laborers: Background to the Rulings', *Nippon.com*, 3 July 2014; Retrieved from http://www.nippon.com/en/in-depth/a02703/.

Qui, P., Zhiliang, S. and Lifei, C. (2013) *Chinese Comfort Women: Testimonies from Imperial Japan's Sex Slaves* (Vancouver: UBC Press).

Ruff-O'Herne, J. (1994) *Fifty Years of Silence* (Sydney: Editions Tom Thompson).

Russell, D. E. H. and Van de Ven, N. (1976) *Crimes Against Women: Proceedings of the International Tribunal* (Millbrae, CA: Les Femmes Pub).

Sakamoto, R. (2001) 'The Women's International War Crimes Tribunal on Japan's Military Sexual Slavery: A Legal and Feminist Approach to the "Comfort Women" Issue', *New Zealand Journal of Asian Studies*, 3, 49–58.

Soh, C. S. (2003) 'Japan's National/Asian Women's Fund for "Comfort Women" ', *Pacific Affairs*, 76(2), 209–233.

Soh, C. S. (2008) *The Comfort Women: Sexual Violence and Postcolonial Memory in Korea and Japan* (Chicago; London: University of Chicago Press).

Spivak, G. C. (1988) 'Can the Subaltern Speak?', in G. Nelson and L. Grossberg (eds.) *Marxism and the Interpretation of Culture* (Urbana: University of Illinois Press), pp. 271–313.

Stepakoff, S., Reynolds, G. S., Charters, S. and Henry, N. (2014) 'Why Testify?: Witnesses' Motivations for Giving Evidence in a War Crimes Tribunal in Sierra Leone, *International Journal of Transitional Justice*, 8(3), 426–541.

Stover, E. (2005) *The Witnesses: War Crimes and the Promise of Justice in The Hague* (Philadelphia: University of Pennsylvania Press).

Tanaka, Y. (2002) *Japan's Comfort Women: Sexual Slavery and Prostitution During World War II and the US Occupation* (London: Routledge).

Walzer, M. (ed.) (1995) *Toward a Global Civil Society* (Providence: Berghahn Books).

Women's International War Crimes Tribunal for the Trial of Japan's Military Sexual Slavery (2001) *Judgement on the Common Indictment and the Application for Restitution and Reparation*, 4 December 2001, The Hague, The Netherlands; http://www.internationalcrimesdatabase.org/Case/981/The-Prosecutors-and-the-Peoples-of-the-Asia-Pacific-Region/.

Yoshimi, Y. (2000) *Comfort Women: Sexual Slavery in the Japanese Military During World War II*, trans. S. O'Brien (New York: Columbia University Press).

13
Seeking Informal Justice Online
Vigilantism, Activism and Resisting a Rape Culture in Cyberspace

Anastasia Powell

Introduction

What does it mean to seek, or indeed to achieve, justice in response to rape? The contributions in this volume explore the meanings and mechanisms of justice in response to sexual violence 'beyond the criminal law'. Taking as already evident that sexual violence is first, extremely prevalent; second, overwhelmingly (though not exclusively) perpetrated by men against women and girls; and third, that formal justice as represented by conviction and state punishment is remarkably rare, this chapter explores social practices of informal justice that are emerging via communications technologies and in online spaces. 'Informal justice', as used here, refers specifically to practices that seek redress for harms in settings operating *outside of the state* and its institutions.

In this chapter, I first explore case study examples of online vigilantism, testimonials and truth telling by rape victim-survivors. Then I draw on Nancy Fraser's (2007, 2009) framework of justice as redistribution, recognition and representation as well as an adaptation of 'bearing witness' (see Henry, 2010), to conceptualise the modes of informal justice such online engagements represent. In doing so, I do not intend to advocate that feminists should abandon projects of law reform and restorative or 'innovative' legal and non-legal state responses to sexual violence; nor to minimise the role and responsibility of states to address the sexual, and indeed gender-based, violence that is systemic globally. Rather I contend that the modes of informal justice being sought online by victim-survivors of sexual violence can serve both to validate women's individual and collective experiences, and ultimately challenge the gendered misrecognition at the heart of 'rape culture' and many women's victimisation.

Outing rapists and harassers: Vigilantism, activism or justice?

Since 2006, in the rural Banda District of Uttar Pradesh in Northern India, women wearing bright pink saris and wielding bamboo sticks have visited the homes of accused wife abusers demanding that the men stop using violence.[1] Sampat Pal, the founder of the Gulabi Gang, which now boasts over 20,000 members, is prepared to act on that threat; beating men who refuse to heed the warning and taking justice into the gang's own hands when the law and police fail to respond (Fontanella-Khan, 2013). The Gulabi Gang are well known for their violent assaults on husbands: vigilante action that achieves justice on behalf of women victims of domestic violence, at least in the short term. However, the group's activities also include: counselling women victims of domestic violence; organising protest rallies and sit-ins; and advocating on women's behalf to local police in order to pursue longer-term action and social change (Sen, 2012). Scholars such as Atreyee Sen (2012, p. 3), while acknowledging that the marginalised women who make up the pink sari movement 'walk a tightrope between legally reprehensible and socially condoned action', suggests that their vigilantism 'procures a legitimate space when viewed and examined through the model of ethical violence, and related to understandings of the proportionate punishment for crimes against women'. Reflecting on various case studies of vigilantism in India's poorest districts, Nandini Sundar (2010, p. 117) similarly argues that vigilantism by such subaltern groups represents not only a challenge to the legitimacy of the state, but also reflects the persistent failure of the formal justice system. She suggests that:

> Even as incidents of vigilantism from below can be criticized for the absence of due process, they show the way in which the formal process and the rule of law are marked by hierarchies of gender, caste and class.

Violent vigilantism in response to domestic violence, such as that in northern India, emerges in the specific contexts of state and institutional failure to take reports or investigate, let alone prosecute, crimes of violence against women. In some cases, women who attempt to report crimes, such as rape or domestic violence, are met with further violence and harassment from police themselves, or from their broader community (Carrington, 2014; Just Associates and Nobel Women's Initiative, 2012). For the poorest and most marginalised women, the risk of being raped and/or murdered is particularly high, and the perpetrators of these crimes do so with impunity. These women's use of violence is therefore in part explainable, even socially and morally condonable, within the context of the extreme danger in which they live their lives and in response to which they have little other recourse to action.

If vigilantism in response to violence against women emerges in the face of state inaction and the relative impunity of men who use violence, then related actions in the United States can be understood as differing in degree rather than kind. For example, in October 2012, at an anti-rape rally in Oakland, California, protestors held banners proclaiming: 'Crucify your rapist. YOLO' (You Only Live Once); 'Don't f–k with us, we'll cut you up. Girl gangs here to f–k shit up!'; and 'Feminist vigilante gangs – we bash back!'.[2] In March 2012, Landen Gambill, a student at the University of North Carolina, publicly disclosed her experience of rape at the hands of her ex-boyfriend (although never specifically naming her perpetrator), after her case was dismissed by the University's Honor Court (Kingkade, 2013). In a further example in May 2014, a list of 'Rapists on Campus' was being scribbled on women's bathroom walls and distributed as paper flyers by students at Columbia University, featuring the names of perpetrators who were found to be 'responsible' for sexual assaults by the university administration, but who nonetheless remained on campus (Ryan, 2014).

Scribbling the names of alleged rapists on the bathroom wall, distributing posters or flyers, or otherwise outing men who use violence against women is not in and of itself a new form of either individual redress or collective activism. As Filipovic (2012, n.p.) has observed:

> Rape remains woefully under-reported and shamefully stigmatised. Narrating our own histories without anyone else's approval or endorsement is what initially brought sexual assault out of the shadows. Continuing to speak the truth is what keeps the light on.

Feminist strategies involving victim-survivor testimonies of sexual violence, or naming and shaming alleged rapists, once occupied the liminal spaces of women's independently run 'zines', consciousness-raising gatherings or the proverbial bathroom wall (see Salter, 2013). However, the rapid uptake of communication technologies and online spaces has since enabled modes of vigilantism and activism to be produced more quickly, communicated to a wider globally networked audience, and potentially with greater reach to mainstream media audiences.[3] Indeed, communications technologies, such as social networking platforms (e.g. Twitter, Facebook), blogging services (e.g. Tumblr, Bloggr), dedicated activist projects and online communities (e.g. Project Unbreakable, Everyday Sexism, Hollaback!) and even video- and image-sharing platforms (e.g. YouTube, Instagram), provide an array of formats for engaging in vigilante and anti-rape activist strategies. While the tools, as described above, are diverse and continue to develop and adapt to their various uses, the strategies themselves gravitate towards familiar forms of 'soft vigilantism' such as 'outing' perpetrators, as well as victim-survivor testimonials and truth telling, each explored in more detail below.

Outing perpetrators

On 22 April 2010, Chloe Rubenstein, a 19-year-old American university student, posted a note on her Facebook page naming two students as rapists:

> ATTENTION WOMEN. We should all be aware! Stay away at all costs. They are predators and will show no remorse for anyone. If you have been effected [*sic*] by either one of these sickos please feel free to talk to me. With enough help we can take them down!
>
> (see Hess, 2010)

According to media reports, Rubenstein (a victim-survivor herself) was motivated to name the men who had raped women she knew at campus parties, as a way to warn her friends and show support for victims. After a few days, and reaching her 968 Facebook friends, Rubenstein removed the post stating: 'I don't clear my status because I'm scared. I clear it for legal reasons...' (Hess, 2010).

In June 2012, Savannah Dietrich, a 17-year-old from Kentucky (USA), named the two boys who had sexually assaulted her after they were sentenced to 50 hours' community service for their crimes (see Salter, 2013 for a detailed discussion). Dietrich's actions were in direct violation of the court, which had suppressed the details of the case including the boys' names, since they were juveniles at the time of the offence (Salter, 2013). The boys had taken photos during the assault and sent them onto their friends, the news spreading through Dietrich's high school, publicly humiliating her in addition to the original assault. The injustice that these two young men could publicly name, shame and humiliate her, while she was court-ordered not to name them, reportedly prompted Dietrich to take matters into her own hands. In a post on her Facebook wall, she wrote: 'If reporting a rape only got me to the point that I'm not allowed to talk about it, then I regret it. I regret reporting it' (Hess, 2012, n.p.).

On 29 October 2012, Brie Lybrand, a 27-year-old beauty and fashion vlogger, named her father on YouTube as having raped her repeatedly between the ages of 4 and 13 (Adams, 2012; Berry, 2012). In her video testimonial, Lybrand describes her father's physical violence towards her mother, her brother, as well as years of sexual assault against her.[4] As Lybrand's account found its way into the mainstream media, questions were raised about its truthfulness, to which she responded by tweeting photos of her mother's bruised face, and police reports (Berry, 2012). At the time of writing, the video is still available online and has been viewed over 1,400,000 times.

On 23 February 2013, Tucker Reed, a University of Southern California (US) alumnus, posted the full name and picture (alongside her own) of her rapist, as well as details of her rape on her Tumblr blog 'Covered in Band-Aids' (Reed, 2013; Shilling, 2013). Reed was assaulted by her then boyfriend of two years, and according to media reports, had been unsuccessful in pursuing the matter through her university's administration despite having surreptitiously recorded his admission. On her blog she wrote:

> You don't owe the boy who hurt you a single thing. You don't owe him silence. If you feel you want the world to recognize that what happened to you was wrong, don't let anyone try to talk you out of standing up and speaking out.
>
> (Shilling, 2013)

Reed has since deleted the blog, though has written publicly about her account for XOJane (Reed, 2013) among other feminist media and, due to the inherent share-ability of Internet content, there are still re-posts of some of her original statements widely available online.[5]

These are just some of the cases that have gained the attention of feminist and mainstream media, yet a search on Twitter, Facebook, Tumblr and YouTube for 'outing rapists' and other similar key terms presents many other examples of women taking justice into their own hands. Whether foremost about seeking 'justice' or 'revenge' (Salter, 2013), what is striking about the naming and shaming of rapists in the four accounts described here is that the victim-survivors appear to have been emboldened to speak out, after months or years of silence, as a result of a renewed injustice: such as frustration at repeat offenders on campus, the inaction of university administrative processes, the 'slap on the wrist' of formal justice or, in Brie Lybrand's case, the fact that her rapist father subscribed to her YouTube channel enabling him to watch his daughter's vlogs online 14 years after she escaped his abuse (Berry, 2012).

Victim-survivor testimonials

While in the instances described above victim-survivors overtly identify themselves and their rapists, many more accounts of sexual violence are shared online without naming and shaming perpetrators. Sometimes remaining completely anonymous, but sometimes not, victim-survivors are describing the nature of sexual assault and harassment that they have experienced which, when combined, can produce powerful and all too familiar narratives of perpetrator tactics and the aftermath of abuse. For example, on countless Tumblr blogs, victim-survivors of sexual assault post their first-hand accounts of the abuse.[6] Many post anonymously, and many are disclosing the abuse for the first time. There are thousands of written testimonies, some are just a few lines, others a few paragraphs. Some are essays of narrative, piecing together the before, during and after of sexual assault. Reading through the posts, it is not long before patterns start to emerge; common are accounts of childhood abuse from a relative or family friend, rape by a boyfriend, date and acquaintance rapes and, less commonly, stranger assaults. Many of the posts begin by thanking the moderators for creating a space in which to tell their story, for instance:

> ... thank you for this website which allows me to get my story out without having to be public about who I am.
>
> (Anonymous, SurvivorStories.Tumblr.com, January 2014)

Contributors can show their support by 'liking', re-blogging and adding comments to each other's posts. Supporters, who openly disclose that they have not experienced sexual assault themselves, also post to the sites thanking contributors for their courage and decrying the 'rape culture' (discussed further below) that has allowed the violence to happen in the first place.[7]

Written testimonials are one way for victim-survivors to share their experiences with the world. Yet with the proliferation of photo- and video-sharing networks, and the increasing ease with which photos and video can be taken, often on a smartphone, tablet or laptop and instantly uploaded to an online audience, it is perhaps of little surprise that many victim-survivors are not only voicing their experiences, but also putting a face to their story. One such example is Project Unbreakable, a photography project that aims 'to give a voice to survivors of sexual assault, domestic violence, and child abuse'.[8] Created in October 2011 by then 19-year-old photographer Grace Brown, the project began with Brown's photographs of victim-survivors, mostly people she knew, holding posters with handwritten quotes from the words spoken to them by their attackers (Malone, 2012). In the beginning, most held the posters in front of their faces, contributing anonymously. Now there are thousands of photographs, some taken by Brown herself as she travels around the United States continuing her project. Many are self-images taken and submitted by victim-survivors themselves and often revealing their identities, standing with expressions of defiance and strength. The project began as a way of raising awareness of sexual assault but, as the Tumblr site describes, it also 'provides a way of healing for violence survivors'. Indeed Brown accounts for the healing that is made possible in this way:

> A survivor can tell their story of abuse to someone but the words are never really said. They bury themselves in a pit in their stomach . . . it's very important that they not hold onto those words because they are incredibly powerful.
>
> (Malone, 2012)

The posters do not name perpetrators, though some identify the victim–perpetrator relationship as a sibling, an uncle, a neighbour, a family friend, an employer, an ex-boyfriend and so on. As such the truth telling in these victim-survivor photo captions is arguably not about revenge or vigilantism but rather about healing, and even redress, through the public disclosure of the wrong and its acknowledgement by an online community of supporters.

Video testimonials are another powerful tool for victim-survivors wanting to break their silence and provide an account of their experience. A common format is the 'card story' or 'note card story' on popular video-sharing platform YouTube.com. Note card stories are 'self-disclosing videos or confessions, using a new frame for telling one's own story audio-visually to the public by combining "old" (handwritten messages) and "new" media (video, computer mediated communication)' (Misoch, 2014, p. 2). They most often take the form of a self-recorded home video, with the subject sitting in front of the camera displaying handwritten cards to relay their message, while a favourite song plays as theme to their disclosure. One of the most famous examples is the note card story of 15-year-old Canadian schoolgirl Amanda Todd who, in October 2012, took her own life after being pressured into sharing intimate images by an Internet predator and subsequently targeted by online bullies (BBC, 2014; Misoch, 2014). Her note card story – which went viral after her death and has had over 19 million views – details her experience of online abuse and her struggle with depression and self-harm.[9]

In the last few years the format has become an increasingly popular one within online culture, with millions of note card stories disclosing everything from sexual victimisation, to bullying, to struggles with mental health and suicidal thoughts, all to a dispersed and unknown online audience (Misoch, 2014). A search for key terms such as 'my rape story' reveals hundreds of thousands of videos made by victim-survivors of sexual violence who share their accounts and the impact of the abuse, often ending with a statement about their survival.

'Soft vigilantism' and feminist activism

The preceding examples of soft vigilantism are not dissimilar to the strategies employed in 1970s feminist activism, with public disclosure of sexual violence victimisation simultaneously a personal and political act. Indeed, Carrie Rentschler (2014, p. 68) describes such online vigilante practices as constituting a ' "feminist response-ability" to rape culture via social media that blends testimonial, advice giving, and cultures of support'. Following Kelly Oliver (2001, p. 15), 'response-ability' contains both 'the condition of possibility of response... and the ethical obligation to respond and enable response-ability from others'. 'Response-ability' suggests more than witnessing, but an imperative to take action; to change the conditions of a society in which the actions of perpetrators are often tolerated and condoned, while victims are overwhelmingly disbelieved and silenced. As such, for victim-survivors and their supporters who 'bear witness' to sexual violence (discussed further below), testimonies of victimisation simultaneously serve as vigilantism and activism. Yet if public disclosure of sexual violence victimisation online demands 'response-ability' from others, which public or which others, are listening and responding?

Rather than representing a singular online forum that engages in public discourse with a broad audience, social networking sites (SNSs) and online spaces are better described as networked publics that provide various opportunities for counterpublic communications (boyd, 2011; Renninger, 2014; Salter, 2013). Such conceptualisation of the constitution of SNSs and online spaces builds on the work of Nancy Fraser (1990) who, in critique of Habermas' notion of a singular public sphere of communicative action, suggests that subordinated social groups form their own parallel public spheres, which she refers to as *subaltern counterpublics*. Fraser describes the emancipatory potential of these counterpublics which, she says, are not separatist enclaves but rather 'aspire to disseminate one's discourse into ever-widening arenas' (1990, p. 67). Indeed, Fraser (1990, p. 68) asserts that in stratified societies in which the democratic ideal of participatory parity is not fully realised for subordinated groups, subaltern counterpublics serve a dual function:

> On the one hand, they function as spaces of withdrawal and regroupment; on the other hand, they also function as bases and training grounds for agitational activities directed toward wider publics... This dialectic enables subaltern counterpublics partially to offset, although not wholly to eradicate, the unjust participatory privileges enjoyed by members of dominant social groups in stratified societies.

Indeed, sexual violence remains a taboo topic in public discourse, a private shame, borne disproportionately by victim-survivors whose experiences are actively and repeatedly *invalidated*: by perpetrators, by communities and by public institutions who routinely fail to provide formal justice (see Clark, Chapter 2; Salter, 2012). The documentation and wide dissemination of testimony and eyewitness accounts of sexual violence and harassment via communications technologies and online networking may in turn enable new practices of collective validation, recognition and informal justice (Fileborn, 2014; Rentschler, 2014; Salter, 2013). As such 'the apparent willingness of some girls and women to seek out alternative modes of discourse and redress suggests a perceived shortfall in the adequacy of institutional responsiveness to sexual violence and gender justice' (Salter 2013, p. 229). Building on Michael Salter's (2013) observation: how might testimonies of sexual violence victimisation serve as more than contestations and counter-discourses (which might be adequately understood as feminist activism) but rather as mechanisms of informal justice?

Justice in (online) recognition?

Previously I have discussed victim-survivors' engagement with communications technologies as *technosocial* practices facilitating informal justice (Powell, 2013; 2015). Recognising that technologies are socially constituted and embedded in social relations, I suggest that these are more than mere tools for achieving recognisable forms of vigilantism, activism or justice, but rather that these practices themselves have shifted or developed through their interaction with SNSs and online spaces; and in turn, have shifted the meanings and possibilities of citizen-led or informal justice (Powell, 2014). Such an argument is contingent on a framing of 'rape justice' beyond the securing of convictions and carceral punishment of offenders often pursued by feminist criminologists and law reformers (Powell, 2015; see also Gotell, Chapter 4). Indeed, in light of the persistent failure of conventional, state-sanctioned justice in response to sexual violence (and gender-based violence more broadly) we must, I contend, consider that some victim-survivors' justice needs (see Clark, Chapter 2) may be met through their engagement with online counterpublics in ways rarely fulfilled in formal, criminal justice settings.

For many victim-survivors of sexual violence, justice is given meaning through the opportunity to tell one's account of victimisation in a public hearing, to have that account validated by a jury of one's peers, and acted upon in a way that seeks to hold the perpetrator accountable, correct the harm and/or prevent its recurrence. Despite the promise that justice will follow one's 'day in court', the criminal justice system has routinely failed victim-survivors of sexual violence, not least due to the well-documented attrition rates that mean very few rape and assault cases ever make it to court, and even fewer (approximately 5–10 per cent) result in a conviction (see Daly & Bourhours, 2010; Kelly et al., 2005; Lievore, 2005). The very format of the hearing offered by the criminal justice system is, some have argued, antithetical to the justice needs of victim-survivors. As poignantly described by Judith Herman (2005, p. 574):

> Victims need social acknowledgement and support; the court requires them to endure a public challenge to their credibility. Victims need to establish a sense of power and control over their lives; the court requires them to submit to a complex set of rules and bureaucratic procedures... Victims need an opportunity to tell their stories in their own way, in a setting of their choice; the court requires them to respond to a set of yes-or-no questions that break down any personal attempt to construct a coherent and meaningful narrative.

In short, victim-survivors' justice needs include: *participation*, *voice*, *control*, *validation* and *vindication* (Clark, 2010; Daly, 2014) at the same time as criminal justice processes sideline, silence, disempower and doubt accounts of rape victimisation. Testifying to one's experience of rape in online counterpublics, where victim-survivors can have control over the extent and nature of their participation; tell their account in their own voice; and receive validation, even vindication, by a community of peers who understand the nature of sexual violence, is potentially a powerful mechanism for seeking justice.

Telling one's story is furthermore commonly held as crucial not only for an individual's psychological recovery from trauma (see Brison, 2002; Harney, 2001), but for the collective recognition and action that is promised when others 'bear witness' to victim-survivors' experiences (see Henry, 2010; Rosenberg, 1996; Solinger et al., 2010; Todorova, 2011). In a criminal trial, the jury are tasked with being impartial observers, and ultimately to decide on the veracity of the evidence and the truthfulness of victim accounts. In the people's court of online counterpublics, however, victim-survivors engage in an alternate format of 'truth telling'; a public narrative to which audiences are not mere observers, but are tasked with validating accounts of rape and placing the burden of correcting the harm back onto perpetrators and society more broadly. In effect, 'bearing witness extends beyond seeing through practices of enacting responsibility' (Tait 2011, p. 1220). Likewise, in her account of victim-survivor testimonies of wartime sexual violence, Nicola Henry (2010, p. 1098) describes 'bearing witness' as:

> ... a form of 'truth telling': a ritualistic public narrative that has the potential to curb the scourge of impunity, restore dignity to survivors, and contribute to the elusive possibility that such crimes will never happen again.

The capacity to narrate one's experience of sexual victimisation online, and share this with a community of one's peers, thus serves not only to fulfil some of the justice needs of individual victim-survivors but arguably also helps correct the collective injustices of *misrecognition* (Fraser, 2007, 2009).

In her threefold conceptualisation of justice, Nancy Fraser (2009) describes the injustices of *maldistribution* (or the inequality in distribution of economic resources), *misrecognition* (or the institutionalised patterns of unequal cultural value) and *misrepresentation* (disparity in political participation). These three dimensions of injustice are, according to Fraser, not reducible to each other in either form or source though they may often co-occur and be mutually reinforcing. Moreover they require simultaneous concerted action to redress, a broad political project that seeks reform along all three dimensions of injustice. Ultimately, the concept of justice proposed by Fraser requires *parity of participation*: social arrangements based on equal distribution, recognition and representation, and that permit all members of a society to interact fully with one another as peers 'throughout the whole of social life' (Fraser, 2007, p. 29).

Fraser (2007, p. 26) further describes the injustices of *gender misrecognition* as constituting pervasive, cultural, gender-specific practices of status subordination that result in women's

> ... sexual harassment, sexual assault and domestic violence; trivializing, objectifying and demeaning stereotypical depictions in the media; disparagement in everyday life; exclusion or marginalization in public spheres and deliberative bodies; and denial of the full rights and equal protections of citizenship.

By her account, rape, and indeed sexual violence and harassment more broadly, are injustices grounded in cultural, discursive or status inequality, in which women are routinely devalued, depreciated and disrespected. Correcting such injustices requires a feminist politics of recognition,[10] aimed at overcoming women's status subordination, by examining and dismantling the 'institutionalized patterns of cultural value [that] constitute women as inferior, excluded, wholly other, or simply invisible' (Fraser, 2007, p. 31).

The combination of the prevalence of sexual violence against women, its minimisation and denial through the practices of state institutions, as well as in public discourse, mainstream media and popular representations, constitute what feminists have long identified as a 'rape culture' (Powell & Henry, 2014; see also Buchwald et al., 1993; Burt, 1980; Gavey, 2005). Rape culture has arguably become a shorthand for the injustices of misrecognition that subordinate women as the targets of men's sexual aggression, silence victims, minimise and/or deny their experiences of victimisation and justify and/or excuse the actions of perpetrators. The term has found renewed favour among the networked counterpublics of online anti-rape activism. The individual testimonies of rape victim-survivors, alongside street harassment and 'Everyday Sexism',[11] are each validated as evidence of the persistence of women's victimisation and subordination within rape culture.

As such, testimonies of sexual victimisation in online counterpublics function both as individual informal justice and collective recognition in response to rape, as well as eliciting a promise to address its underpinnings in rape culture (Rentschler, 2014). Furthermore, rather than merely an expansion of conventional feminist vigilantism and activism, the persistence, replicability, scalability and searchability (boyd, p. 46) of SNSs, as well as the networked participatory engagement between victim-survivors and an audience of peers, enable these new *technosocial* practices of informal justice (see Powell, 2015). They are 'new' not so much in their fundamental nature (as victim-survivor testimonies have long formed a basis for vigilantism and feminist activism), but rather in their capacity to expand the *participation* of victim-survivors (whose accounts were previously marginalised); to provide multiple and diverse formats for testimonials in victim-survivors' own *voice* (through short and long blogging platforms, photo as well as video testimonials, and creative forms); to garner greater *validation* by a globally connected online audience; and *vindication* in the acknowledgement of the social and political significance of the individual's victimisation (Powell, 2015; see also Clark, Chapter 2).

(Im)Possibilities of informal justice online

The subaltern counterpublics of feminist online spaces simultaneously represent possibilities, as already discussed, and impossibilities for informal justice in response to sexual violence. In her analysis of victim-survivor testimonies in the aftermath of wartime sexual violence, Henry (2010) provides a nuanced account of the 'impossibility of bearing witness' that is particularly relevant to the discussion here. Drawing on Giorgio Agamben (1999), Henry first identifies the impossibility of language to adequately convey the pain and suffering actually experienced. Indeed the 'unspeakability' of rape is elsewhere acknowledged as a contributor to trauma and a barrier to the recovery of victim-survivors (see Herman, 1997), as well as an impediment to formal justice (see Henry, 2011; Jordan 2011). Words do not only fail to describe suffering, but the persistent taboos surrounding sexual violence itself and differing cultural values related to speaking about sexual matters often prevent victim-survivors from being able to clearly convey the nature of the violation they have experienced (Henry, 2010). This appears also to be true in many online testimonies, where victims refer to being 'forced', to being touched 'down there', or made to touch 'it', but rarely are explicit in their accounts of the sexual violence itself (such as in SurvivorStories.Tumblr.com). Rather, their accounts include statements regarding the nature of the relationship, the trust that was violated, that they felt fear and/or panic, and that the assault has had a lasting impact on their lives. But *how* they felt fear, or *what* it is like to be frozen with panic, or the *ways* in which their life is affected, escape description. Of course, informal justice may not be contingent on the experience of victim-survivors being accurately conveyed to non-victim audiences. It would be simplistic then, to assert that the 'unspeakability' of rape itself renders justice, whether formal or informal, an impossibility. But to the extent that justice requires *voice* (for victim-survivors to be able to express their experience in their own words without external restriction) and *validation* (for an audience of peers to endorse victim-survivor accounts as true) as earlier discussed, then language can arguably be seen as simultaneously representing possibilities and impossibilities for informal justice online.

It is not only the deficiency of language that represents inherent contradictions for informal justice. 'Bearing witness', as discussed earlier, is relational, involving the victim-survivor who describes their experience as well as an audience who listens and who ultimately has the ability (or 'response-ability') to validate the account, support the victim and act to prevent the recurrence of these crimes (see also Jordan, 2011). Still, as Henry (2010) describes, many victim-survivors of rape fear and experience the doubt and disbelief of others; listeners whose only response is to deny, minimise or blame the victim. Certainly, as my colleagues and I have argued elsewhere, communications technologies have also been taken up as tools for gender-based hate speech in both online and terrestrial space (Henry & Powell, 2014, 2015), extending the harm of sexual violence through further harassing, humiliating, shaming and blaming victim-survivors of sexual violence. Fileborn (2014), Renninger (2014) and Salter (2013) all likewise acknowledge the double-edged sword for victim-survivors in publicly disclosing experiences of sexual violence online, in which they may be subject to further trauma as a result of the antagonism and victim-blaming of online harassers. The responses of such audiences are clearly antithetical to either the healing or justice needs of victim-survivors.

A third impossibility that Henry (2010) articulates is the very structure of institutional, to which I would add cultural, settings that presuppose narratives or testimonies of sexual victimisation to follow particular patterns or scripts. This 'violence of rhetoric' (De Lauretis, 1985; see also Hesford, 1999, 2004) precludes the possibility of victim-survivors having *control* over the form and content of their account which, as is well documented in legal settings, must conform both to the question–answer format of cross-examination and the culturally expected experience of a rape victim (Henry, 2010; see also Young, 1998). While online counterpublics are not as restrictive as legal settings in terms of either the *participation* of victim-survivors or the manner in which they can express their *voice*, they are not unproblematically liberatory for women either. There remain truth-telling conventions in online disclosure cultures that are evident in the victim-survivor accounts that attract 'likes', 're-blogs' and comments by supportive audiences, and those that are never responded to – painful narratives that are sent out into the ether (Fileborn, 2014). For example, on SurvivorStories.Tumblr.com, narratives that resolve in telling of the victims-survivors' success, such as her study or employment achievements, her newfound 'love' and/or the ability to 'enjoy sex again', are met with approval indicated by the number of likes and comments on the posts. Likewise, narratives expressing struggles with depression, symptoms of post-assault trauma, and self-harm, are met with likes and comments indicating support to 'hang in there' and often referrals to telephone support or counselling lines. Arguably such narratives mesh with dominant scripts of expected responses of rape victims. Others, however, are less conforming. One victim-survivor, for example, speaks of the lasting impact of childhood sexual assault that prevents her from enjoying sex unless it replicates the power imbalance of the abuse she experienced. She describes feeling 'dirty', 'broken' and 'disgusting', and ends with 'Does anyone else feel like this? Please tell me I'm not alone...'. Despite a handful of 'likes', no comments affirm her experience, or refer her to support.

Conclusion

Communications technologies offer a provocative assortment of tools and platforms for facilitating vigilantism, activism and informal justice. This chapter has explored the modes of informal justice being sought online by victim-survivors of sexual violence. Victim-survivors of rape and other forms of sexual violence and harassment are not only able to document and share their experiences in new ways, but also to connect with an ever-expanding global network of like-minded anti-rape activists and supporters. Such engagements can serve to validate women's individual and collective experiences of sexual violence. Indeed, in a culture that routinely silences, trivialises the harm and blames victims of rape while empathising with alleged perpetrators, it is little wonder that women have turned to subaltern counterpublic online spaces to voice their experiences and claim informal justice. Victim-survivor testimonials represent evidence of, and a call to respond to, the explicit (prevalence of sexual violence) and implicit (rape supportive attitudes and practices) signifiers of rape culture and indeed the cultural misrecognition of women as targets for sexual violence.

There are contradictions, even dangers, inherent in testifying to sexual violence in online environments, both for individual victim-survivors and women collectively. Failed by deficiencies of language, the unevenness of audience responses (and response-ability), targeted by online harassers, and cultural conventions that limit the form and content of truth telling, sharing one's account of sexual victimisation online simultaneously makes informal justice a possibility and an impossibility. Nonetheless, speaking the truth about experiences of sexual violence serves to 'keep the light on' the persistence of these violences, and to challenge the gender misrecognition at the heart of women's victimisation. For some victim-survivors at least, to remain silent about their experience is not an option. In the face of a formal justice system that frequently denies participation, voice, control, validation and vindication, truth telling in online counterpublic spaces can meet some of these justice needs, and while it may not hold individual perpetrators to account, seeking informal rape justice online contributes to the responsibilisation of a society, its culture and institutions that continue to fail victims.

Notes

1. See www.gulabigang.in.
2. YOLO is the abbreviated form for 'You Only Live Once'. Photographs from the rally, depicting this and other banners, were posted on the Tumblr site. See fuckyeahanarchistbanners.tumblr.com and searchable under the hashtag #feminist vigilante march.
3. For instance, some scholars (e.g. Harris, 2010; Martin & Valenti, 2012; Munro, 2013) and media commentators (e.g. Cochrane, 2013; Valenti, 2007) are heralding the arrival of 'feminism 2.0' or a 'fourth wave' of feminism signified by the uptake and reach of feminist activism online and into mainstream media discourse.
4. See https://www.youtube.com/watch?v=B1iUog2lL8k.
5. See, for instance, http://larosaknows.com/post/49051114845/covered-in-band-aids-what-does-a-rapist-look.
6. See, for example, SurvivorStories.Tumblr.com, survivorschat.tumblr.com, rapeculturemakesmeangry.tumblr.com, notgoquietly.tumblr.com.
7. A further example and alternative short-format for accounting for sexual victimisation is through so-called 'hashtag activism', such as on Twitter, where victim-survivors have disclosed their experiences of abuse under #BeenRapedNeverReported, #yesallwomen, #whyileft and #whyistayed, among others.

8. See projectunbreakable.tumblr.com.
9. See https://www.youtube.com/watch?v=ej7afkypUsc.
10. Fraser (2007) distinguishes these feminist politics of recognition from what she describes as the standard perspective of identity politics. By Fraser's account, what requires 'recognition' is not the equal value of a feminine gender identity (i.e. not 'valorizing femininity' per se), but rather dismantling those cultural patterns of value that impede gender parity as full partners in all social interaction.
11. See, for example, Hollaback.com and EverydaySexism.com.

References

Adams, R. (2012) 'Brie Lybrand, New Orleans Beauty Guru, Posts Video Claiming She Was Raped By Her Father', *Huffington Post*, 6 November.

BBC (2014) 'Man Charged in Netherlands in Amanda Todd Suicide Case', *BBC News*, 18 April.

Berry, S. (2012) 'A Message to My Rapist', *Sydney Morning Herald*, 8 November.

Brison, S. J. (2002) *Aftermath: Violence and the Remaking of a Self* (Princeton, NJ: Princeton University Press).

boyd, d. (2011) 'Social Network Sites as Networked Publics', in Z. Papacharissi (ed.) *A Networked Self: Identity, Community and Culture on Social Network Sites* (New York: Routledge), pp. 39–58.

Buchwald, E., Fletcher, P. R. and Roth, M. (eds.) (1993) *Transforming a Rape Culture* (Minneapolis, MN: Milkweed Editions).

Burt, M. R. (1980) 'Cultural Myths and Supports for Rape', *Journal of Personality and Social Psychology*, 38(2), 217–230.

Carrington, K. (2014) *Feminism and Global Justice* (London: Routledge).

Clark, H. (2010) ' "What Is the Justice System Willing to Offer?": Understanding Sexual Assault Victim/Survivors' Criminal Justice Needs'. *Family Matters*, 85, 28–37.

Cochrane, K. (2013) 'The Fourth Wave of Feminism: Meet the Rebel Women', *The Guardian*, 11 December.

Daly, K. (2013) 'Reconceptualizing Sexual Victimization and Justice', in I. Vanfraechem, A. Pemberton and F. Mukwiza Ndahinda (eds.) *Justice for Victims: Perspectives on Rights, Transition and Reconciliation* (London: Routledge), pp. 378–395.

Daly, K. and Bouhours, B. (2010) 'Rape and Attrition in the Legal Process: A Comparative Analysis of Five Countries', *Crime and Justice*, 39(1), 565–650.

De Lauretis, T. (1985) 'The Violence of Rhetoric: Considerations on Representation and Gender', *Semiotica*, 54(1–2), 11–32.

Fileborn, B. (2014) 'Online Activism and Street Harassment: Digital Justice or Shouting into the Ether?' *Griffith Journal of Law and Human Dignity*, 2(1), 32–51.

Filipovic, J. (2012) 'The Ethics of Outing Your Rapist', *The Guardian*, 10 November.

Fontanella-Khan, A. (2013) *Pink Sari Revolution: A Tale of Women and Power in the Badlands of India* (London: Oneworld Publications).

Fraser, N. (1990) 'Rethinking the Public Sphere: A Contribution to the Critique of Actually Existing Democracy', *Social Text*, 56–80.

Fraser, N. (2007) 'Feminist Politics in the Age of Recognition: A Two-Dimensional Approach to Gender Justice', *Studies in Social Justice*, 1(1), 23–35.

Fraser, N. (2009) *Scales of Justice: Reimagining Political Space in a Globalizing World* (New York: Columbia University Press).

Gavey, N. (2005) *Just Sex? The Cultural Scaffolding of Rape* (London: Routledge).

Harney, M. (2001) 'In the Aftermath of Sexual Abuse: Making and Remaking Meaning in Narratives of Trauma and Recovery', *Narrative Inquiry*, 10(2), 291–311.

Harris, A. (2010) 'Mind the Gap: Attitudes and Emergent Feminist Politics Since the Third Wave', *Australian Feminist Studies*, 25(66), 475–484.

Henry, N. (2010) 'The Impossibility of Bearing Witness: Wartime Rape and the Promise of Justice', *Violence Against Women*, 16(10), 1098–1119.

Henry, N. (2011) *War and Rape: Law, Memory, and Justice* (London: Routledge).

Henry, N. and Powell, A. (2014) 'The Dark Side of the Virtual World', in N. Henry and A. Powell (eds.) *Preventing Sexual Violence: Interdisciplinary Approaches to Overcoming a Rape Culture* (Basingstoke: Palgrave Macmillan), pp. 84–104.

Henry, N. and Powell, A. (2015) 'Embodied Harms: Gender, Shame and Technology Facilitated Sexual Violence in Cyberspace', *Violence Against Women*, 21(6), 758–779.

Herman, J. (1997) *Trauma and Recovery: The Aftermath of Violence – From Domestic Abuse to Political Terror* (New York: Basic Books).

Herman, J. L. (2005) 'Justice From the Victim's Perspective', *Violence Against Women*, 11(5), 571–602.

Hesford, W. S. (1999) 'Reading Rape Stories: Material Rhetoric and the Trauma of Representation', *College English*, 192–221.

Hesford, W. S. (2004) 'Documenting Violations: Rhetorical Witnessing and the Spectacle of Distant Suffering', *Biography*, 27(1), 104–144.

Hess, A. (2010) 'De-Friendly Fire: American University Student Makes Facebook Rape Accusation', *Washington City Paper*, 6 May.

Hess, A. (2012) 'Can Twitter Help Rape Victims Find Justice?', *The XX Factor*, 23 July.

Jordan, J. (2011) 'Silencing Rape, Silencing Women', *Handbook on Sexual Violence*, 253–286.

Just Associates and Nobel Women's Initiative (2012) *From Survivors to Defenders: Women Confronting Violence in Mexico, Honduras and Guatemala* (Just Associates and Nobel Women's Initiative).

Kelly, L., Lovett, J. and Regan, L. (2005) *A Gap or a Chasm?: Attrition in Reported Rape Cases* (London: Home Office Research, Development and Statistics Directorate).

Kingkade, T. (2013) 'UNC Sexual Assault Survivor Faces Honor Code Violation After Speaking Publicly About Abuse', *Huffington Post*, 25 February.

Lievore, D. (2005) *Prosecutorial Decisions in Adult Sexual Assault Cases* (Canberra: Australian Institute of Criminology).

Malone, L. (2012) 'Project Unbreakable: From Victim to Victor', *Sydney Morning Herald*, 13 March.

Martin, C. and Valenti, V. (2012) *New Feminist Solutions Volume 8. #FemFuture: Online Feminism* (New York: Barnard Center for Research on Women, Columbia University).

McAfee, N. (2005) 'Bearing Witness in the Polis: Kristeva, Arendt, and the Space of Appearance', in T. Chanter, and E. Plonowska Ziarek (eds.) *Revolt, Affect, Collectivity: The Unstable Boundaries of Kristeva's Polis* (New York: State University of New York), pp. 113–125.

Misoch, S. (2014) 'Card Stories on YouTube: A New Frame for Online Self-Disclosure', *Media and Communication*, 2(1), 2–12.

Munro, E. (2013) 'Feminism: A Fourth Wave?', *Political Insight*, 4(2), 22–25.

Oliver, K. (2001) *Witnessing: Beyond Recognition* (Minnesota: University of Minnesota Press).

Powell, A. (2013) 'Seeking Rape Justice: The Role of Communications Technologies in Legal and Non-Legal Responses to Sexual Violence', paper presented at *The Australian and New Zealand Society of Criminology annual conference*, 1–3 October 2013, Brisbane, Australia.

Powell, A. (2014) 'Pursuing Justice Online: Citizen Participation in Justice via Social Media'. *TASA 2014 Conference Proceedings: Challenging Identities, Institutions and Communities*, 24–27 November, The University of South Australia, Adelaide.

Powell, A. (2015) 'Seeking Rape Justice: Formal and Informal Responses to Sexual Violence through Technosocial Counter-Publics', *Theoretical Criminology*, Online First, 1–18.

Powell, A. and Henry, N. (2014) 'Framing Sexual Violence Prevention', in N. Henry and A. Powell (eds.), *Preventing Sexual Violence: Interdisciplinary Approaches to Overcoming a Rape Culture* (Basingstoke: Palgrave Macmillan), pp. 1–21.

Reed, T. (2013) 'After Being Failed by My College's Administration, I Posted My Rapist's Name and Photo on the Internet', *XO Jane*, 26 April.

Renninger, B. J. (2014) ' "Where I Can Be Myself... Where I Can Speak My Mind": Networked Counterpublics in a Polymedia Environment', *New Media & Society*, Online First.

Rentschler, C. A. (2014) 'Rape Culture and the Feminist Politics of Social Media', *Girlhood Studies*, 7(1), 65–82.

Rosenberg, S. (1996) 'Intersecting Memories: Bearing Witness to the 1989 Massacre of Women in Montreal', *Hypatia*, 11(4), 119–129.

Ryan, E. (2014) 'Here's The "Rapist List" Flyer Being Anonymously Handed Out At Columbia', *Jezebel*, 13 May.

Salter, M. (2012) 'Invalidation: A Neglected Dimension of Gender-Based Violence and Inequality', *International Journal for Crime and Justice*, 1(1), 3–13.

Salter, M. (2013) 'Justice and Revenge in Online Counter-publics: Emerging Responses to Sexual Violence in the Age of Social Media', *Crime, Media, Culture*, 9(3), 225–242.

Sen, A. (2012) 'Women's Vigilantism in India: A Case Study of the Pink Sari Gang', *Online Encyclopedia of Mass Violence*; Retrieved from: http://www.massviolence.org/women-s-vigilantism-in-india-a-case-study-of-the-pink-sari

Shilling, M. (2013) 'Outing a Rapist', *Ms Magazine Blog*, 10 April.

Solinger, R., Fox, M. and Irani, K. (eds.) (2010) *Telling Stories to Change the World: Global Voices on the Power of Narrative to Build Community and Make Social Justice Claims* (London: Routledge).

Sundar, N. (2010) 'Vigilantism, Culpability and Moral Dilemmas', *Critique of Anthropology*, 30(1), 113–121.

Todorova, T. (2011) '"Giving Memory a Future": Confronting the Legacy of Mass Rape in Post-conflict Bosnia-Herzegovina', *Journal of International Women's Studies*, 12(2), 3–15.
Valenti, J. (2007) *Full Frontal Feminism: A Young Woman's Guide to Why Feminism Matters* (Emeryville, CA: Seal Press).
Young, A. (1998) 'Waste Land of the Law, the Wordless Song of the Rape Victim', *Melbourne University Law Review*, 22, 442–465.

Index